Electronically Stored Information

The Complete Guide to
Management, Understanding,
Acquisition, Storage,
Search, and Retrieval

Second Edition

T0382738

Electronically Stored Information

The Complete Guide to Management, Understanding, Acquisition, Storage, Search, and Retrieval

Second Edition

David R. Matthews

CRC Press
Taylor & Francis Group
Boca Raton London New York

CRC Press is an imprint of the
Taylor & Francis Group, an **informa** business

AN AUERBACH BOOK

CRC Press
Taylor & Francis Group
6000 Broken Sound Parkway NW, Suite 300
Boca Raton, FL 33487-2742

First issued in paperback 2020

ISBN-13: 978-1-4987-3958-0 (hbk)
ISBN-13: 978-0-367-65848-9 (pbk)

Library of Congress Cataloging-in-Publication Data

Names: Matthews, David R., author.
Title: Electronically stored information : the complete guide to management, understanding, acquisition, storage, search, and retrieval / David R. Matthews.
Description: Second edition. | Boca Raton : Taylor & Francis, 2016. | Includes bibliographical references and index.
Identifiers: LCCN 2016002528 | ISBN 9781498739580 (hard cover : alk. paper)
Subjects: LCSH: Electronic discovery (Law)--United States. | Electronic records--Law and legislation--United States. | Electronic data processing--United States. | Electronic data processing--Management.
Classification: LCC KF8902.E42 M38 2016 | DDC 005.7068--dc23
LC record available at http://lccn.loc.gov/2016002528

Visit the Taylor & Francis Web site at
http://www.taylorandfrancis.com

and the CRC Press Web site at
http://www.crcpress.com

Contents

FOREWORD		ix
PREFACE		xi
ACKNOWLEDGMENTS		xiii
AUTHOR		xv

CHAPTER 1 WHAT IS ELECTRONIC INFORMATION, AND WHY SHOULD YOU CARE? 1

1.1	Introduction	1
1.2	Electronically Stored Information and the Federal Rules of Civil Procedure	1
	1.2.1 Changes to the Federal Rules of Civil Procedure	3
	1.2.1.1 Rule 1: Scope and Purpose	3
	1.2.1.2 Rule 16(b)(5) and (6): Pretrial Conferences; Scheduling Management	3
	1.2.1.3 Rule 26	4
	1.2.1.4 Rule 37 Safe Harbor	11
	1.2.1.5 Rule 34(b) Producing Documents Procedures	13
	1.2.1.6 Rule 33(d) Interrogatories to Parties	15
	1.2.1.7 Rule 45 Subpoena	15
	1.2.1.8 Form 35	15
	1.2.2 Federal Rules of Evidence	16
	1.2.2.1 FRE 502	17
	1.2.2.2 FRE 901	17
	1.2.2.3 FRE 802	18

	1.2.3	Case Law Examples	18
		1.2.3.1 Social Media Cases	20
		1.2.3.2 Spoliation Cases	23
		1.2.3.3 Rulings of Judge Scheindlin: Zubulake, Pension, and National Day Labor	29
		1.2.3.4 Reasonably Accessible Cases	36
		1.2.3.5 Metadata Cases	40
		1.2.3.6 Claw-Back and Privilege Cases	41
		1.2.3.7 Preservation/Production Cases	44
		1.2.3.8 Attorney Competence Cases	48
	1.2.4	Other Federal Rules That Affect Electronic Data	49
1.3	Problems with ESI as Discoverable Evidence		50
1.4	Why and How This Affects the Practice of Law		55
1.5	How This Affects Business Organizations		59
1.6	Effects on Government Entities		60
1.7	What This Might Mean to You as an Individual		60

CHAPTER 2 TRANSLATING GEEK: INFORMATION TECHNOLOGY VERSUS EVERYONE ELSE — 63

2.1	Introduction	63
2.2	Role of IT	63
2.3	Information Technologist's Perspective	72
2.4	Information Technology as an Ally	76
2.5	Translating Geek	77

CHAPTER 3 WHERE IS ELECTRONICALLY STORED INFORMATION? IT'S EVERYWHERE! — 79

3.1	Introduction	79
3.2	Basics	80
3.3	Database Systems	87
3.4	E-Mail Systems	91
3.5	File and Print Servers	94
3.6	Instant Messaging Services	99
3.7	Mobile Devices	101
3.8	Physical Access Records	105
3.9	Telecommunications	109
3.10	Cellular Devices	119
3.11	Digital Video	126
3.12	Internet or Online Data	130
3.13	Storage Media	144
3.14	Internet of Things (IOT) or of Everything (IOE)	147
3.15	Event and System Logs	148
3.16	Desktop Computer Facts	149
3.17	Metadata and Other Nonapparent Data	154
3.18	Conclusion	157

CHAPTER 4   WHO'S IN CHARGE HERE? ALLIES, OWNERS,
AND STAKEHOLDERS   159
- 4.1   Introduction   159
- 4.2   The (Long) List of Stakeholders   159
  - 4.2.1   Information Technology Professionals   159
  - 4.2.2   Legal Staff   162
  - 4.2.3   Records Managers   163
  - 4.2.4   Auditors   163
  - 4.2.5   Human Resources   164
  - 4.2.6   Department Heads, Vice Presidents, and Executives   164
  - 4.2.7   Physical and Information Security Personnel   165
- 4.3   Ownership of Data   165
- 4.4   Data Control Considerations   170
- 4.5   Required Skill Sets and Tools   173

CHAPTER 5   THE HUNT: RECOVERY AND ACQUISITION   177
- 5.1   Introduction   177
- 5.2   Where, Oh Where, Has My Data Gone?   178
  - 5.2.1   Applications as a Vital User Interface   178
  - 5.2.2   Hidden or Restricted Access Data   183
  - 5.2.3   Encrypted Data   188
  - 5.2.4   Deleted or Corrupted Data   190
  - 5.2.5   Proprietary Data or Data Stored on Obsolete Media   191
- 5.3   Privileged, Sensitive, and Inaccessible Data Management   196
- 5.4   Proving Ownership and Integrity   203
- 5.5   Marking Time: How Time Is Recorded and Ensuring Integrity   211
- 5.6   Legal and Forensically Sound Acquisition   215

CHAPTER 6   KEEPING YOUR TREASURES: PRESERVATION
AND MANAGEMENT   223
- 6.1   Introduction   223
- 6.2   Securing the Data   223
- 6.3   Access Control and Management   226
- 6.4   Organization and File Management Techniques   232
  - 6.4.1   Day-to-Day Organization   232
  - 6.4.2   Management of Data over Time   236
  - 6.4.3   Response to Litigation or Audits   238
- 6.5   Safe Storage Issues and Considerations   241
- 6.6   Litigation Hold   246
- 6.7   Spoliation: The Loss of Relevant Data   248
- 6.8   Automated Technical Solutions   250

CHAPTER 7 SHARING IS GOOD: DISSEMINATION AND
           REPORTING   255
           7.1 Introduction   255
           7.2 Format Issues: Original or Usable?   255
           7.3 Mediums for Transfer   259
           7.4 Creating Readable Reports   261
           7.5 Tips for Depositions and Expert Witness   264
           7.6 Conclusion   266

APPENDIX I: LINKS AND REFERENCES FOR MORE INFORMATION   267

APPENDIX II: FORMS AND GUIDES   273

APPENDIX III: LINKS TO TECHNICAL SOFTWARE SOLUTIONS   291

INDEX   293

Foreword

Matthews has approached e-discovery from a fresh, new perspective—one that is understandable to the layperson as well as the technologist. *Electronically Stored Information: The Complete Guide to Management, Understanding, Acquisition, Storage, Search, and Retrieval* will guarantee that you know more about e-discovery than you thought possible. A must read for anyone in the information technology and legal professions, the book provides invaluable information to be proactive or reactive in responding to requests of electronically stored information. The flow of the book from the first chapter to the last is clear, simple, and thorough—any attorney who desires to become a technically savvy advocate for his or her corporate legal department or law firm will have this book at hand. This book goes a long way in removing the intimidation factor between IT, the corporate legal department, and outside counsel. This book should be required reading for anyone in a computer science, information technology, or law-related program, and is now part of the Digital Forensics and the Law course I instruct. If you want to get up to speed on e-discovery and actually understand what you read, you'll buy this book.

Steve Hailey
President/CEO
CyberSecurity Institute
Digital Forensic Examiner and Educator

Preface

Welcome one and all. That is not just a pleasantry, but my way of letting you know that whether you are an attorney, judge, paralegal, business manager or owner, or just one of the ever-growing population of computer users, you will all benefit from what follows.

We all live in a new world in which we are surrounded in an ever-deepening fog of data. The data define who we are, for better or worse. The data contain information about our livelihoods, our education, our finances (or lack thereof), our health (or lack thereof), our history, and probably our future.

And yet very few of us understand how the data are created, where data are stored, or how to retrieve or destroy data (if that is indeed at all possible!). This book is for all of you, whatever your need or interest. In it we will discuss the reasons you need to know about electronic data as well as get into great detail about the how, what, when, and where of what is known in legal circles as ESI, or electronically stored information.

You can use this as a reference and simply go to the chapters you are interested in, or read through if you like. I try to keep it entertaining and simple to understand, even when we get into some pretty esoteric engineering concepts. I am pretty sure no one is planning to earn his or her computer science or electrical engineering degree with this book, so concepts will be as simple as possible and related to stories and illustrations that will help make sense of these sometimes difficult ideas.

So read on without trepidation, dear reader. I promise it will be enlightening, and perhaps even fun. If nothing else, you will have some interesting new ways to entertain your geek friends or impress your non-geek friends at your next party.

Acknowledgments

This book could not have been written were it not for the many patient and supportive people in my community in the Puget Sound area of Washington State.

There are too many to name them all, but the many information security, legal, and computer forensics professionals with whom I have shared these ideas have been extremely generous with their thoughts, wisdom, and advice.

I especially thank my colleague and mentor, Michael Hamilton, who has given me the support to learn more about these issues and the time to collaborate with others. He is a font of knowledge and just an all-around good friend and person.

I also want to add a big thanks to my original Information Security mentor and guru, Kirk Bailey. I will not forget the day when, in answer to my question of what would be the most beneficial skill to learn, he said "forensics." It changed my life in many ways.

I would also like to acknowledge my good friend, colleague, and mentor, Steven Hailey, whose gracious generosity, incredibly deep wisdom and assistance I can always count on whenever I get stuck.

And of course I need to thank my family for putting up with those long hours of husband and daddy being hunched over the computer trying to get this all done.

Author

David Matthews has worked in the information technology (IT) field since 1992. He began working for the City of Seattle as the technology manager for the Legislative Department (City Council) in 1998. In early 2005, he was selected to be the first Deputy CISO for the city. In his work for the city, he developed and created an incident response plan that is compliant with the National Incident Management System (NIMS)/Incident Command System (ICS); updated and extensively rewrote the city's information security policy; and created and taught training courses on information security and forensics. He created an IT primer for the city's law department as part of his collaboration with them on e-discovery issues.

In 2012, he was recruited by Expedia, Inc. to develop and lead their global cyber incident response team. He created and exercised a plan that integrated with their network response and disaster recovery plans and led a team located both in the United States and India. He retired in 2014 and is now doing consultant work mostly with local governments and critical infrastructure to enhance their cyber response and resiliency capabilities.

He is a participant and leader in regional information security organizations. He was the public-sector co-chair of the U.S. Computer Emergency Readiness Team (US-CERT)/Department of Homeland Security (DHS) sponsored North West Alliance for Cyber Security

(NWACS). With NWACS, he has worked with the Pacific Northwest Economic Region (PNWER) nonprofit to sponsor information security training for Supervisory Control and Data Acquisition (SCADA) operators and managers, a risk management seminar, four regional cyber response exercises, and four Blue Cascades disaster scenario exercises.

He is the founder and co-chair of an organization called the Cyber Incident Response Coalition and Analysis Sharing (CIRCAS) group. This is an organization with participants from the public, private, academic, law-enforcement, military, and non-profit sectors with the mission to develop information and resource sharing capabilities to better protect everyone. That organization has been written into a new Cyber Annex to the State of Washington's Comprehensive Emergency Management Plan and is working to develop resource typing that will allow state emergency management to call upon public and private resources during a cyber emergency.

Matthews is also an active participant in many local, national, and international information security, forensics, and e-discovery organizations. He is the former chair and still an active member of the local Critical Infrastructure Protection subcommittee of the Regional Homeland Security team, and is also a member of the American Bar Association's Science and Technology and Electronic Discovery committees. He published an article on active defense in the Information Systems Security Association (ISSA) journal and has presented at many emergency management and information security conferences. His most recent presentation on e-discovery, called "New Issues In Electronic Evidence," has been presented to records managers and information technology and security audiences in corporations such as REI and Starbucks, was presented as a peer-to-peer session at RSA, and was given as a continuing legal education course for the U.S. Attorney's office in Seattle and the City of Seattle's law department.

He holds the titles of Certified Information Systems Security Professional (CISSP), Certified Information Security Manager (CISM), Digital Recovery Forensics Specialist (DRFS), and Cyber Security Forensic Analyst (CSFA).

Matthews is a native of the Seattle area whose interests spread much further than IT or even information security. He is an avid reader, writer, hiker, biker, gardener, and a black belt in Shitoryu karate. He and his wife live with their three children north of Seattle.

1

WHAT IS ELECTRONIC INFORMATION, AND WHY SHOULD YOU CARE?

1.1 Introduction

The best place to begin our discussion about electronic evidence is to make sure we understand what is meant by the term *electronically stored information* (ESI). Because that is a term most often used in a legal context, we begin by looking at the rules that define how electronic evidence is used in a civil court case. We will also talk about other laws and rules that deal with electronic evidence in legal matters.

From there we take a look at case law, as that is extremely important to understanding the ever-evolving ways data are changing the legal landscape.

Finally, we'll spend some time looking at how this fog of data affects you personally or as part of an organization or a professional.

1.2 Electronically Stored Information and the Federal Rules of Civil Procedure

One of the most likely reasons you might be interested in ESI is if you are involved in a civil lawsuit. Of course, if you are an attorney or paralegal, that is perhaps more likely than if you are just Mr. or Ms. John Q. Citizen. But as a business owner or manager, the chances are actually pretty likely that you or your organization might be involved in some type of legal action (Figure 1.1). In my former careers in both the public and private sectors, the organizations I worked with often dealt with over 400 legal issues per year. Most of those were settled without any need to go to court, and some

Figure 1.1   Legal documents in the electronic world have become ubiquitous and overwhelming.

of them included criminal or other courts besides civil law. But any organization or individual can find themselves in court.

This chapter specifically discusses the Federal Rules of Civil Procedure (FRCPs) because they were amended in December 2006, and have been revised several times since then to specifically address ESI and to better define the ways ESI needs to be handled. However, it is important to understand that rules in any legal action are going to be similar to those we will discuss here. Because these rules offer good examples of what to expect in other legal actions, we specifically look at all of the pertinent sections of the FRCPs.

We also spend some time looking at rules of evidence, because those have also been evolving to address the new frontier of electronic evidence. We spend time considering some case law as well, because that is the crux of the way this evolving area of law is changing and growing.

We begin with a run-through of the specific rules that were amended in December 2006 as well as some of the more pertinent and interesting changes and clarifications that are being considered in the current set of amendments (final changes and amendments to the FRCP were approved by the Supreme Court and Congress and published in December 2015).*

---

* Lange, Michele (October 7, 2014). Part III—FRCP amendments: The long and winding road. The eDiscovery Blog. Retrieved from http://www.theediscoveryblog.com/2014/10/07/part-iii-frcp-amendments/.

For the first time, in 2006, these rules outlined a specific responsibility of organizations to identify electronically stored data that might be relevant in a case and specify if the organization feels it is reasonably accessible. Organizations are also expected to identify data that might be relevant but that they consider not reasonably accessible. These are important considerations, and we spend more time talking about this concept later.

First, though, here is a quick breakdown of the rules that were changed or are being revised. We follow each of these with a more in-depth look and consider how the rules affect you and the organizations you work with.*

1.2.1 Changes to the Federal Rules of Civil Procedure

1.2.1.1 Rule 1: Scope and Purpose The current change to the first rule, while not specific to e-discovery or electronic evidence is nevertheless significant. In the new rule, the language has been changed to emphasize how important it is for the parties to cooperate. Specifically it says "These rules … should be construed, administered, and employed by the court and the parties to secure the *just, speedy, and inexpensive determination* of every action and proceeding" (emphasis added).

This is, in effect, laying down the theme of the new rules. You will see this theme reflected throughout the amendments. Parties and the courts need to consider, first and foremost, how to apply the rules to ensure the most even playing field, at the least expense and burden possible.

1.2.1.2 Rule 16(b)(5) and (6): Pretrial Conferences; Scheduling Management The changes to Rule 16(b) in 2006 were designed to give the court a way to define rules about disclosure, privilege, and the ways that discovery of electronic evidence will be conducted. For instance, what kinds of electronic data will be considered work product (discussions between attorneys and their clients, or work that counsel is doing

---

* Cornell University Law School, Legal Information Institute, Federal Rules of Civil Procedure (as amended to December 1, 2010): http://www.law.cornell.edu/rules/frcp/. Retrieved February 11, 2011.

on behalf of their client that should not be disclosed). The rule also discusses the methods that should be employed by all parties to manage the discovery of their electronic data.

These discussions and agreements take place in what are called the Rule 16 pretrial meet and confer conferences, where both sides get together and discuss what electronic evidence they expect to acquire and preserve for the case at hand, how they would like it to be produced, and the general management of what is called the electronic discovery or e-discovery process. Agreements are made between the parties, and those agreements are recorded and become an important part of the case at hand. We look at some case law later where the agreements that were made in these pretrial meetings were used by the court to decide on the correct ruling on a question of evidence.

The bases of the agreements that come out of the Rule 16 meetings are established by Rule 26, which is discussed next and which governs the provisions of discovery and the duty to disclose.

In the current amendments, there are two changes to Rule 16(b). The first is in Section (3)(B)(v), and this is again indicative of the theme of cooperation. It states that the scheduling order may "direct that before moving for an order relating to discovery the movant must request a conference with the court." As noted, this is to encourage the parties to work things out in an efficient and cooperative way.

The second is again in Section (3)(B), but in (iv) and it relates to *claw-back*. Claw-back rules are about when a party can basically say, "oops" and ask the other party to return some evidence it produced (or the court to not admit it in the case) that should have been protected.

In this section, the changes refer to the Federal Rule of Evidence 502, which we'll discuss later. Basically, it simply allows for any agreements reached under that rule of evidence to also be considered in whether produced evidence should be able to be "clawed" back.

1.2.1.3 Rule 26 General Provisions Governing Discovery; Duty of Disclosure Rule 26 has received a lot of attention in the most recent set of amendments. We'll look more specifically at those changes and their significance.

However, in 2006, one of the first changes was in 26(A)(ii), which states parties must provide: "a copy—or a description by category and location—of *all documents, electronically stored information, and tangible things* that the disclosing party has in its possession, custody, or control and may use to support its claims or defenses, unless the use would be solely for impeachment" (emphasis added).

The term *electronically stored information* was added to specifically call out the fact that this evidence was now considered as important as any other type of evidence.

Specifically, in 26(f), parties are required to meet and confer about ESI early on and discuss things such as

- What the parties will rely on as relevant electronic evidence (what types of electronic data such as e-mail, documents, etc.—see Chapter 3 for detailed descriptions of the types of electronic evidence)
- How that data will be stored and preserved by each party
- Whether the data are considered reasonably accessible
- What will be considered privileged or work product
- What formats will be expected for production of the data (e.g., will the parties produce the data with or without metadata?—see Chapter 3 for more on metadata—and will they produce final drafts or all drafts, and will the production be in the format that the data is stored in natively, or in some other format that the parties agree on?)

That last point can be extremely important. Again, when we look at case law, we see examples of this coming up in rulings because one party does not like the way documents were produced, but the other party points to these agreements and argues (and the courts agree) that they did what they were asked to do.

In order for attorneys to follow the prescripts of Rule 26, they now have a stated duty to understand their client's information technology (IT) systems and their policies and procedures for records retention.

This will require those of you who own or manage a company, or manage IT or records for an organization, to work closely with your counsel to help them understand how your systems and policies work. The courts will hold you and your attorneys responsible under Rule 26 for any electronic evidence that is relevant to the case, so working together to clarify what electronic data are relevant and accessible is of paramount importance (and you should not wait until you have a legal case at hand before discussing this).

It is equally important to ensure that you and your legal representatives understand where the data are physically and logically and how the data will be accessed, acquired, and preserved in a forensically sound manner (to preserve the integrity and nonrepudiation of the evidence). In Chapter 3, we take a detailed look at all of the different types of electronic evidence and where and how they are stored. This is information you should use as you explore and discuss with your attorneys the specific electronic data for which you are responsible.

In a survey commissioned by the Deloitte Forensic Center and conducted by the Economist Intelligence Unit (EIU),* it was found that 40% of respondents did not feel like their organization's IT and legal staff communicated well and 35% did not have a team to respond to e-discovery requests. In fact, in many cases, the people who should have known about e-discovery issues were found to be painfully unaware of the issues. This serves to further point out the depth of this problem and the importance of you and your organization coming to grips with it as soon as possible.

If you have reason to consider data inaccessible, you will need to do a good job of explaining and documenting why that is the case.

Rule 26(b)(2) was amended to specifically address this issue. It basically says that if relevant electronic data are not "reasonably accessible" because the data would cost too much to produce or be too much of a burden or are simply no longer available, then you are not required to produce the data as evidence. It also attempts to set some procedures for how to shift costs if data are considered inaccessible.

Unfortunately, the term "reasonably accessible" is not specifically defined in the rules. However, there is considerable case law that gives some idea of what the courts are expecting.

Data that are live, online on servers, desktops, laptops, and so forth, at the time of expected litigation will be considered accessible of course. But also, data that are well documented and organized,

---

* Deloitte, E-Discovery: Mitigating risk through better communication: http://www.deloitte.com/view/en_US/us/Services/Financial-Advisory-Services/Forensic-Center/26d4c52d2bdf8210VgnVCM200000bb42f00aRCRD.htm. Retrieved February 15, 2011.

such as indexed backup tapes that can be retrieved without undue burden to your organization, have been deemed reasonably accessible. Information that can be gleaned via query to a database has been ruled accessible as well.

Finally, what is called near-line data, defined as data stored on removable media, such as the backup tapes we referred to earlier, or just CDs and DVDs, USB sticks, or even external, removable hard drives, are most often considered reasonably accessible.

Data that have not been well indexed or documented or that have been fragmented or corrupted in some way and would require extensive work to convert or recover in order to be used as evidence may be considered not reasonably accessible. Also, data that have been deleted or overwritten may be considered not reasonably accessible. However, it is important to recognize that this is a relatively gray area, and we see examples of that when we look at case law. It is very important, again, to work with your counsel to decide what you and your organization feel is and is not accessible and to carefully document your reasoning. The opposing party has the right to ask the courts to evaluate any claims you make that some data are inaccessible. They can make what is called a motion to compel production if they feel the evidence that you are claiming is inaccessible is important to their case. Then it becomes your responsibility to convince the court that the data are really inaccessible or that the production of the data would be an overly expensive burden.

Even then, as we see in some of the cases we look at later, the courts can decide that the evidence is important enough to the case that the burden is worth the trouble. They may, however, use what is known as cost shifting and compel the requesting party to pay for all or part of the cost of recovery to balance out the issue of burden.

There is another important point to understand in this respect, however. Courts will consider your policies and procedures and how well they are documented and followed.

This is extremely important, especially the parts about how those policies are followed. Having good policies is an important first step, but if no one in your organization knows those policies or follows them because they are too complex or they were never trained, the courts are going to be looking at what actually happens, not at what you say should happen (Figure 1.2).

Figure 1.2   Policies are worth little if they are too complex or too numerous to be understood and followed.

For instance, if you have a policy that all e-mail is deleted after 45 days, but your organization only "remembers" and follows that policy after you receive notice of litigation (thereby deleting some possibly relevant electronic evidence), the courts are going to be less than sympathetic to your claim that those e-mails are not reasonably accessible.

Further, if your organization's failure to follow good practices has resulted in important electronic evidence being a burden to access, the courts are likely to be unsympathetic to your claims. They are also less likely to shift the cost or resource burdens to the other party if the reason the data are inaccessible is because of your own poor practices.

Here is a good example of what I am referring to.

I heard a story of a consulting organization that was contracted to work with a company to assist with the indexing and organization of all of the archived data. When they arrived they asked the company IT staff if they had a backup system in place. The IT person explained that yes, indeed they did. Their process was to take laptops that they were no longer using and back up all of the important documentation onto those laptops once a month. Then they would store those laptops in their warehouse.

Now, this was a relatively large organization with a lot of different departments, all of which followed this rather unique process for archiving records. The consultants asked to be shown the warehouse.

Imagine the looks on their faces when they were shown a rather large room stacked with laptops with no labels, no indexing or organizing system, and not even a dating procedure. They obviously had their work cut out for them.

The reason this organization called on these contractors was because they had recently been sued and their attorneys had informed them that they might be responsible for producing archival information about their company and its practices.

It would probably be realistic for them to claim that data were not reasonably accessible, don't you agree? Yet, I can almost promise you that this is a case where the courts would come down on the side of their opposition if the data were considered important to the case. The courts would be very likely to expect this organization to accept the burden of whatever costs and resources were required in order to locate, preserve, and produce that electronic evidence. And that is simply due to their poor practices.

Again, this is something to be cognizant of as you discuss this in your organization. Be sure you are following accepted best practices for your records management and that everyone in your organization is aware of those practices and following them carefully.

If you happen to be the requesting party in a case similar to this, it can be to your benefit to have quality computer forensic resources either in house or by contract. We discuss forensics procedures and capabilities later in the book. That may give you an advantage over your opponents by virtue of your ability to access data that might otherwise be considered inaccessible, such as deleted, corrupted, or even encrypted data.

Another part of Rule 26 (26(b)(5)) was changed to address how electronic data that were inadvertently produced can be retrieved.

This is called the claw-back provision, but as with all of these issues, it can be difficult in real-life cases to establish that information should have been privileged or considered work product and should not be allowed to be entered as evidence. In some cases, the courts have ruled that privilege is waived by the data having been released, and because of its relevance or importance to the opposing party's case, you are not allowed to recover it or disallow it as evidence.

We spend more time discussing the work product doctrine and attorney–client privilege later in this book (see Chapter 5), because this is a very important part of evidence law that will be helpful for you to understand as you deal with e-discovery issues. It is also an evolving part of the law as courts learn to deal with the ramifications of electronic evidence.

Finally, Rule 26(f) requires everyone to get together early on to agree on the protocol for electronic discovery.

This is an important discussion for you and your counsel to have ahead of time. If you go into the Rule 16 meet and confer with a good plan of action, understanding what protocols and formats of electronic evidence are most easily available to you and most advantageous to your overall case and use of resources, you will be ahead of the game.

By understanding the what, when, where, why, and how of all the electronic data you own (which is the point of this book after all), you can make good decisions about what kinds of agreements you hope to make during the meet and confer conference.

All of the protocols and agreements based on these rules will be adopted as a court order under the Rule 16 meet and confer, so understanding their ramifications and being well prepared can be a huge help for you as an individual or for your organization, should you be involved in litigation.

In the current amendments to Rule 26, we note an emphasis on proportionality. This is in direct response to the ongoing escalation of costs associated with discovery—for the most part engendered by the incredible growth in the quantity of electronic data.

In the amendment to Rule 26(b)(1), regarding the scope of evidence that should be discoverable, it states that discoverable evidence should be "proportional to the needs of the case, considering the importance of the issues at stake in the action, the amount in controversy, the parties' relative access to relevant information, the parties' resources, the importance of the discovery in resolving the issues, and whether the burden or expense of the proposed discovery outweighs its likely benefit."

Again, this is an effort by the writers of the rules to create a level playing field and (hopefully) to keep the expense of discovery under control.

The new amendment goes on to note, however, that this evidence need not be admissible but can still be discoverable if everyone agrees.

The only other amendment to Rule 26 related to proportionality is to Rule 26(b)(2)(C)(iii), wherein they basically just refer back to the above when discussing when the court should "limit the frequency or extent of discovery."

In Rule 26(C)(1)(b), they have amended the wording to address the allocation of costs by including "or the allocation of expenses" in the specific terms a court can add to a protective order.

Once again, the writers are hoping to give the court tools whereby it can encourage responsible and inexpensive options for discovery from all parties.

Finally, as in Rule 16(b)(3)(B) above, the new amendments in Rule 26(f)(3) include a reference to the Federal Rule of Evidence 502 as another reason that can be included in an agreed-upon order for production as a remedy for the accidental production of privileged data. This would be included as part of the "Discovery Plan" that is outlined in this rule.

1.2.1.4 Rule 37 Safe Harbor When you are thinking about what is reasonably accessible, you also need to consider a concept called spoliation. This might be thought of along the lines of "the dog (or computer) ate my homework (or e-mail)."

You might be accused of (and sanctioned for) spoliation if you go into court with bad arguments for relevant electronic evidence being not reasonably accessible because you allowed it to be deleted or lost or damaged somewhere along the way, when you should have realized it would be important to a case that you should have known was coming (all of these "should haves" are important and as usual pretty ambiguous, so we talk about them more later).

I think spoliation was best described in a case known as *Mosaid Technologies, Inc. v. Samsung Electronics Corporation* from the New Jersey District courts in 2004 as follows: Spoliation is "the destruction or significant alteration of evidence, or the failure to preserve property for another's use as evidence in pending or reasonably foreseeable litigation."*

---

* Applied Discovery, Online Law Library, Case Summary, *MOSAID Techs. Inc. v. Samsung Elecs. Co.*: http://www.applieddiscovery.com/ws_display.asp?filter=Case% 20Summaries%20Detail&item_id=%7B781012C0-1342-4A84-8BA9-9BC1FC9 FDE57%7D. Retrieved February 25, 2011.

There is that "reasonably foreseeable" language again. You have to love the courts for piling on this type of ambiguous language that gives attorneys and all of us plenty of opportunities to guess what they might mean. We talk a lot more about this later, and you will see examples when we look at case law of how various court cases have treated this idea. It is a great idea to consider all of these cases and work with your legal counsel to decide what you consider a reasonable trigger to foresee litigation so that you are all operating from the same principles.

But when we are considering whether data are reasonably accessible, we might be tempted to the spoliation of evidence by virtue of the assumption that if it is not accessible, it will not need to be produced, and therefore we can ignore it and not worry about its preservation. It is important to understand that the opposite is true. Even if electronic data are not reasonably accessible, if the data are relevant to a case, you have a duty to preserve the data as long as it is possible to do so.

The only "get out of jail free" card in this deck is Rule 37(f) as amended in 2006 to include electronic evidence. This rule, often called the Safe Harbor rule, says that you cannot be sanctioned for spoliation of evidence if you have destroyed that evidence as part of your "routine, good faith" operations and policies.

But let me insert a huge caveat here—one you heard before and will find many times in this book: The courts will look at your practices and not your policies if and when you claim safe harbor under this rule.

Consider, for instance, a case in which an organization claims that important and relevant electronic evidence was lost as a result of its routine, good faith policies to recycle videotape after a given amount of time.

However, during deposition of their IT staff, it is revealed that for the most part they never recycle their videotapes and in fact have video dating back to the ancient days before video was digital. Their policy states that they will recycle videotapes, but that policy had never been followed before now. Suddenly, upon finding this particular tape that might have been damaging to their case, they remembered their policy and had a whole group of tapes recycled.

Obviously, this is not going to fly with the courts, and the Safe Harbor rule is going to fall flat on its face as an excuse. In fact, in case after case we find that this can be extremely difficult to prove unless you have very well-documented and audited policies and procedures.

Rule 37(f) also sets rules for sanctions against parties who refuse to participate in good faith in the discovery conference procedures outlined in Rule 26(f). This is basically the teeth behind the Rule 26 guidelines for the "meet and confer" and is meant to encourage all parties to set a level playing field early in the litigation process to avoid costs and delays later on.

In the current amendments Rule 37(e) has some important new language that better defines how courts should decide whether to sanction parties for failing to provide electronic evidence. In fact, they have changed the word "provide" to "preserve."

This is important, because again it hearkens back to the idea that everyone should be playing fair and this should not take so much time and money. Organizations now will have the duty to *preserve* electronically stored information but only to produce it if it has been agreed upon by all parties as relevant and important to the case.

The second part of this change is also notable in that it notes that if ESI that should have been preserved is lost and not retrievable because reasonable steps were not taken, a court should consider whether that lost evidence actually creates "prejudice" to the other party. In other words, does the loss of that evidence harm the other party's case?

If the court feels that is the case, the amendment goes on to say that it "may order measures no greater than necessary to cure the prejudice ..."

Finally, it clarifies that a bit more by suggesting that if the court finds that there was intent to commit spoliation, the court may impose greater sanctions from instructions to the jury that it should presume the evidence would have been bad for the spoliators case, up to a dismissal of the case or a default judgment.

These sanctions can be significant to a case and we will see case law later in which judges threw the book at bad actors. However, it seems the writers of these new amendments are trying to set some standards to assist courts in making better and more thoughtful decisions about when sanctions are appropriate.

1.2.1.5 Rule 34(b) Producing Documents Procedures　Another important rule that was amended in 2006 was Rule 34(b), which allows the requesting party to set protocols for how it would like electronic documents to be produced. The idea was to ensure that everyone agreed up front how the evidence would be produced and in what format (native format or something more accessible for the parties, with or without metadata, etc.).

Again, this is an important thing to discuss with your attorneys. You can be a big help to them if you have talked beforehand about how data are stored in native format, what is included, and what is stripped away. You can make decisions up front about how you retain information so that it will be the most advantageous to you whether for litigation or just for records retention and archiving purposes. But considering this in the light of possible litigation can be illuminating and may change the decisions you and your organization make.

For instance, your organization may be required by law to retain business-related records for a given period of time. One of my former organizations had to keep contract documentation for a period of 6 years, and other types of business decision documentation for 3 years.

However, the format in which we keep those documents can be equally important to consider. We will probably not store copies of drafts because those might contain edits and comments that the preparers of those documents were considering but that were never meant for public consumption and did not in fact become part of the final documentation.

Understand, however, that those edits and comments might be considered important and relevant to opposing counsel in a legal dispute. And they might equally be considered detrimental to your organization.

This is not to suggest that you should have policies that purposely destroy any documentation that might ever be used against you. That would be both impractical and in some cases illegal. It is just to suggest that as you and your organization are developing records retention policies and procedures, you should carefully weigh the advantages and business needs around what and how you retain electronic data, against the unnecessary retention of metadata, draft documents, and so forth, which might be used against you at some point in the future.

In the more recent changes, the language in Rule 34(b)(2)(B) has been clarified to say that if a party objects to production, it must "specify the grounds for objecting." And that it is permitted, if agreed to, for parties to respond with copies of documents or ESI instead of originals.

Once again, the more your attorneys understand about how and where data are stored, the better they will be able to address these requests during the Rule 34 agreements.

Finally, Rule 34(b)(2)(C) is amended to clarify that if you are making an objection to responding to an evidence production, you must state whether any requested evidence is being withheld based on your objection.

This is again to ensure that everyone is very clear about what is being produced and why, and to try to give the courts some ammunition for discouraging parties from playing "hide the ball." Before and without that language change there have been cases where an objection was made, responsive evidence was withheld, but no one noticed or tried to remedy the situation until it was too late.

1.2.1.6 Rule 33(d) Interrogatories to Parties   In the 2006 amendment to the rules, the change was simply intended to ensure that electronic records were included when business records were requested. This can allow parties to provide answers to interrogatories (sets of written questions asked by the opposing party during the pretrial discovery process that must be answered in writing under oath within a specified time) via electronic media such as e-mail or electronic documents.

1.2.1.7 Rule 45 Subpoena   This rule simply made it clear that subpoenas to produce evidence should include electronic evidence. This basically intended to put an end to any arguments about whether electronically stored information should be considered "documents" in a court of law.

1.2.1.8 Form 35   One other change was made in December 2006 to the Federal Rules of Civil Procedure—that was in the standard form for discovery agreements, Form 35 (Figure 1.3). Basically, this template was revised to include a reminder that electronically stored information needed to be considered and included in all discovery agreements.

Form 35 Fed.R.Civ.P.

Report of Parties Planning Meeting

[Caption and Names of Parties]

1. Pursuant to Fed.R.Civ.P. 26(f), a meeting was held on _(date)_ at _(place)_ and was attended by:

(name) for plaintiff(s)
(name) for defendant(s) _(party name)_
(name) for defendant(s) _(party name)_

2. Pre-Discovery Disclosures. The parties [have exchanged] [will exchange by _(date)_] the information required by [Fed.R.Civ.P. 26(a)(1)] [local rule ___].

3. Discovery Plan. The parties jointly propose to the court the following discovery plan: [Use separate paragraphs or subparagraphs as necessary if parties disagree.]

Discovery will be needed on the following subjects: _(brief description of subjects on which discovery will be needed)_

All discovery commenced in time to be completed by _(date)_ . [Discovery on _(issue for_

Figure 1.3   A small sample of Form 35. The full text is included in Appendix II.

1.2.2 *Federal Rules of Evidence*

The other important rules to think about when considering electronic evidence in a court case are the Federal Rules of Evidence (FREs). As with the FRCPs, though these apply to federal cases, these rules are generally accepted in all types of court cases, and their precepts can be considered and applied to any type of litigation that you might encounter.*

We consider a few of these that are specifically relevant to your better understanding and management of electronic evidence. However, please realize that these are a relatively complex set of rules and I am not an attorney. The intention is to simply give a general layperson's idea of what these might mean to you and your organization, but not a legal education.

These rules often address the important understanding of privilege and the work product doctrine. We spend much more time on these issues when we discuss recovery and acquisition of electronic evidence in Chapter 5.

---

* Cornell University Law School, Legal Information Institute, Federal Rules of Evidence: http://www.law.cornell.edu/rules/fre/. Retrieved March 11, 2011.

1.2.2.1 FRE 502   FRE 502 specifically addresses the attorney–client privilege and gives protection from inadvertent disclosure, similar to what is discussed in FRCP Rule 26(b)(5) and in the changes to Rule 16(b)(3)(B) and Rule 26(f)(3), as noted earlier. If you notice your mistake quickly enough, you can use this rule of evidence to ask the courts to disallow the use of electronic information that should not have been disclosed to the opposing parties because it was work product or privileged. Rule 502(b) allows you to request the return of inadvertently produced privileged or work product evidence if you took reasonable steps to prevent the error and noticed it relatively quickly and responded promptly.

Again, this is a place where preparation and good procedures make all the difference. If you or your organization have a good records management process in place that everyone knows about and follows carefully, it will be much easier to winnow out the relevant electronic data for any type of litigation or even for an audit or other records request.

By creating and sustaining good records retention practices you will be less likely to inadvertently disclose evidence that should be treated as privileged. You will also need to have and practice good and thorough discovery procedures. We spend time outlining those procedures and the tools and skills necessary later in the book. For now, suffice it to understand that, as always, the more you can put in place up front and the more you practice and refine those processes, the better you will fare when it comes time for litigation or other records production needs.

When we look at case law we see some good examples of how this process works for or against a party in court depending most often on the quality and efficacy of their practices and procedures.

1.2.2.2 FRE 901   Another of the FREs that is important to understand is FRE 901. This is basically the rule that requires that any evidence admitted in court be authenticated in some manner.

This goes to the heart of nonrepudiation and the integrity of electronic evidence, and this is another subject we spend more time on in later chapters because of both its complexity and importance.

Electronic evidence, unlike physical evidence and the documentary evidence that was dealt with historically, presents huge challenges when it comes to being able to prove its authenticity and that it has not been tampered with in any way.

This is another case where excellent forensics capabilities can be an important advantage to you or your organization. A good computer forensics expert has the tools, expertise, and experience to be able to establish authenticity to a much greater degree of certainty than is possible without those resources. Again, we discuss this in greater detail later in the book.

1.2.2.3 FRE 802   Finally, FRE 802 is called the Hearsay Rule. There is a dynamic and ongoing discussion in the courts about how this rule should be applied to electronic evidence. Hearsay is defined in Rule 801 as "a statement, other than one made by the declarant while testifying at the trial or hearing, offered in evidence to prove the truth of the matter asserted."

Rule 802 states that hearsay is not admissible as evidence, except, and there follows a group of exceptions (that we will not delve into here), which might allow a statement into evidence that was not made by a declarant (i.e., someone making a sworn statement in court under penalties of perjury) while testifying at the actual trial.

Electronic evidence by its very nature could nearly always be considered hearsay, so there are many cases where that evidence has been challenged and the courts have had to decide whether it is admissible under one of the exceptions to the hearsay rule.

We spend more time with this later as well, when we look at some case law. But this is an evolving area of the law and a great example of how the world of electronic data has changed and challenged the legal landscape.

1.2.3 Case Law Examples

In the next section we talk about recent rulings that affect e-discovery and electronic evidence. The thing to note about these is that most are relatively recent rulings. This gives you an idea of how fast this area of law is changing and evolving. It is meant to impress upon you the need to stay in tune and up to date with these cases so you can be of service to your organization in understanding their liabilities and responsibilities.

However, it is also important to understand how case law is applied in deciding cases. Each area of the country has different federal court districts, as well as local and state jurisdictions. Cases used as precedent will be chosen first within their own jurisdictional areas and type of cases so that they are judged to be most similar.

For instance, a civil case would not usually rely on a criminal case ruling, nor would a case in the federal district of New York be likely to take into account a ruling that happened in a California local jurisdiction. Even if it was in federal court in California, a court in New York would give it less weight than a case found more locally.

It should be noted, though, that certain federal district courts, such as the South District of New York, have a well-established expertise specific to electronic evidence rulings. For that reason, those cases are often quoted as precedent setting even though they might not be specifically related to the jurisdiction of the case at hand.

The point of understanding and referring to case law as part of litigation is to understand the precedent that has been set in similar types of cases, in similar communities, and with similar arguments. The further you get from those similarities, the less weight a court is likely to put on the conclusions that were arrived at in the referenced cases.

Yet that in no way diminishes the excellent understanding and perception of the evolving nature of legal perceptions around electronic evidence that can and should be gained by a close study of the most recent cases. The cases quoted below have all made a difference in the way courts in all jurisdictions are thinking about electronic evidence and the rules that surround them. I include the court references in the quotations, however, so that you can better understand from whence these cases derive and their relative relevance to your particular jurisdiction.

Since I completed the first edition of this book, many more cases have been added to this list and the precedent continues to evolve. Of course, new technologies are adapted more and more, and that also affects the case law.

In this new edition, I have broken the different cases down into categories so that you can reference specific areas of interest.

Figure 1.4   This case is one of many that involved social media sites.

1.2.3.1 Social Media Cases

1.2.3.1.1 Bass v. Miss Porter's School (D. Conn. 10/27/09) Defining Relevancy* This case involved the bullying and harassment of a student using the social media website Facebook (Figure 1.4).

The plaintiff's attorneys for Bass decided they would provide limited documentation of the Facebook activities of their client and argued that the rest were irrelevant to the case.

However, on review, the court disagreed and ended up ordering the production of all Facebook documentation.

In this case, the court felt that the plaintiff should not be the one to decide relevance. The judge suggested that the issue of relevance is in the eye of the beholder and that Facebook usage is like a snapshot of the user's relationship and state of mind. Thus, the court felt that all available electronic data from the Facebook archives and pages of the plaintiff should be included as evidence.

The lesson here is that courts are the ultimate arbiter of what is relevant evidence. That means that as an attorney, manager, organization, or even an individual, you have the responsibility to be able to locate, acquire, preserve, and produce any electronic evidence that might be relevant to a case if you have reason to believe litigation is possible. Even if you do not think it is relevant, the courts or your

---

* The relevance of Facebook evidence: http://bowtielaw.wordpress.com/2009/11/02/in-the-eye-of-the-beholder-the-relevance-of-facebook-evidence/. Retrieved March 9, 2012.

opposing counsel might disagree, so your duty is to preserve anything that might possibly be construed as relevant (a challenging thought!).

1.2.3.1.2 Crispin v. Christian Audigier, Inc. (C.D. Cal. 2010) Private Information   This is another case involving social media sites. In this breach of contract, copyright infringement case, the defendants were asking the court to allow subpoenas that were requesting all of the information from any social media sites that the plaintiff had accounts with.

However, this case went a little differently from the last one in that the court held that messages from social media sites were subject to the Stored Communication Act and chose to quash any subpoenas that were seeking private messages.

The court's ruling was based on its interpretation of the Stored Communications Act. The Stored Communications Act is a federal law that basically guarantees the privacy of communications stored on electronic media depending on the method of communications, transmission, and storage of that data. The act requires the operators of that storage media to obtain permission from the originators of the data before releasing it.

With that in mind, the court in this case ruled that depending on the plaintiff's privacy settings, the data requested by the defendant in its subpoena would probably be considered private.

However (and this is an important qualification), the court also said that if the plaintiff's privacy settings were adjusted in a way that allowed the general public to access the messages, the court might allow acquisition of those messages.

There is an important lesson here for those of you using social media or for any organizations that either allow or encourage their employees to use social media. It is imperative to be aware that your data will only be considered private if you have actually taken the correct steps to ensure it is not available to the general public. Once again, this takes us back to one of the main themes of this book: your actions are what will really count in the end.

1.2.3.1.3 Romano v. Steelcase (N.Y. Sup. Ct. 2010) Another Social Media Privacy Case   In this case, the defendant, Steelcase, sought the plaintiff's current and historical Facebook and MySpace pages including deleted information.

The plaintiff argued that its social media information should be considered private. But here again we have a good example of how different judges will make different rulings based on the facts of the case and their own understanding of the prevailing laws.

This time the court ruled that the plaintiff had no reasonable expectation of privacy because Facebook and MySpace specifically did not guarantee "complete privacy" in their user contracts—you know, those long legal documents that you have to click "Yes" on whenever you sign up for a new account or load up some software. How many of you have ever actually read one of those? They are legally binding contracts, so we should all read them carefully, but hardly anyone ever does.

Here is a case where that contract was actually called upon to decide a legal matter. So they really are important even though they are ridiculously verbose and difficult to get through.

As noted previously, every case will be different depending on many factors. In this case, the court felt that the information was material and relevant, and the defendant's need for access outweighed the plaintiff's privacy concerns. Using the contract as legal support, the court therefore ruled against the plaintiff and they had to produce all of the documentation from their social media sites as requested.

1.2.3.1.4 Lester v. Allied Concrete Company (Circuit Court VA, September, 2011) Original Award Reduced Due to Withholding of Facebook Evidence   In this case, the plaintiff had won a wrongful death suit and was awarded $10 million. However, in his final ruling, the judge took $4.13 million off of the award and agreed to an additional $722,000 in legal fees to the defendant when he found that the plaintiff and his attorney purposely deleted photos from Lester's Facebook account and withheld information about those photos.

The court, on finding that the attorney had advised his client to delete those photos, required the attorney to pay $522,000 of the legal fees himself. This is considered to be possibly the largest ever sanction against an attorney.

The lesson here is that social media data are absolutely electronically stored information under the rules and are being treated that way in court. It will be important to consider that and ensure you have done what is necessary to preserve that evidence if you are involved in a court matter.

1.2.3.2 Spoliation Cases Some of the following cases are older, but I wanted to include them to illustrate specifically the kinds of ways the courts address spoliation. If you do not remember what that is, check back a little in this chapter where we discussed the federal rules.

Other newer cases are also noted here, as they illustrate the evolution of the way courts are addressing spoliation issues.

1.2.3.2.1 Coleman v. Morgan Stanley (Florida Cir. Ct. 2005) This case resulted in a default judgment against Morgan Stanley. They were ordered to pay $604 million in compensatory damages and $850 million in punitive damages for failure to produce 2000 backup tapes.

1.2.3.2.2 Brown v. American Home Products Corporation Diet Drugs (E.D.Pa. 08/28/2000) (Fen-Phen litigation) You may remember this case. It involved the selling of a weight loss drug that, as it turned out, could cause some serious side effects, such as lung disease.

They were sanctioned for spoliation because they did not produce relevant e-mails. You can see why they might have preferred not to when you read this quote from one of the defendants to their attorney: "Am I off the hook or can I look forward to my waning years signing checks for fat people who are a little afraid of some silly lung problem?"*

1.2.3.2.3 Wachtel v. Health Net, Inc. (NJ District Ct 2006) In this case, facts were taken as established, which means the court instructed the jury to assume the facts that were presented by the plaintiff's counsel were true even though the evidence no longer existed (because it had been destroyed). The defendant's exhibits were stricken from evidence, and their witnesses were barred.

Further, the courts required the defendant to pay reimbursement of plaintiff's fees and costs, and to pay for a discovery master. A discovery

---

* Fen-Phen article: http://articles.philly.com/1999-08-01/business/25482928_1_fen-phen-ahp-pondimin, pg 1. Retrieved March 9, 2012.

master is a very well paid individual who is an expert in discovery, and the court was basically telling the defendant that because they were obviously inept at locating, preserving, and producing relevant evidence, they were now ordered to pay for an expert to assist them.

Finally, the court fined the defendants for discovery violations. Basically, the courts took a very dim view of the incompetence or actual intransigence of the defendants and their attorneys and threw every spoliation sanction possible at them.

1.2.3.2.4 Zubulake v. UBS Warburg (S.D. N.Y. 2003–2005) This is one of the most important cases regarding electronic evidence and e-discovery. We spend more time with this and two other rulings by Judge Scheindlin, who wrote this ruling and who has come to be known as one of the experts in electronic law. She was one of the first to really consider many of the issues surrounding our new world of electronic data and its effect on our legal system.

This was a suit brought by Zubulake against UBS for gender discrimination, failure to promote, and retaliation. This case lasted many years and has several different rulings, all of which set important precedents for the treatment of electronic evidence and electronic discovery.

In this case, the judge ordered an adverse inference instruction to the jury, telling them to assume that the e-mails that were not produced by the defendant, UBS, would have negatively impacted their case. She said that the defense counsel was partly to blame for not locating and producing those e-mails for several reasons. One was that they failed to continue to monitor their clients and ensure their clients understood that they were required to preserve relevant e-mails as evidence under a litigation hold even though it went on for years. The defendants were required to pay $29 million in damages.

1.2.3.2.5 Medcorp, Inc. v. Pinpoint Tech., Inc. (D. Colo. 6/15/10) In this case, the court found that the plaintiff willfully spoliated 43 hard drives. A special master was assigned to assist the court with the discovery and preservation of relevant electronic evidence. He found that the plaintiffs had destroyed 43 hard drives that most likely contained important evidence for the case.

The special master ordered adverse inference to the jury, suggesting that the court inform the jury to assume that the evidence that was destroyed would have adversely affected the plaintiff's case. The judge agreed and also ordered the plaintiff to pay all the defendant's expenses to the tune of a payment of $89,365.88.

1.2.3.2.6 KCHServs., Inc. v. Vanaire, Inc. (W. D. Ky. 7/22/09): Trigger to Reasonably Expect Litigation In this case, the plaintiff, KCH Services, was the maker of a software application. They learned that Vanaire was using their application without having licensed it, and they called and spoke to one of the vice presidents at Vanaire. The person from KCH informed the Vanaire VP that they had reason to believe Vanaire was using their software without a license. The vice president at Vanaire did what some would consider a reasonable thing and ordered all of the unlicensed software to be deleted from their company's computers.

However, here's the rub: that phone call from KCH to Vanaire was considered notice of litigation by the court. They basically said to Vanaire, "You should have known that KCH is a very litigious organization and that when they called you like that, it was extremely likely that litigation would follow."

Vanaire tried to argue that under the Safe Harbor rule (I'm sure you remember reading about that under Rule 37(f) in the Federal Rules of Civil Procedure section earlier in this chapter), they should not be sanctioned. They said that this was part of their "routine and good faith" business practices.

The court disagreed and said the deletion in this case was not covered by the Safe Harbor rule because Vanaire should have realized by virtue of that phone call that they would be sued and that therefore that application being on the computers would be considered relevant evidence that must be preserved and produced in court.

The court ordered adverse inference instruction to the jury, basically telling them to assume that the plaintiff's claims of Vanaire's having used the software without license were true even though there was no evidence existing on the computers anymore.

The lesson here is to really think about what can and should be considered a trigger for a reasonable expectation of litigation. Spend time working with your legal counsel to set those expectations and the procedures that you will follow to put a litigation hold in place to preserve the relevant electronic evidence.

1.2.3.2.7 Olson v. Sax (E. D. Wis. 6/25/10): Safe Harbor Rule In this case, the plaintiff, Olson, was terminated for theft of company property. The actual theft was recorded on videotape on July 22, 2009. The plaintiff, Olson, sued for wrongful termination.

In discovery the tape was requested by the plaintiffs, but the defendants informed the court that it had been erased. They claimed protection from sanctions under the Safe Harbor rule because the recycling of their digital videotapes was done automatically in their normal course of business (Figure 1.5).

What is particularly interesting about this is that the court said the defendants were or should have been aware of the possible litigation by August 11, 2009, and the tape had not yet been overwritten at that time. So, based on the last case we discussed, one would assume they should be sanctioned for spoliation of evidence.

However, in this case the court declined to impose sanctions absent evidence that the destruction was in "bad faith." The judge basically said that because they did not purposely spoliate the evidence, there was no justification for sanctions.

The lesson here is that different courts can and will make different decisions based on the facts of the case and the judge's discretion. Do not think this is ever cut and dried. It is important to read the entire

Figure 1.5 Caught on tape, but where is the tape?

case sometimes to try to get an idea of what the facts in the case were and to try to understand why the court makes its decisions.

The bottom line is that these are just human beings, and their decisions will be based on their best understanding of the law and precedent, as well as on the facts of the case at hand. So do not assume you know how a case will be decided simply based on your understanding of precedence in past cases.

1.2.3.2.8 Kipperman v. Onex Corp. (N.D. GA. 5/27/10): A Textbook Case The judge in this case called it a "textbook case of discovery abuse,"* so obviously this one belongs in this book, which may be used as a textbook. Basically, the defendants in this case did everything wrong in their very poor e-discovery processes. The lesson here is that you can no longer slide through, professing ignorance of electronic evidence and the rules that now surround that evidence in modern courts. The judges just will not stand for it.

The court in this case ruled the defendants were guilty of incomplete discovery, deliberate misrepresentations to the court, and multiple failures to abide by court orders. They were slapped with over $1 million in monetary sanctions that they were ordered to pay to the plaintiffs to cover all the attorney fees the plaintiffs had paid due to the defendant's intransigence. Ouch.

1.2.3.2.9 United Central Bank v. Kanan Fashions, Inc. (N.D. Ill. 9/21/11): Spoliation Sanctions That Hurt the Party but Not Their Attorney In this case, we get to see what happens when you try to fool the judge. The defendants, Kanan Fashions, had a server with relevant information stored on it that was slated to be sold as part of an acquisition. However, they were told numerous times by their attorneys that they had a duty to preserve it due to the court case they were involved in with the United Central Bank.

They "forgot" and let the server be sold and moved to a company in Dubai where it was subsequently reimaged and "lost" to production for the case. The court called this "elaborate spoliation" and recommended sanctions against the defendants.

---

* ralphlosey.files.wordpress.com/2009/06/kipperman-v-onex-corp.doc, pg. *18–16. Retrieved March 9, 2012.

The judge declined to sanction the attorneys because they were lied to and kept in the dark about the server being sold and sent away.

Bottom line: it is always the responsibility of the organization in the end. If you do a good job as an attorney and document that you did so, you can avoid sanctions.

1.2.3.2.10 Pension Comm. of Univ. of Montreal Pension Plan v. Bank of Am. Secs., LLC (S.D.N.Y 1/15/10)   This is another case ruling by Judge Scheindlin (of Zubulake fame). In this case, the judge addresses electronic evidence preservation obligations and spoliation in great detail.

She includes some important discussions on the culpability of the litigating parties for the preservation and production of evidence, as well as burdens of proof for the parties to comply with in presenting their evidence. Finally, she discusses appropriate remedies when these guidelines and rules are not followed.

In the next section, we spend some quality time looking at both Zubulake and Pension, as well as a new ruling by Judge Scheindlin because of the relevance of her thinking. Her guidance regarding electronic evidence, e-discovery, and this whole new world of data and its legal ramifications is extremely important and illuminating in our understanding of the direction the courts will take.

1.2.3.2.11 Crews v. Avco Corp., No. 70756-6-I, 2015 WL 1541179 (Wash. Ct. App. Apr. 6, 2015): Willful Disregard Can Put You in Contempt In this more recent Washington State case, the defendants were held in contempt and basically had the book thrown at them with severe sanctions, including that all allegations against the defendant were deemed admitted and that all of the defendant's defenses were stricken. The court found that their "continued disregard and violation of the discovery and contempt orders" was willful. Ultimately, the jury awarded one plaintiff $17,283,000 (the other plaintiff settled after the compensatory damages phase).

The defendant tried to rely on their document retention policy as an explanation for not producing evidence, but the court disagreed, at first because they did not produce the retention policy and then because, when they got around to it, the policy was far too vague to specifically support their assertion that it had been the reason for their not retaining the relevant evidence.

The lesson here is that if you are going to rely on your data retention policy to assert inaccessibility, you had better be very familiar with what it actually says and ensure that you have followed it to the letter.

1.2.3.3 Rulings of Judge Scheindlin: Zubulake, Pension, and National Day Labor Most of the following cases, except for the National Day Labor case (more about production and preservation), can be categorized broadly as being related to spoliation. However, Judge Scheindlin's rulings tend to cover a large area of electronic evidence law.

Judge Shira Scheindlin, the U.S. District Judge in the Southern District of New York (SDNY) located in Manhattan, is one of the most respected and referenced judges when it comes to understanding the evolving world of electronic evidence and e-discovery. Beginning with her landmark rulings in Zubulake, she has been one of the most thoughtful and forward-thinking jurists around all of the many issues that face the legal system in this changing environment.

Even though her decisions and opinions are not necessarily binding outside of her jurisdiction, the obvious wisdom and thoughtful consideration she brings to these issues is highly respected and is used by judges nationwide as guidance.

We therefore look more closely here at these three cases and the specific issues that were raised in each of them, as well as at Judge Scheindlin's treatment and opinions of those issues.

1.2.3.3.1 Zubulake v. UBS Warburg (S.D.N.Y. 2004)* As we discussed previously in the section on spoliation sanctions, Zubulake was a groundbreaking case on many fronts. Judge Scheindlin considered and wrote some very wise opinions on e-discovery issues well before the federal rules were amended in 2006. It is thought that many of the changes made to those rules had their precedent in the thoughts and opinions rendered in Zubulake.

---

* Zubulake VI decision details: http://www.ediscoverylaw.com/2005/03/articles/
 case-summaries/zubulake-vi-court-rules-on-various-motions-in-limine-and-
 precludes-admission-of-certain-evidence-unless-defendants-open-the-door/.
 Retrieved March 9, 2012.

Laura Zubulake was an up-and-coming manager in her company, UBS Warburg. By all accounts she was an aggressive, hardworking person doing what she needed to in a male-dominated society and workplace to get ahead. She began to lose out on promotions and to get poor performance reviews and was finally terminated.

She filed an employment discrimination suit and in that suit she argued that there was e-mail evidence between some of the managers and other employees that would prove her case.

In the first and third Zubulake rulings, the court considered and wrote precedent-setting opinions on two specific issues related to e-discovery and electronic evidence. Those were the issues of what should be considered accessible and not reasonably accessible, and how to shift costs appropriately when there was a cost and resource burden involved in the production of evidence.

Zubulake was able to produce over 450 pages of what she considered to be relevant e-mails. However, the defendants produced only 350 pages of documents total, of which only 100 pages were of e-mail. The plaintiff asked that UBS locate more e-mail by searching backup tapes and other archives.

But UBS argued that was an undue burden and would be a huge expense. They requested that the courts rely on a former ruling called Rowe (*Rowe Entertainment, Inc. v. The William Morris Agency*—SDNY 2002) that had set forth an eight-factor test to decide who should pay costs. The defense felt that, based on that precedent, any costs incurred to recover and produce the requested e-mails should be shifted to the plaintiff.

However, Judge Scheindlin disagreed. She felt that the older decision unfairly favored the shifting of costs away from the responding party and that its eight factors were used too much like a checklist, while she advocated a seven-factor list with the factors listed in order of importance and cost-shifting decisions being weighed accordingly.*

The court also connected this discussion to the idea of accessibility because the judge argued that the burden of producing documentation

---

* Case Law Update and E-Discovery News, Recent E-Discovery and Computer Forensics Court Decisions, 3(August; 8), 2003: https://www.krollontrack.com/newsletters/clu_0803.html. Retrieved April 6, 2011.

is often predicated on the ease of access. If recovering and producing electronic evidence was unduly burdensome and expensive, it would affect the balance of the decision on who should pay.

So, beginning with accessibility, in these first and third opinions, Judge Scheindlin described five categories of electronic storage, the first three of which she considered reasonably accessible. If you read the earlier part of this chapter, you will notice the similarities to what we already discussed in this regard.

She described the following three types of data storage that she considered reasonably accessible:

1. Online data on hard drives or other media used regularly in the course of business
2. Near-line data such as CDs or DVDs (and now we would include USB drives)
3. Off-line storage such as magnetic tape as long as it was easily recoverable and recovered and used on a regular basis in the normal course of business (today we might also include data stored on the Internet or "cloud")

Then she described two more that could be considered not reasonably accessible:

1. Backup tapes, especially if they were not normally accessed and it required a burden of time, resources, and money to do so
2. Fragmented, erased, and damaged data

In her subsequent discussion of the shifting of costs, she set forth the following seven-factor test that, as noted previously, she listed with the most important factors first:

1. The extent to which the request is specifically tailored to discover relevant information
2. The availability of such information from other sources
3. The total cost of production, compared to the amount in controversy
4. The total cost of production, compared to the resources available to each party
5. The relative ability of each party to control costs and its incentive to do so

6. The importance of the issues at stake in the litigation
7. The relative benefits to the parties of obtaining the information

In these rulings, the court decided to first ask the defendant, UBS, to produce all of the relevant e-mails that it had on servers, CDs, and five backup tapes as requested by the plaintiff and at its (the defendant's) expense. The judge said she would decide on cost shifting after they reviewed the contents of the backup tapes and considered the seven factors listed above.

Of course, when the restoration was complete, both parties asked the court to force the other party to pay the full cost of recovering the backup e-mails. The defendant estimated the cost for restoration of the evidence at close to $20,000, but said the full costs would be over $270,000 including the money it would cost for their attorneys to review the evidence. Judge Scheindlin applied her seven-factor test and reached the conclusion that the plaintiff should have to pay 25% of the cost of the restoration only, excluding the attorney review costs.

1.2.3.3.2 Pension Committee of the University of Montreal Pension Plan v. Banc of America Securities, LLC (S.D.N.Y. 2010)* Pension is an interesting twist and reiteration of the precepts put forth in Zubulake. The plaintiff, the University of Montreal, filed this suit asking for $550 million in losses that resulted from the liquidation of two hedge funds managed by the defendants. There were actually 96 separate plaintiffs being represented in this case.

The defendants argued that there were some large gaps in the electronic documentation produced by 13 of the 96 plaintiffs, and they asked the court to issue sanctions for failure to preserve and produce both electronic and paper documentation. These defendants, called the Citco Defendants in the decision, asked for dismissal of the complaint, which would have been the ultimate sanction, or whatever sanction the court deemed appropriate.

The judge ruled pretty much in the defendant's favor and wrote a very detailed and lengthy decision that goes a long way to helping

---

* Gibbons, Zubulake Revisited: Pension Committee of the University of Montreal Pension Plan v. Banc of America Securities, LLC: http://www.gibbonslaw.com/news_publications/articles.php?action=display_publication&publication_id=2983. Retrieved April 6, 2011.

describe what actually amounts to negligence, gross negligence, and willful, bad faith actions when it comes to e-discovery issues. She discusses how these different levels of culpability for spoliation of evidence should be used to decide the levels of sanctions and describes the different remedies that can be used to punish the party responsible for the spoliation of evidence.

She particularly chastises the plaintiffs in this case for their failure to issue a written litigation hold in a timely manner. She writes that this can be construed as gross negligence, depending on when they should have known there would be litigation. And of course because in this case the plaintiff is the party that brought the suit, they should be expected to have known well ahead of the actual filing of the claim that there would be litigation. Therefore, their failure to issue and maintain a written litigation hold that resulted in the loss of relevant evidence is especially egregious.

She discusses the different types of conduct that can result in different levels of culpability for the spoliation of evidence, including any place where a party fails its duties to preserve, acquire, review, or produce relevant evidence. Depending on the circumstances, the culpability might be considered gross negligence as in the case of the plaintiff not issuing a written litigation hold, or the failure to collect relevant data from the key players in a case. However, she said that not gathering records from every employee in an organization, while it might miss relevant data, would probably only be considered negligent. She did not try to define an exhaustive list of what might be considered culpable behavior because she noted that each case will be different and it will be up to the courts to weigh the differing factors and make decisions appropriate to the facts of the case.

In this case, she found that several of the plaintiffs had been grossly negligent, resulting in the spoliation of relevant evidence, and issued an adverse inference to the jury regarding those specific plaintiffs, telling the jury that it "may, if it chooses, presume that the lost evidence would have been favorable to the Citco Defendants," and if they decided to make those presumptions and "the plaintiffs-spoliators do not adequately rebut them,"* they may infer that the evidence would have been favorable to the defendants.

---

* 2010 U.S. Dist. LEXIS 4546 at pg 105–08. Retrieved March 9, 2012.

The judge also ordered the plaintiffs to pay the defendant's costs for bringing the motion and the attorneys' fees and deposition costs, and so forth. With some of the "spoliators" that she did not find grossly negligent, she nevertheless ordered them to pay for further discovery to produce the evidence that was lost. In one particular example, she said that one plaintiff should have searched the handheld device for relevant e-mail and made sure all of its employees were instructed to preserve any relevant evidence. Not doing so resulted in the failure to produce 22 e-mails that the Citco Defendants specifically asked for.

The lesson here is that thanks in part to Judge Scheindlin and to other evolving case law, it is no longer acceptable to shirk your duties to preserve and retain electronic documentation.

All courts, especially the federal courts, are coming to expect attorneys and organizations and even individuals to have a very firm grasp on all of their electronically stored information. If you do not know where your data lives, how to access, store, and preserve it in a sound manner, and produce it when required, you will be held culpable and could face some severe sanctions, either in litigation or from regulatory or tax revenue agencies. Yet, it is not expected that anyone will be perfect in this knowledge and compliance. Judge Scheindlin made that point in her decision, basically saying that as long as you make a good-faith effort and establish and follow good practices you will be in pretty good shape.

1.2.3.3.3 National Day Laborer Organizing Network v. U.S. Immigration and Customs Enforcement Agency (S.D.N.Y.–7 Feb, 2011)* This case is particularly interesting because it is actually a freedom of information act (FOIA) case in which the plaintiff, which advocates for day laborers, was seeking information from several different federal organizations including Immigrations and Customs Enforcement (ICE).

The plaintiff was requesting documentation regarding the "Secure Communities" program that was established as a way for the federal government to collaborate with state and local law enforcement on immigration laws.

---

* RSA Conference, New e-discovery case emphasizes attorney collaboration: https://365.rsaconference.com/blogs/ediscovery/2011/03/17/new-e-discovery-case-emphasizes-attorney-collaboration. Retrieved April 6, 2011.

What is interesting in this case is Judge Scheindlin's perspective that a FOIA request for documentation could be "informed" by the Federal Rules of Civil Procedure, specifically Rule 34, which as you know from reading previously, is the rule that describes what evidence should be discovered and produced in a trial. She said that when a litigant produces documentation "in the twenty-first century," the amended FRCP should be referenced to understand what should be expected.

This case fit well into the electronic evidence questions because the dispute was specifically about what ESI the government should have to produce and how it should be produced.

The plaintiff's first complaint to the court was that though they requested the documents in native format, the government produced them in pdf format, which made them unsearchable. This also stripped any metadata from the ESI and lumped all of the requested documentation into one large pdf file, so there was no way of telling easily where one document ended and another one began.

During the case, the plaintiff offered to discuss these issues or any other problems the government had with the requested production, but the government counsel ignored those offers.

The court agreed with the plaintiff on all three issues. The judge wrote that producing the documents in a pdf format was "an inappropriate downgrading of ESI." Not producing files in a native format made them impossible to search.

She also agreed that the metadata should have been produced, saying, "By now, it is well accepted, if not indisputable, that metadata is generally considered to be an integral part of the electronic record."

Finally, she said that producing the evidence in one lump document made it unreasonably burdensome for the plaintiffs to use the information effectively in trial.

Judge Scheindlin also made a point of emphasizing the importance of cooperation between the parties, specifically when it came to e-discovery issues. She pointed out that the entire dispute and resulting loss of time and resources could have been avoided if they "had the good sense to 'meet and confer,' 'cooperate' and generally make every effort to 'communicate'" to resolve the form of production issue.

Judge Scheindlin pointed out that this is not a new issue and that in case after case it has been established that attorneys must take the time and make the effort to cooperate and "fulfill their obligations to each other and the court."

The lesson here is that courts in all jurisdictions and areas of law will expect litigants and their counsel to work together to produce usable and complete electronic evidence. The judges will have higher expectations and less patience for attorneys who do not recognize the necessity of these practices and the justification for following them to ensure that justice is served.

1.2.3.4 Reasonably Accessible Cases

1.2.3.4.1 Spieker v. Quest Cherokee, LLC (D. Kan. 7/21/09): It Is the Practice In Spieker v. Quest, the plaintiff Spieker filed motion to compel production—meaning that they were asking the courts to force or compel Quest to produce evidence they felt was important to the case even though Quest did not agree.

The defendant Quest was basically claiming that the electronic data being requested was not reasonably accessible and not relevant. They said that they did not have the means to extract that information. They claimed that the software tools to do so were only recently purchased and had never been tested. Therefore, the time and effort it would take to test the software and use it to extract the requested information would be extensive and unreasonably expensive.

The court ruled against them, both because it felt the data were relevant and because they felt that the defendant's cost estimates were "grossly exaggerated." The court did not buy their argument that it would be so difficult just because they had never done it before.

What really sunk their argument, though, was the testimony of one of their IT managers in deposition. The IT manager testified that, contrary to their claims, they had tested and used the new software extensively and that the extraction of the relevant electronic evidence would be relatively simple.

The lesson in this case is the same one we emphasize over and over again: It is the practice—not the policy—that counts! Or, in this case, it matters more what you actually do than what you say you do. The IT manager helped the court's argument by admitting that they had indeed used the software that the company claimed was unused and untested.

1.2.3.4.2 Valeo Electric Sys., Inc. v. Cleveland Die and Mfg. Co. (E.D. Mich. 6/17/09): Production of Evidence as Requested in Meet and Confer In this case, the plaintiff Valeo produced electronic evidence files (270,000 pages) as kept in the ordinary course of business and provided two indices of the files to the defense. The defendant argued that they had to open every one of the 270,000 documents to review them for the case and that was an undue burden. They asked the courts to compel the plaintiff to reproduce the evidence and put the documents into 28 different categories to make it easier for them to work with.

The court ruled that the plaintiff had satisfied its burden to produce the evidence under Rule 34 and denied the defendant's request.

The lesson here is to be sure you go into your meet and confer with a good understanding of how you will promise to produce evidence and that you come out of that with everything well understood. In this case, the court came down on the side of the party that had produced data in a form they used in the ordinary course of business in spite of the defendant's argument that it was unusable to them.

This is important because it is based on the agreements made between the parties at the beginning of the trial. If the defendant had specifically requested a different type of production and the plaintiff had agreed in their discovery meetings, the courts would probably have ruled in favor of the defendant. But since that did not happen and the plaintiffs did what they were required to do, the court did not ask them to reproduce their data to satisfy the defendant.

1.2.3.4.3 Takeda Pharm. Co., Ltd. v. Teva Pharm. USA, Inc. (D. Del. 6/21/10): Not Reasonably Accessible? This is an interesting case in which the defendants asked for ESI for a period of 18 years. The plaintiffs argued that they felt this request was for evidence that was "not reasonably accessible" (duh!).

The court agreed with the plaintiff, but it ruled that the data were relevant and very important to the interests at stake in the case, and that there were very substantial financial stakes. So the motion to compel was granted, but the defendant had to pay 80% of the costs of production.

The lesson here is to be careful what you ask for! The court has the ability to do what is known as cost shifting (Figure 1.6). This means that if there is a financial burden involved for whatever reason, the

Figure 1.6   The judge decides with cost shifting who pays for what.

courts can take into consideration several different factors to decide who should pay. In this case, they felt that if the defendants really needed that much data and the data were really important to them, they should be willing to put up the majority of the money to pay for the cost of recovering and producing that data.

1.2.3.4.4 United States ex rel. Carter v. Bridgepoint Educ., Inc., 305 F.R.D. 225 (S.D. Cal. 2015): It's Important What You Agree to Produce and How   Here the court was dealing with requests from the plaintiff that the defendants provide ESI contained on backup tapes and produce the data in native format including metadata.

The defendants argued, and the court agreed, that the tapes were inaccessible and decided that if the plaintiffs demanded production, they could pay for it (cost-shifting decision). The court also said that TIFF images were reasonable and the defendant should not be required to produce data in native format or produce metadata.

Discussing the question of the backup tapes' inaccessibility, the court wrote "regardless of the cause of their inaccessibility, '[b]ackup tapes are considered an inaccessible format, and, thus, shifting the costs of producing data from backup tapes may [always] be considered'" and that "Plaintiffs may feel free to decry Defendants' contentions that it will take years and millions to restore this ESI to Native form, but these declamations do not disprove Defendants' assertion that the Backup Data has become inaccessible as part of their typical data retention schematic. And such ESI has been held, by dozens of jurists, to be inaccessible as a purely technological matter."

In its discussion on the ruling regarding cost shifting the court said it was "based on both the Backup Data's minimal apparent relevance and Defendants' adherence to a [sic] common ESI policies." In support of its conclusion, the court noted that, pursuant to its "prior dictates," the defendants had restored the contents of one tape, thus providing the plaintiffs with access to many potentially relevant e-mails. Further, regarding the plaintiffs' insistence on production in native form, the court reasoned that TIFF images were "widely used" and, noting that the plaintiffs had not "discounted" the fact that the "Defendants' storage practices accord with much of corporate America's approach to storage of non-active data for business purposes" and that "almost every bit of probably relevant ESI will still be provided … in a commonly utilized electronic form."

So, basically the court is saying that whether the plaintiff agrees or not, this court does not believe the rules require the defendants to produce inaccessible ESI in a format that is preferred by the plaintiff. The rules only require production in its usual format, and the plaintiffs should have to pay if they want to push for production of inaccessible ESI.

The court also found the plaintiff's request for metadata lacking in that they had not asked for it up front and they gave no "precise reason why the metadata of any ESI [was] specifically relevant to a claim or a defense." The court was "unpersuaded by Plaintiffs' threadbare reasoning for forcing the production of any metadata belonging to ESI already provided by Defendants."

The court concluded:

> Having waded through this case law, this Court is driven to one conclusion: had the Parties adhered to the spirit of Rule 26(f)(3)(C), nearly every dispute dissected in this lengthy order may have been avoided. Unfortunately, they did not strive to avoid later difficulties or ease their resolution via compromise and accommodation; unfortunately, access to ESI that may have been more broadly available based on compromise and mutual understanding of the costs and complexities involved will now be delimitated by court order rather than these adversaries' agreement.

Accordingly, the court ordered that the "Plaintiffs' requests for the production of the Backup Databases, the Active Emails in Native, and the Metadata are DENIED without prejudice."

1.2.3.4.5 United States ex rel Guardiola v. Renown Health (D. Nev. Aug. 25, 2015) You have a responsibility to be cognizant of the requirements of ESI storage and retention and maintain some competence and capability to do so correctly.

In this case, the defendants argued that the retrieval of relevant e-mail from backup tapes would be an undue burden. Their contention that it would cost more than $100,000 did not impress the court.

The "relators" in this case (Guardiola) had requested specific e-mails from a "gap period." The defendants held that the e-mails in question were only stored on backup tape per their retention schedule and that they relied on a third party for archival and storage. They stated that the costs to engage that third party to locate and restore those e-mails was too great.

However, the court replied that the defendants should bear some responsibility for the consequences of the decision to use an "archival/ backup solution that did not maintain ESI in an indexed or otherwise searchable manner." The court ruled to compel production and did not agree to shift costs (so the defendant was still responsible for the cost of production).

The lesson here is that you cannot count on poor practices to relieve you of your duty to produce relevant evidence in a timely manner. The courts now expect that all organizations should be aware of their responsibilities for maintaining and managing ESI.

1.2.3.5 Metadata Cases

1.2.3.5.1 O'Neill v. the City of Shoreline (Wash. 9/27/10): Metadata Are Data and Home Computers Are Evidence In this case, the deputy mayor of the city of Shoreline, Washington (a suburban city to the north of Seattle), reported to the city council about an e-mail complaining of improper conduct by a city employee. The plaintiff who was supposedly the author of the e-mail claimed she did not send it to the deputy mayor and asked the court to compel the defense to produce the e-mail and its metadata so they could see who did send it to the deputy mayor and when it was sent.

The defense argued that first, only a copy of the e-mail was available which did not contain the metadata, and second, that metadata should not be considered part of the relevant electronic evidence.

This ended up going to the Court of Appeals and finally to the Washington State Supreme Court. The Supreme Court upheld the Court of Appeals' decision agreeing that the plaintiff was entitled to the metadata.

Further, and most compelling of all, the court ruled that the city of Shoreline was responsible for searching the deputy mayor's personal hard drive from her home computer.

This example hits close to home—very close to home, as I live in Shoreline and know several of the people in this case pretty well. Even though it has been pretty well established in case law that metadata count and the data are considered relevant evidence, this is a landmark ruling for Washington State that creates a firm precedent.

It is also quite interesting that they suggest the public-sector organization was responsible for preserving and searching the personal computer of one of its employees. This is another thing that has been in question and that now looks like it will be expected in future cases, at least in this jurisdiction.

1.2.3.6 Claw-Back and Privilege Cases

1.2.3.6.1 Williams v. District of Columbia (D.D.C. 8/17/11): When "Claw-Back" Rules Can Fail You In this case, we get an example of what happens when an organization is not careful about its production of electronic evidence and how the "claw-back" provisions we spoke of earlier work (or do not work) in real life.

The defendant in this case inadvertently produced an e-mail that should have been considered privileged. They realized their mistake and sent a request to the counsel for Williams, the plaintiff, asking for the e-mail to be returned. However, they never received a response and they either forgot about the matter or failed to follow up. Two years later, the e-mail showed up as evidence in the case and they asked the court to exclude it because it was privileged and pointed to their earlier request.

The judge ruled against them saying that the rule of evidence clearly "requires a party who has inadvertently produced a privileged document to *'promptly' take reasonable steps to rectify the error*" (emphasis added).*

---

* www.ediscoverylaw.com/uploads/.../Westlaw_Document_Williams.doc, p. 1. Retrieved March 9, 2012.

The judge in this case did not feel that waiting 2 years to deal with the inadvertent production of electronic evidence could be construed as prompt and reasonable steps.

This is very important to understand as you are assisting with your legal team's production of data. First, it is important to carefully review what is being produced to ensure it is not privileged or part of the work product, and second, it is equally important to encourage and support a prompt response if you find that mistakes were made, as they often are. Especially when dealing with the large volumes of data inherent in electronic evidence discovery, it is very easy to make mistakes. The courts will forgive those mistakes and work with you if you follow the rules, but as noted here, they can also work against you if you fail to do so.

1.2.3.6.2 Pacific Coast Steel, Inc. v. Leany (D. Nev. 9/30/11): Losing Privilege   Yet another important and recent case shows us how easy it can be to lose the right to claim attorney–client privilege by virtue of unwise actions. The defendant Leany worked for Pacific Coast Steel and then went to work in another organization. Pacific brought a case against him for his taking of intellectual property belonging to them to his new employers.

In the case, his computer from his work at Pacific was admitted as evidence. His attorneys argued that the data on that hard drive should be considered privileged as there was information on it about his communications with his attorneys.

The court disagreed based on the company's published policies saying that there was no expectation of privacy for any data stored on a company computer. The court ruled that, by storing data on that computer about his move and even discussions with his attorneys, he waived all rights to privilege claims.

The lesson here is that with well-designed policies and procedures that are published and followed, a company can protect itself from liability and possibly a loss of important evidence in a trial.

Another lesson comes from the fact that the courts said that had the defendant done anything to protect that data, such as encrypting it, or purposefully deleting it, he might have had an argument to retain his privilege because he had taken steps to protect the privacy of the information. However, lacking those precautions, he had no good reason to expect privacy of the data stored on a computer owned by the company he was working for, especially after being explicitly notified and implicitly agreeing to a lack of that expectation of privacy.

1.2.3.6.3 Holmes v. Petrovich Development Company, LLC (CA Court of Appeals, October, 2011): Employee's E-Mail Sent from Work Not Privileged This is another example where someone lost their attorney–client privilege by virtue of a very well-written and published privacy and acceptable use policy on the part of an organization.

The plaintiff Holmes e-mailed her attorney using her personal e-mail from her work computer to ask about discrimination. When she was terminated, the company she worked for, Petrovich, preserved the data from her computer and eventually those e-mails were used in the court matter.

The plaintiff argued that they should be considered attorney–client privileged material and not admitted. However, the court disagreed based on the strict and well-publicized privacy and acceptable use policy of Petrovich in which it clearly stated that employees were not allowed to use company devices for personal e-mails, which eliminated any expectation of privacy.

The lesson here for organizations is to ensure you have a rock solid policy and that you can show evidence of your employees being aware of it. On the other hand, this is another good lesson in not assuming attorney–client privilege.

1.2.3.6.4 Kyko Global Inc. v. Prithvi Info. Solutions Ltd., No. C13-1034 MJP, 2014 WL 2694236 (W.D. Wash. June 13, 2014): Sale of Seized Computer at Public Auction Did Not Waive Privilege where Steps Were Taken to Prevent Disclosure In this Washington State ruling after settlement against a number of defendants, the plaintiffs obtained a Writ of Execution resulting in one of the defendant's personal computers and other property being seized. Subsequently, one of the plaintiff's counsel outbid the defendant's counsel at public auction and purchased the computer. They sent the computer to a third-party forensics expert for analysis.

The defense argued that this violated ethics rules and the computer should be returned. This also raised the question of whether the computer's sale at public auction should waive attorney–client privilege for any data discovered on the computer.

The court ruled against the defendant, saying that their purchase of the computer was not wrong, nor did the forensics examination violate state law about mining for metadata (RPC 4.4(a)).

As to waiver of privilege, the court stated that since the original owner had gone to some lengths to remove all data by reformatting the hard drive and installing a new operating system, that privilege should not be waived.

1.2.3.7 Preservation/Production Cases

1.2.3.7.1 Pippins v. KPMG LLP (S.D.N.Y. 10/7/11): How Much Data Do You Really Have to Keep? The defendant in this case, KPMG, preserved over 2,500 hard drives when it realized that there would be a case. KPMG asked the court to allow it to destroy some of those drives, saying it was too great a burden to have to preserve so much data.

The court denied their request because they failed to establish that the data contained on those drives were not relevant to the case or that they had evidence that could be produced from another source (the evidence on them was not "duplicative").

The judge decided that it would be prudent to retain all possibly relevant materials, thus establishing a hard lesson for some: You may be required to preserve and manage huge amounts of electronic evidence in this new world of exponentially growing capacities for storage of data.

1.2.3.7.2 National Day Laborer Organizing Network v. U.S. Immigration and Customs Enforcement Agency (S.D.N.Y.–7 Feb, 2011) This case was already discussed at length in Section 1.2.3.3, "The Rulings of Judge Scheindlin." Please refer to that section for details on this case, which includes specific discussion about preservation and production of evidence.

1.2.3.7.3 United Corp. v. Tutu Park Ltd., No. ST-2001-CV-361, 2015 WL 457853 (V.I. Jan. 28, 2015): No, You Don't Have to Keep Everything Forever In this case, Kmart (a party with the defendant) had production requests from the plaintiff for information as far back as January 1, 1991. They produced what they could but made a good argument to the court for the data that were not reasonably accessible. They explained that a combination of retention policy, their Chapter 1 bankruptcy, their merger with Sears, and various changes and updates to databases, software, and hardware resulted in the limited scope of their production.

The court accepted their explanation as reasonable and felt that they had made a "diligent attempt to comply." Therefore, they declined to hold Kmart in contempt or grant any sanctions as requested by the plaintiffs.

1.2.3.7.4 LordAbbettMun. Income Fund., Inc. v. Asami, No. C-12-03694 DMR, 2014 WL 5477639 (N.D. Cal. Oct. 29, 2014): Applying Proportionality to Preservation, Court Grants Permission to Dispose of Computers In this case, both parties had agreed to preserve 159 computers and split the cost. However, when the defendants were granted a summary judgment in their favor, they declared they would no longer contribute to the preservation but would not agree to the plaintiff's disposal of the computers in case they were needed for evidence on appeal.

The plaintiffs argued (and the court agreed) that there had been more than adequate time for the defense to establish if those computers held any relevant information and that the plaintiff's investigations had indicated these were never used by the actual custodians of relevant information.

The court also considered the "proportionality principle" as referenced in the FRCP (26(b)(2)), which applies to the duty to preserve evidence, and decided that the burden of preservation outweighed the likely benefit. For those reasons, the court allowed the plaintiffs to dispose of the computers.

1.2.3.7.5 Procaps S.A. v. Patheon Inc., No. 12-24356-CIV, 2014 WL 800468 (S.D. Fla. Feb. 28, 2014); No. 12-24356-CIV, 2014 WL 1047748 (S.D. Fla. Mar. 18, 2014): Court Orders Forensic Examination for Inadequate Preservation and Collection, Confirms "Basic Rule" that Custodians Must Be Consulted for Input on Search Terms This includes two decisions of note. First, due to what the court agreed were deficient efforts to preserve and collect ESI (including the failure to issue a litigation hold, travel to Colombia where the data were based, and failure to meet with IT or enlist assistance from a consultant), the court ordered the plaintiff to pay for an extensive forensic examination by a neutral third party.

In the second opinion, the court agreed with the defense in its concerns about the plaintiff's attorney's lack of communication about how search terms were derived. They cited the fact that the plaintiff's counsel only initially used eight search terms all in English while the company and its employees all speak Spanish. The court confirmed a "basic rule" that "outside counsel must carefully craft the appropriate keywords with input from the ESI custodians."

1.2.3.7.6 In re Domestic Drywall Antitrust Litig.,: F. Supp. 2d—, 2014 WL 1909260 (E.D. Pa. May 12, 2014): Courts Expect Legal Teams to Be Cognizant of the Capabilities of Current ESI Tools "Ignoring the capabilities which ESI allows the parties to search for and produce factual information in a case of this nature is like pretending businesses still communicate by smoke signals."

The judge makes an important statement here when the plaintiffs tried to contend that review of the large number of documents was burdensome. The court ruled that because of the existence and use of ESI tools that with search terms are able to quickly find relevant evidence, this should not create a large expense and the plaintiffs must proceed to provide the facts requested.

1.2.3.7.7 Federico v. Lincoln Military Housing, LLC, No. 2:12-cv-80, 2014 WL 7447937 (E.D. Va. Dec. 31, 2014): Delayed Production OK If You Really Tried and Got It (mostly) Right Eventually The class action case plaintiffs (Fedirico) alleged personal injury and property damage resulting from mold in their military housing.

The defense moved to have the case dismissed based on the delay and incomplete production of social media content from the plaintiffs. The judge agreed only to the payment of attorney's fees and did not dismiss the case, due to the eventually produced nearly complete record.

Even though it was well understood by all parties at the beginning of litigation that the plaintiffs were heavy users of e-mail and social media, their initial production was sparse. This led the defense to "move to compel" greater production and the plaintiffs agreed, stating that they would need to hire outside help due to the voluminous and complex nature of the production.

They asked the court to shift the cost of that expert to the defense. The court declined to do so and, once again, the plaintiffs failed to meet a deadline to produce the data. They agreed to a new production date and were finally able to meet the "nearly complete" standard sought by the judge.

The defendants also asked for sanctions due to the failure to produce text messaging. The plaintiffs argued that the text messaging would not have been relevant and that it had been irretrievably lost before they were made aware it would be sought in discovery. However, again the court found that there was no reason to believe anyone acted in bad faith and that before the data were sought or they had reason to believe there would be litigation, the data were deleted by providers in the "routine, good-faith operation of an electronic information system"—Rule 37.

1.2.3.7.8 Various New Cases Regarding Emojis* Emoji images have been entered as evidence in a handful of cases. In a case before the Supreme Court in December 2014, a man convicted for threatening his ex-wife on Facebook said the threats were not meant to be taken seriously.

As evidence, his lawyers showed a violent tirade that was punctuated with a smiley face and a tongue sticking out.

In January, in the federal court trial of Ross Ulbricht, a California man charged with running an online drug trafficking site called Silk Road, emojis again played a role.

Ulbricht's lawyer argued that prosecutors failed to include a smiley face that was part of an Internet post when they read the text to the jury.

"The judge actually found that the emojis should be read into the testimony and that the jury should have the ability to read the texts or online messages themselves so that they could see the emojis in context," Dalia TopelsonRitvo says.

1.2.3.7.9 When Can/Should an Employer Wipe an Ex-Employee's Mobile Device?† The dispute in *Rajaee v. Design Tech Homes, Ltd.* illustrates

---

* Emoticons as evidence: http://kbia.org/post/next-witness-will-yellow-smiley-face-take-stand. Retrieved December 2, 2015.

† Wiping personal data from terminated employee's iPhone: http://scholar.google.com/scholar_case?case=17791284937819645574&hl=en&as_sdt=6,44. Retrieved December 2, 2015.

this point nicely. In that case, the employee claimed that he had to have constant access to his e-mail in order to do his job. His employer did not provide him with a mobile device so he used his own personal iPhone 4 to do his job.

His iPhone was connected to his employer's network server to allow him to remotely access the e-mail, contact manager, and calendar provided by the employer. The employer and employee later disagreed over who connected the device to the network or whether it was authorized.

The employee resigned his employment and, a few days later, his former employer's network administrator remotely wiped his iPhone, restoring it to factory settings and deleting all the data—both work-related and personal—from the iPhone.

The employee then sued his former employer, claiming that the employer's actions caused him to lose more than 600 business contacts collected during his career, family contacts, family photos, business records, irreplaceable business and personal photos and videos, and numerous passwords.

He asserted claims for violation of the Computer Fraud and Abuse Act, Electronic Communications Privacy Act, and various claims under Texas state law.

The lawsuit was filed in August 2013. Due in large part to fine lawyering by the folks who represented the employer, they were able to get the case dismissed in November 2014. While this was a "win" for the employer, that win came at a significant cost.

1.2.3.8 Attorney Competence Cases

1.2.3.8.1 Chen v. Dougherty (W.D. WA. 7/7/09): Attorney Gets a Slap for Incompetence   Here is a sad example of how a court can react to poor practices by attorneys. In this case, the plaintiff prevailed in the trial and asked the courts to award them attorney fees. As is usual in such a request, they stipulated their hourly rate and the number of hours they spent on the case.

The court agreed that those costs should be paid; however, the judge reduced the rate considerably for one attorney with the statement that her "inhibited ability to participate meaningfully in electronic discovery" was indicative of "novice skills in this area" and not "experienced council."*

That had to hurt. The lesson here is once again to recognize that courts will not tolerate incompetence in the production and management of relevant electronic evidence.

1.2.3.8.2 Brown v. Tellermate Holdings, Ltd., No. 2: 11-cv-1122, 2014 WL 2987051 (S.D. Ohio July 1, 2014): Counsel's Failure to "Examine Critically" Client's Representations about "Existence and Availability of Documents" was "Overriding Reason" for Discovery Problems The judge in this case called out both parties' counsel for inadequate management and participation in the preservation of ESI. The court specifically observed that with the defense "significant problems arose in this case for one overriding reason: counsel fell far short of their obligation to examine critically the information which Tellermate gave them about the existence and availability of documents requested by the Browns. ... As a result, they did not produce documents in a timely fashion, made unfounded arguments about their ability and obligation to do so, caused the Browns to file discovery motions to address these issues, and, eventually, produced a key set of documents which were never subject to proper preservation."

Accordingly, the court ordered that the defendant was precluded from "using any evidence which would tend to show that the Browns were terminated for performance-related reasons" and also ordered monetary sanctions, to be paid jointly by the defendant and counsel.

1.2.4 Other Federal Rules That Affect Electronic Data

There are three other federal rules that affect the way federal jurisdictions treat electronic evidence. They are beyond the scope of this

---

* Attorney fees cut due to lack of eDiscovery knowledge: http://www.ediscoverylaw.com/2009/07/inhibited-ability-to-participate-meaningfully-in-electronic-discovery-results-in-reduction-of-rate-of-recoverable-attorneys-fees/. Retrieved December 2, 2015.

book, but I wanted to at least reference them here so that you would
be aware of them:

- Electronic Communications Privacy Act or ECPA (1986)*
- Stored Communications Act (1986)—part of ECPA
- Daubert ruling—a case that specifically discusses the criteria
  for expert witnesses

1.3 Problems with ESI as Discoverable Evidence

When we need to use ESI in a court of law, or if we just need to
understand how to find it and deal with it for whatever reason, we
have to think about how it is different from any other type of data or
information.

In the old days, if you wrote a contract with someone, or made
some other kind of agreement, you would probably write it up on
paper and after agreeing to everything, everyone would get copies
and everyone would sign the copies in ink as proof of your agreement and intention, as well as proving the integrity of the documents.
To maintain that integrity, those documents might be witnessed and
notarized by a third party and possibly stored in a secure place so they
could not be altered.

Proving the integrity of that type of evidence was relatively
straightforward. As we discussed in the last section when we looked
at rules of evidence, in order for a court of law to admit evidence for
consideration, it has to be shown to be both legitimate and relevant.
Proving a paper document to be legitimate is a matter of proving it
was not altered after the fact and that it says what you are suggesting
it says in a correct and understandable way.

Think about how that is different when you are talking about electronic evidence.

Almost everything we do is now recorded electronically. The first
big difference between ESI and evidence in the past is the sheer
volume of data.

---

* *The New York Times*, 1986, Privacy law is outrun by the web: http://www.nytimes.
com/2011/01/10/technology/10privacy.html?pagewanted=1&_r=1. Retrieved April 6,
2011.

In the past, a large and complicated case might require boxes and boxes of documentation that the poor paralegals would have to work their way through to find the relevant and important evidence. But now, with electronic data being accepted as evidence, the quantity of documents or other types of evidence, even for the simplest cases, is often orders of magnitude greater. If you had to store it in boxes, it would fill thousands of acres of warehouses.

It is said that currently every one of us generates gigabytes of data every day, and that number continues to rise exponentially (for an explanation of gigabytes and other large increments of electronic data, see Chapter 3).

Given that exponential growth in electronic data worldwide, we can assume that the quantity of electronic evidence will continue to grow, and that is one of the most important and relevant problems we all have to deal with when working with ESI (Figure 1.7).

Another big difference is in the data. Electronic data by its nature is dynamic. It can be changed in nonapparent ways by the simple action of accessing it, viewing it, or moving it. That nonapparent information that can become part of electronic data is called metadata. We will have a much longer and detailed look at metadata later because it can be hugely important to understanding electronic evidence.

This dynamism also creates problems with the integrity of electronic data. It is relatively easy to manipulate electronic data to make it seem to reflect a different reality than it might have originally. And it can be extremely difficult to verify or prove that such manipulation has occurred.

Figure 1.7   Poor paralegals are being buried in electronic data.

In an article on MSNBC's Open Channel,* Steven Teppler, a partner in the Chicago law firm Edelson McGuire and co-chair of the American Bar Association's Digital Evidence Committee, is quoted as saying that there is a growing movement of legal professionals who feel that digital evidence should be deemed "hearsay." He goes on to say, "Unless we change the rules of evidence to require a higher level of reliability, you have this built in problem where people say, 'It comes out of the computer, therefore it must be reliable.'"

But that does not account for the fact that programmers create the software that instructs those machines to generate data, Teppler said.

"Computers will repetitively create bad information if they are programmed incorrectly," he said. "Just because a computer generates it doesn't mean it's true."

As noted in this article and seen more and more often in court cases, being able to prove the integrity of electronic information can be extremely difficult but at the same time very relevant to the case at hand.

In the same article, Mike McCullough, a retired Phoenix police detective and president of the Southwestern Association of Technical Accident Investigators, notes that this whole issue is being treated very differently in different jurisdictions. He says, "Right now it depends on the state, depends on the judge ..." and "A lot of information has to be established to show that it's reliable."[†]

So, this is becoming one of the most important and challenging issues for dealing with and presenting electronic evidence.

Let us consider some examples based on real-life scenarios.

A software engineer working in Company A creates a new application that he is really proud of. Company A is not interested in the application and he asks for and receives documentation in an e-mail saying that the company grants him the intellectual property rights to that application.

---

* Open Channel, msnbc.com, Mike Brunker, Digital evidence becoming central in criminal cases, November 11, 2011: http://openchannel.msnbc.msn.com/_news/ 2011/11/11/8743687-digital-evidence-becoming-central-in-criminal-cases. Retrieved April 11,2011.

† Digital evidence key in criminal cases: http://insidedateline.nbcnews.com/_news/ 2011/11/11/8753776-digital-evidence-becoming-central-in-criminal-cases?lite. Retrieved December 2, 2015.

The engineer chooses to go to work for a different company (Company B) and they are very excited to promote his application. As it turns out, the application is quite popular and Company B begins to make a tidy profit from it.

Company A notices and brings a lawsuit claiming that the engineer gave them the rights to the software. In court, they produce an e-mail with a date and time stamp earlier than the one the engineer possesses that says he actually did release his rights to the software. Of course, the engineer never saw or received that e-mail, so he and his new company and their attorneys are rather unhappy.

But riding to the rescue is the wonderful and amazing computer forensics expert. Company B's expert takes apart the plaintiff's (Company A's) president's computer hard drive and discovers something interesting. At a certain point the computer's clock does an odd thing. It suddenly seems to shift back a few months for just an hour or so, and then shifts back to normal time. And what do you know—there seem to be traces of a familiar looking e-mail that was created during that little time glitch.

Voila! Mystery solved. In subsequent testimony it is discovered that Company A's IT administrator, under direct orders from the president of the company, set the clocks back long enough for the fake e-mail to be generated, then corrected them again afterwards.

Thus the metadata that showed the time and date on the fake e-mail were altered to make it seem to have been sent before the real e-mail.

As noted previously, this was a relatively simple thing to do because this was electronic evidence, and it would have been difficult to figure out if not for the expertise and skills of the computer forensics expert.

Here is another example. Years after a nasty divorce, the ex-wife, Jane, was having trouble getting her ex-husband to pay for medical expenses. She maintained that he agreed to pay all medical expenses in their divorce agreement, but he sent her a paper copy of what he claimed was the section of the agreement regarding medical expenses that said he only agreed to pay half. That was not what she remembered, but she could not find her own copies.

So, Jane contacted her attorney, but his office said he had moved his practice to another state and it would take some time to locate her documentation. They suggested she go to the county where it was recorded and ask their records archivist for copies.

Jane went to the county archives and was able to bring up a copy on their microfiche as the original documents had all been on paper, and so were preserved in that medium. But to her surprise she found that the copy her ex-husband had sent her was the same as what she found in these records.

She was baffled by this discrepancy, so she went back to her old attorney's office and asked them to keep looking for the original documents. A little time passed, but eventually they called her and said they had them and she could come in to pick them up.

When Jane did so, the mystery deepened because her recollection had been correct. The original documents from her attorney showed that her ex was responsible for the medical costs just as she had thought. She made an appointment with one of the new young lawyers at her previous attorney's office, and when she got there she explained the entire conundrum to her.

Her new attorney (let us call her Jill) looked everything over and thought about it for a while. Then she took the copies that our heroine had made from the microfiche and looked at them again very closely. She even took out a magnifying glass, and with their originals right next to the copies Jill compared them back and forth.

Finally, she looked up and said, "Jane, I think I know what's going on but we're going to have to get the actual original documents from the county archives to be sure."

Over the next few days, Jill took some time to visit the archives and do a search and eventually she was successful and found the original documents stored away deep in the archives. She brought them back to her office and called a different kind of forensics expert: one whose services were not needed as much anymore. His expertise was in validating the integrity of paper documents.

The next day, she called Jane and asked her to come in. They agreed to meet that afternoon.

When Jane arrived in Jill's office there was an older gentleman sitting there with two sets of documents in front of him, as well as several odd looking devices and vials. He introduced himself as Herman Everly and told Jane he was a documents expert.

Jill told him to go ahead, and he proceeded to demonstrate to Jane how he could tell that the originals from the archives had been tampered with, and even approximately how long ago.

With that the mystery was solved and a new lawsuit was born. The suit did not need to go far, though. As soon as Jill showed Jane's ex-husband's attorneys the report from her document expert, they quickly settled to avoid Jill's promise to press charges for fraud.

As these two cases illustrate, paper documentation created different issues that in some cases were easier to deal with and in some cases created confusion. In both cases, the experts made all the difference, and things could very well have gone the opposite way had those experts either been unavailable or less qualified.

Though we have moved to a world where nearly all documentation is electronic, the issues of relevance, integrity, and availability remain as important as ever. And they are now more difficult in many ways than they were in the past. There is a high level of expertise and training required to understand, analyze, and clearly explain whether electronic documentation is relevant to a case, is what it purports to be, has not been tampered with, and can be counted on to prove or disprove an assertion. In a later section on nonrepudiation and electronic evidence integrity, we will discuss this issue in even more detail.

1.4 Why and How This Affects the Practice of Law

Think about the very basic reason there is something called the "practice of law." Would you agree that at its most ideal it is meant to be a way to find the truth of a matter and serve justice? OK, if you have dealt with lawyers and lawsuits or other legal matters, you might be inclined to think otherwise, but for the sake of the argument let us agree the ideal is at least that the purpose of the law is to find the truth and mete out justice to the parties involved (Figure 1.8).

If we can agree to put aside our admittedly justified skepticism and work with that ideal definition, we can take some time to consider how this ideal is affected by the introduction of electronic evidence to the mix. OK—will you go there with me? Thanks.

So, to affect justice, a court of law has to establish, as best as possible, what happened, when it happened, how it happened, and to whom, or by whose actions.

Let's think about each of those points one at a time in the light of electronic evidence.

Figure 1.8   The point of litigation is to weigh the evidence and mete out justice.

How might one decide what happened using electronic data? There are myriad ways depending on the case, so let's look at some examples.

If you are lucky enough to live in one of those wonderful communities that adopted red light cameras and you get a ticket for going through a red light, the traffic court might use a digital photo of your license plate from your car to show that what happened was you did not make it through the intersection on time.

Sticking with your automobile, you may be aware (and will certainly be so by the time you finish this book) that almost all modern vehicles have computers installed that not only help your car or truck run right and save gas, but also keep track of a lot of the things your vehicle is doing, such as speed when you are in a crash, braking and steering, and even whether you had your seatbelt on. These data sets are increasingly being brought into court to prove or disprove culpability and liability issues.

If someone worked for an organization that developed some new experimental manufacturing product and signed a noncompete agreement, and then went to work for a competitor who suddenly began manufacturing the same product, the court or the complaining party (the plaintiff in a court case) might very well bring forward the electronic version of that agreement to prove their assertion of breach of contract.

What about establishing when something happened? Electronic evidence is possibly unique because in many cases there will automatically be a time stamp affixed to any type of electronic data. Even if that "metadata" with the time stamp is not actually part of a document or piece of data, there will most always be an application or device that created the data and whose log files will contain information that establishes the time and date on which the data were created, altered, moved, or even deleted.

Again, let's think of some examples. Say a person is accused of robbing a bank. The robbery took place at 1:35 P.M. on Monday afternoon. During the trial, the defendant's attorney is able to produce a video recording of his client buying Twinkies in a convenience store two towns away. The time stamp on the video tape shows 1:27 P.M. on Monday. The store is more than a half-hour away from the bank in the best of traffic. The time stamp has created a perfect alibi (unless the prosecutor can prove the time stamp is faulty or the video has been tampered with, but that gets into a whole different discussion on data integrity that I promise we get into later).

Or consider the noncompete agreement we talked about earlier. What if the employee was able to show that he had a more recent document releasing him from that contract with regard to a specific product? Again, this entire argument would revolve around the time the agreements were created, so the integrity and reliability of the time stamps or other time assertions would be paramount.

Finally, how something happened and to or by whom is quite often a question that will be answered by documentation, a photo and/or video evidence, and so forth. As long as there is the ability to prove the integrity of the data, the electronic evidence is likely to be of immense value and importance to proving or disproving the assertions of the parties in a case.

We are now seeing more and more research on ways to verify that electronic evidence has not been tampered with. In a report in an article from Duke University's *Duke Today* called "Was This Web Photo Altered?—New software for the Android phone tracks editing of images, then authenticates web postings,"* an application called YouProve is discussed. With this application loaded into a device, any changes made to an original are tracked and can be revealed later.

---

* *Duke Today*, Ashley Yeager, Was this web photo altered, November 3, 2011: http://today.duke.edu/2011/11/youprove. Retrieved April 11, 2011.

This issue of integrity is so important that we can look forward to much more research and many more applications to address it in the future.

Let's consider a few examples of this concept.

Think about an injury case being brought by a plaintiff who hurt himself when an elevator door closed on his leg.

The organization to which the elevator belonged might have video of the incident. There might be witnesses both for and against the claim who were in the elevator at the time or right outside. Any of them might have pictures or video of the incident that they took with their cell phones. The elevator maintenance company might have maintenance records or incident records. Any responding emergency organizations would have records, as will the plaintiff if he or she had any resultant medical procedures. All of these records would very likely be considered relevant and producible as evidence in court to try to establish what happened, when, and to whom.

If the integrity of any of those records can be proven or disproven by virtue of corroborating evidence, technology, forensic tools, and so forth, that will be extremely important to the parties involved.

Or consider a case where the defendant is accused of wrongful termination of an employee. Any human resource records relating to the employee's behavior would absolutely be relevant. Other electronic evidence that might be of interest might include

- Performance reviews by the employee's managers
- Records of when the employee logged into and out of his computer
- Records of when the employee went into or out of the building
- Records of the employee's personal Internet or telephone usage while at work
- Any disciplinary issue documentation

And finally, we can consider all of the recent issues that have arisen with alleged police use of force. Those events as well as protest events around the world are now showing up every day on the news. What is the most likely medium for those reports? Cell phone video, over and over again.

Now, it is imperative that attorneys understand these new tools that everyone owns and that inevitably create important evidence that can and will affect cases. Legal professionals must be competent and either have or hire expertise in all of the new social media, wearable computers, and mobile devices that are out there and in common use.

The bottom line for the legal profession is to have a good understanding of all the places and ways that possibly relevant electronic evidence can be stored, retrieved, preserved, and produced, and perhaps even more importantly, how to preserve and prove the integrity of that evidence.

1.5 How This Affects Business Organizations

If you own or manage a business, electronically stored information must be an integral part of your everyday existence.

Even if you chose to remain in the dark ages of paper and slide rules, your existence as a business is recorded electronically with the jurisdiction in which you are licensed. Your yearly payrolls, benefits, expenses, and so on, are all recorded electronically by your accountant and in your tax returns. Your employees may be commenting electronically on their satisfaction or lack thereof in their Facebook pages or blogs. Your customers are very likely keeping records of your transactions either for their own business or financial records, or online in comments or reviews.

It is more likely that you established yourself electronically and are using all of the wonderful electronic business tools available to you. Thereby you are creating electronic data all day every day that will be important to you in keeping records of your finances, profits and losses, expenses, payroll, benefits, intellectual property, contracts, provisioning, ordering, manufacturing, shipping, retail and wholesale costs, pricing, and so forth.

No matter what your business, you will likely be subject to records retention rules and accounting records requirements. And as noted before, anyone can end up in court under a myriad of circumstances, all of which will require you to understand your electronically stored information, know where it lives, who has control of it, and how to access, retrieve, and store it in a forensically sound manner.

Any organization that buys and sells using credit cards, for instance, is subject to the Payment Card Industry (PCI) standards. These include requirements around how and where you store and transport your customer's electronic credit card information. There are numerous other regulations, depending on the type of organization, with similar requirements. So, it is not just for the sake of being prepared for litigation that one should understand electronic data, but to comply with regulations.

And finally, every business, no matter its size or sector, must manage its records well in order to be efficient and profitable.

If you do not have a good records management process and policy in effect, you do not have the very foundation of all business management and practice. Everything we discussed before now can be either enhanced or degraded based entirely on the quality of that basic foundation of records management. It cannot be stated strongly enough how important a high-quality records management process is to any business, and the new world of electronic data that surrounds us adds to the complexity and challenge and especially to the importance of those practices.

So, as a business manager or owner it behooves you to understand the information we discuss in detail in this book.

1.6 Effects on Government Entities

Like businesses, government entities and the hardworking folks who serve in the public sector will have records retention rules they are subject to.

Because most all government organizations, at least in the developed countries, are beholden to their citizens and operate under the mantle of transparency, they also have a responsibility to maintain good electronic records. Under open government rules, they are responsible for producing records of their activities and business at the request of any constituent. They are also often subject to the auspices of auditing authorities.

And of course, they will almost without fail end up in court. So, once again it is absolutely imperative for government organizations to have a complete understanding and developed procedures of the electronic data they produce and store.

1.7 What This Might Mean to You as an Individual

As we discussed, each of us is surrounded by a growing magnitude of electronic information about ourselves, our families, our work, our hobbies, and so forth. Unless you managed to completely separate yourself from the modern world and stayed entirely off the grid of the current infrastructure, data about you and yours absolutely exist and are growing every day.

You have choices. You can exist in this fog of data in a state of blissful disinterest, and it will continue to grow around you and affect your life for good or bad. You can decide to take at least a little interest and responsibility and do your best to control what is generated, or at least understand it. Or you can really take the time and energy to both understand all of the different types of information that are generated and actively maintain and manage that data.

Of course, this book advocates for the latter course. That is because the very premise of this book is that individuals, just like the organizations, management, and attorneys we spoke of earlier, both have a responsibility and will gain an advantage by virtue of their understanding, monitoring, and management of the data that affect them.

Here are some examples that illustrate that premise. You as an individual are as subject as any organization to a lawsuit. You might also be subject to law enforcement action, credit qualification, qualification for education or for a high-security job, or even a simple background check for a job in the public sector (say as a teacher) or as a volunteer in a school.

In all of these cases, it is nearly certain that electronic data about you and your history, family, associations, former jobs, hobbies, and so forth, will be examined and evaluated. The information that is recorded and presented in these cases could make the difference between your winning or losing a case, being prosecuted for something you did not do, getting a loan, being accepted into college, getting a new job, or being allowed to volunteer at your children's school.

In a court case reported in the November 2011 *ABA Journal*,* a divorcing couple's attorneys were ordered to exchange their passwords for their Facebook and online dating sites. So, data that you create online might very well end up in court, even some of that most embarrassing type.

---

* *ABA Journal*, Privacy Law, Debra Cassens Weiss, Judge orders exchange of facebook and dating website passwords in custody fight, November 8, 2011: http://www.abajournal.com/news/article/judge_orders_exchange_of_facebook_and_dating_website_passwords_in_custody_f/?utm_source=maestro&utm_medium=email&utm_campaign=weekly_email. Retrieved May 6, 2011.

Many of these examples are perhaps somewhat sobering and might make you fear for your privacy. But in an article from NPR online* we see a great example of how this technology and storage of your information is being used for important research.

In the article titled "Swipe a Loyalty Card, Help a Food Detective," the author talks about how the Centers for Disease Control and Prevention and other public health workers can use information stored on grocery store loyalty cards to identify the sources of food poisoning outbreaks. By asking victims' permission to check their electronic records, these researchers were able to find out specifically what groceries they purchased, compare them to the purchases of other victims, and thereby discover the source of the poisoning.

Another example to think about is the use of your stored electronic records for your budget, your accounting for taxes, or even the archiving and storage of important pictures, journals, or any of the other myriad records you create. These electronic records can be extremely important to you emotionally, or for financial accountability and maintenance. Understanding where and how those records are created and stored might very well mean the difference between being able to recover or preserve them when required or just desired.

So, I encourage you to read on and learn all you can about this new world of electronic media.

Everyone has a very real stake in understanding and managing this huge new source of data about themselves, their businesses, or their clients. Hopefully, this book and the chapters that follow can assist you in that understanding.

---

* Nancy Shute, Swipe a loyalty card, help a food detective!, November 17, 2011: http://www.npr.org/blogs/thesalt/2011/11/17/142470536/swipe-a-loyalty-card-help-a-food-detective. Retrieved November 20, 2011.

2

TRANSLATING GEEK
Information Technology versus Everyone Else

2.1 Introduction

In the first chapter, we discussed and established the ways electronically stored information (ESI) changed the world we live in. We looked at how it changed the legal landscape and thus can have a real and long-lasting impact on all of us.

All of that electronically stored information is most often managed and maintained by those wonderful folks in the information technology (IT) field of endeavor. These men and women work on many different types of tasks to ensure that the computer-enabled conveniences and efficiencies that we have all come to depend on continue to work seamlessly (Figure 2.1).

This is a gargantuan challenge, yet many of us do not even realize the amount of work that is constantly going on behind the scenes in the world of IT. And these folks have a lexicon all their own. They speak "geek."

They can and should be one of your most important allies in your ability to manage, understand, locate, acquire, and preserve electronic evidence. In this chapter, we consider their role and perspective and discover the secrets to working with and for them to ensure the best possible outcomes when dealing with ESI.

2.2 Role of IT

As noted above, everything we do these days depends more and more on the ubiquitous IT infrastructure that enables all of our systems and conveniences.

Figure 2.1 Information technology professionals are important allies when dealing with electronic evidence.

Walk through a typical day in your life and think about all of the ways that you interact with technology and computers.

Some of those are obvious, of course. You open your e-mail, or you check on your friend's status on a social media platform. You write reports or fill in spreadsheets for work, and so on.

But there are limitless numbers of other ways that you might not have even considered. So let's take a look.

Your alarm goes off in the morning. Most modern alarm clocks or clock radios these days have some computer technology inside of them that stores your preferences for the sound you want to hear, or just keeps the time correctly. They might also be connected to your media player so you can listen to tunes from your iPod or other MP3 player. But even beyond those obvious possibilities, the electricity running your alarm is entirely dependent on an infrastructure controlled by computers. The hopefully uninterrupted flow of electrical energy to your home on which so many things depend is dependent on a myriad of computer devices (Figure 2.2).

Those computers are integral to every step of the electrical infrastructure:

They control the generation of electricity at the dams or coal or nuclear power plants or solar and wind farms.

They regulate the flow of electricity over and through the grid to maintain the proper levels of power.

They communicate between the different controlling mechanisms in order to coordinate, monitor, and regulate the flow of electricity.

Figure 2.2 Nearly everything we depend on all day long is dependent on the electricity infrastructure.

They allow communications between power traders to enable different markets to buy and sell power where it is needed or where there is excess.

They have many more detailed controls, monitors, and systems that enable this incredibly complex and vital infrastructure to keep working.

So, right away, when that alarm goes off, you tapped into and depended on one of the most sophisticated and important IT systems.

Of course as your day progresses, that electronic infrastructure will be vital to nearly every moment in your life. The eggs you eat for breakfast were kept cold in your refrigerator powered by electricity; the toast is toasted in an electronic toaster. The lights and heat or air conditioning in your home came from that same grid.

Now, this might seem obvious and beyond the point of this book. But in fact as these electronic systems become "smarter" and even more connected to each other through IT, they begin to contain more and more information about your lifestyle and data that might even be discoverable and useful if you or someone else wants to prove something about your life.

For instance, even now, without the great details that are becoming available with smarter meters and grids, there have been cases where power consumption records have been used in court to show the possibility of someone using their home as a marijuana garden. Growing such a crop indoors requires large lights, fans, cooling systems, and so forth, that can be indicated by a larger than normal power bill.

As these technologies become more sophisticated, they are able to be accessed for information on specific uses of electricity in your home and work. The upside of this is an ability to better control the flow of power and regulate conservation efforts. The possible downside might be the ability of utilities and government organizations to pinpoint the specific uses of power and use that information as part of a profile of your life and lifestyle.

But that is just electricity, and I think we can all agree that going through your day, that particular connection to IT will persist and be integral to everything you do, unless you somehow managed to get yourself far up into the wilderness and off the grid (in which case you are unlikely to be reading this book).

Let's keep going and consider the other connections to IT and thus to electronic records as you go through your day.

So, you got through breakfast and headed out the door. Before you did, you might have taken a moment to check the television or your computer to see how the traffic looks or to check the news. That is another connection to IT. Those traffic reports are entirely dependent on computers that are located throughout the highway and transportation infrastructure and that feed back to computer modeling systems to create those traffic maps (Figure 2.3).

And, again, with current television and computer logging technology, there is very likely to be a record kept on those devices that could show what you chose to look at before heading out the door.

Of course televisions are now going all digital, so they are again just a computer system that receives digital signals and translates them to a big screen for your viewing pleasure. As they have gone digital they also created more possibilities of data storage and in some cases will store your preferences, record shows for you, and maintain connections to your computer networks.

So, you make it into your car and start it up. All modern cars now run with computers that regulate the fuel flow, braking systems, performance, emissions, and much more. These all create records that an automobile technician can access for troubleshooting. Newer vehicles also include navigation, security, locks, and controls for lights, horns, and even heating and cooling that can be accessed remotely via the

Figure 2.3 Being able to know how the traffic looks can help you make decisions about when (or whether) to leave.

Internet and a wireless or Bluetooth connection. In fact, some of the latest hacking demonstrations show ways that hackers can gain access to these systems in a car and open the doors, turn the lights off and on, honk the horn, and so forth. And of course, coming soon to a highway near you—driverless cars! All IT all the time.

As we noted in the first chapter, these records from vehicles are being used in court to show culpability or establish liability for an accident. So again, you are in the midst of creating electronic evidence that might well become important to your life.

As we move more and more into the world of computers being a part of everything we do, we have to be aware that with all those fun and exciting conveniences and applications comes the other side of the coin. We also create vulnerabilities and records of our day-to-day lives. The newest computer systems in cars contain records of where you were, what you listened to, and even how many people were in the car and how much luggage you stored (based on weight, stopping distances, etc.). As noted, they are able to record things like how close you were to other vehicles and do a pretty good job of establishing fault in an accident.

This information could be very important and could be data that you might welcome or regret, depending on your situation and perspective.

Before we leave the car, there is one other source of data created as you drive to work. In many cities throughout the United States and in other countries, there are license capture cameras. These are meant to be used by law enforcement to be able to track down terrorists or criminals, or even to search for missing persons.

However, it has been established that in fact all of the data collected from those cameras, and possibly from tolling systems or other traffic control and surveillance systems, are being collected and stored electronically in a database.

Law enforcement can access that database to look for a fugitive or a child abductor. In a recent article in the *ABA Journal*,* it was noted that in one case police sent more patrol cars into an area when they noticed rival gangs' vehicles converging.

Even though there are legitimate and important uses for these surveillance tools, you need to be aware that this is yet another source of information being created about you as you move through your day.

Of course, if you are carrying a smartphone or tablet, records are also being kept about where that device is at all times. Those records exist for the purpose of being able to find a lost device or to serve you local advertising and services, but again they are created and could be used to track where you travel.

Let's say you are a bus or train rider instead of a driver and head to your bus stop to commute to work. Nearly all of those mass transit systems are completely regulated and monitored by computers now. In order to keep them running on time and safe, there are transportation management systems tracking every train and bus. Often these will include GPS systems, digital cameras both on the vehicles and on the

---

* *ABA Journal*, Privacy Law, Debra Cassens Weiss, DC police scan and store license plate images; ACLU suggests need for a warrant, November 21, 2011: http://www.abajournal.com/news/article/d.c._police_snap_and_store_license_plate_images_aclu_suggests_need_for_a_wa/?utm_source=maestro&utm_medium=email&utm_campaign=tech_monthly. Retrieved November 26, 2011.

roads, and other electronic monitoring tools that allow controllers to keep track of every vehicle, track, or roadway and warn operators of problems or assist when something comes up.

In our area, we use a transit card that we pay for on a yearly basis to pay our fares. Those create records of each time they are used, so there is now another record of where you were and how much time you spend commuting and how often you use mass transit. Once again, this can have important and valuable uses for planning and coordination of transportation, but it also might be used to demonstrate your movements.

Let's not forget that the roads and highways and railways are also being monitored, maintained, and regulated by transportation control systems that rely entirely on computers.

The lights and signs that regulate traffic, as well as traffic cameras that monitor and troubleshoot traffic issues, all depend on computer systems and software. All of those create records that might be of importance to a legal case or simply to an understanding of what happened in a certain instance. They might be used to solve a crime, track a missing person, establish fault in an accident, or many other uses.

So, we made it to our workplace finally and there are probably only a few hundred megabytes of data that would demonstrate every move we made since that alarm went off. Let's add some more.

Time for a cup of coffee or tea, wouldn't you say? Once again, the world is changing and more records and IT are coming into play.

Now, if you are so old-fashioned as to actually use cash to pay for your latte, you might avoid creating a record of your own preferences. However, there will definitely be a record created in nearly every case. Almost without fail, the accounting systems used by businesses rely on computers to track their sales. These computers are now tied directly into the registers that take your order, so that latte has been recorded.

But if you, like so many others, use a debit card or a prepaid card from the store you are buying from, electronic records are absolutely created that relate directly to your habits (Figure 2.4). And now, with new applications that allow you to use your smartphones for purchases, you can directly create computer records of everything you buy. Believe me when I tell you that those records are monitored and maintained as marketing tools and might well be requested or required as producible electronic evidence in a court case.

Figure 2.4 Every time you purchase something with a credit or debit card, another electronic record is created.

So, with that latte, you have more than likely tapped into your banking system. The financial infrastructure that we all depend on for storing, maintaining, regulating, and securing our money is again entirely dependent on computers.

Computers track the flow of funds, regulate interest rates and trading, allow you access to your banking information, and with ATMs give you access to cash and information as well.

Again, smart phones are now being used with new applications that allow you to transfer funds, pay your bills, or just monitor your accounts. Records of all your transactions are stored on these little computers and once again can provide a very detailed look at your actions throughout the day.

It is finally time to head into work. If you work in a building with any kind of security, you may have an access card to get into the building or onto your floor or into your work area (or maybe all of those). Those access cards connect to a computer system that tracks your entrances and in some cases your exits as well.

There may well be closed-circuit security cameras anywhere along your route to work or even in your work space. Again, these are tied into computer systems for storage and monitoring, and records are created.

As we already noted, once you sit down at your computer you are creating records of when you arrived and logged in, where you go on the Internet, the e-mail or instant messaging you might take part in, and everything else you do on the computer.

If you go out for lunch and pay with a debit card, you are again plugging into the financial system computers, and your movements are recorded through your access cards and possibly security cameras.

Maybe you decide to go work out at your gym instead. Once again, nearly all organizations will use computers to track when you use their facilities. If you have a membership card, it might be scanned or otherwise recorded and another computer record is created.

Perhaps you are heading off on a business trip, so off you go to the airport. If you take a taxi or an airport van or limousine, their dispatch is all controlled by computers that will have a new record of your trip.

Of course, all airlines rely on computers for ticketing, and the airport will have a wide variety of computer-operated security and monitoring systems that create another set of records as you move through on the way to your flight.

The flight is coordinated, monitored, and regulated by computer-enabled control systems, and more electronic records are created.

Modern airplanes are more and more controlled by computer systems for navigation, speed, autopilot, and so forth. In fact, some of the new jets "fly by wire" and the only job of the pilot is to program the instructions for the computers and monitor what they do (Figure 2.5).

At the end of your day, all of the above activities will happen in reverse as you head home. Maybe you stop at the store for groceries and use your loyalty card to get a discount. Computers will record

Figure 2.5   All air travel begins with, is controlled by, and ends with computer records.

your transactions including what you purchased and how often you have been there.

When you finally arrive at home, you may have one of those nifty smart homes. So, the heat is turned up, the lights turned on, and dinner is warming in the oven. Your refrigerator may be set up to notice that you are getting low on milk and might send you an e-mail, or even order the milk for you in some cases! This new "Internet of Everything," as it has been called, creates a whole new level of data collection, mining, and analysis that can be used for good or ill.

As with all of these computerized systems and conveniences, there are good uses and possibly bad uses that you should be aware of and consider.

This walk-through of your day-to-day life is an illustration of the many ways that you interact with computers and IT, even when you are not sitting at a keyboard. The point as it relates to this book is that each of these interactions creates records that might at some point be important and require you to gain access to them.

To do so, you will need to communicate with the folks who work with IT and find a way to work with them. That will require that you either speak geek yourself, or have an interpreter to assist you with those communications.

For those of you reading this book who are in the IT field, your task is to be able to assist everyone else when they need this type of access. Your job will be to translate that geek in a way that they can understand so they are able to use the data that you created and maintained for them.

In the rest of this chapter we look at the perspective of those in this industry, how they can be an ally, and finally some tips on translating geek.

2.3 Information Technologist's Perspective

The world of IT is a vast and complex arena that includes networks, hardware and software, telecommunications, audio and video, application development, Internet systems, information security, and much more. Each of these areas of specialty requires of their practitioners differing levels of understanding, training, tools, and expertise.

These practitioners range from those in the trenches who are dealing with operational-level issues, troubleshooting, and setup and maintenance, to the other end of the spectrum at the level of chief information officers (CIOs) who are overseeing and managing all of the logistical, budgetary, and business considerations around the IT systems for an organization.

In a mature and relatively large organization there might be any or all of the following within the IT department:

1. Service technicians who do troubleshooting, maintenance, and repair of computers, servers, printers, and network systems
2. Service desk staff who handle user problems either remotely via a network or in person
3. Network management staff who monitor and maintain specific network hardware and monitoring tools
4. Messaging specialists who monitor, maintain, and manage e-mail, instant messaging, and other messaging systems
5. Wiring technicians who make the connections and run the wiring as required
6. Telecommunications specialists who monitor, maintain, and troubleshoot telephone systems including both landlines and cell phones
7. Data center staff who monitor and maintain the hardware, cooling, and electrical systems in larger data centers or server farms
8. Backup technicians who monitor and maintain tape or other backup systems and software
9. Web technicians who monitor, maintain, and design a company's Web presence
10. Application developers who create, test, and disseminate new applications
11. Database managers who design, develop, and maintain the databases of information on which the organization depends
12. Project managers and engineers who design and develop new systems or update older ones
13. Trainers who instruct users on the use of new applications or any computer software the organization uses

14. Records management staff who manage retention policies and assist employees and the organization in the legal or regulatory retention and management of records
15. Information security specialists who monitor IT traffic, develop and enforce policy, train staff on online safety, investigate compromises or employee malfeasance, assist with data retention and recovery, maintain security devices, manage regulatory requirements and security testing, and develop and initiate security strategy
16. Human resource, administrative, and financial staff who support the IT department
17. Cyber risk managers who assess and strategize about ways to mitigate information security risks
18. Security architects who assist the network staff in designing a secure and safe network
19. Incident response teams who monitor the network and respond to data compromise or attacks
20. Computer forensics specialists who are responsible for the preservation, analysis, and production of computer evidence
21. Managers and executive leadership for all of the above

Of course, in smaller organizations, any or all of these roles might be handled by a few people or outsourced to contractors.

The point of enumerating these different roles that come under the title of IT is to impress upon you that there are a myriad of areas of expertise and thus myriad numbers and types of people involved in any IT system.

Each of these specific types of information technologists will have their own language with which they communicate to their peers and with which they manage their day-to-day tasks. A layperson who does not do that type of work, even a person who is in a different part of the IT organization, may very well have no way of understanding what is being discussed or how to communicate with those technicians (Figure 2.6).

From the perspective of information technologists, there are specific problems and tasks that they have to accomplish every day, and the knowledge and language that they and their peers bring to each of those tasks can be very specialized. This is absolutely

Figure 2.6 The technologists might seem to be speaking a different language, but they understand it.

necessary and appropriate in order for them to communicate and work effectively.

Yet there will always be times when someone who is not a part of their specialty will need to understand what they are doing. It might be one of the engineers or project managers who is trying to find new and better ways to run the business. Or it might be someone from a different area of the IT spectrum who needs to coordinate with them for some reason. It might be the managers, executives, or accountants who need to create a business case for budgeting and strategic planning. Or it could be the security specialists who need to understand what might have happened within a system in order to analyze a compromise or develop logical and effective policies.

It could also be the legal counsel or auditors who need to acquire important information and electronic evidence for a legal action or audit.

In any of those cases, the technician may have difficulty finding a way to translate their everyday concepts into a language that someone who is not familiar with those concepts can understand. From their point of view, the systems and language they work with look obvious and clear, but that can be hard to get across to others without some effort and excellent communications skills.

Unfortunately, those skills are not typically taught or even valued in the realms of IT training and recruiting. There are some technologists who chose that career specifically because they were more comfortable working with computers than with people, and whose people skills are thereby relatively lacking.

However, as we are beginning to understand, in this ever more IT-dependent world, these folks are integral to everything we do. Thus, it is important for us to find a way to communicate clearly with and among IT staff of all stripes.

2.4 Information Technology as an Ally

We walked through a typical day in any of our lives and we jumped into the world of information technologists to look at things from their point of view.

The point of all of this was to help us understand how and why these folks can and must be our allies when we attempt to manage our electronic data.

When we get into later chapters and start looking carefully at all of the places data can be stored and from which electronic evidence might need to be acquired, it will become even more obvious that the men and women in the IT field are, in the end, the key to accessing that information. These folks have the day-to-day interactions with that data. They create, monitor, and maintain the systems on which the data are generated and stored.

No one understands better than they how and where the data are maintained. If we have a need to access, acquire, recover, store, or manage any electronically stored information, we will absolutely rely on these folks as our allies in that task.

So, taking the information in this chapter to heart, it behooves all of us to become familiar with as many of these parts of our organization as possible and to understand as best we can their areas of expertise and access.

It is neither important nor possible to become an expert in all of these fields. Yet it is necessary to understand all of the different fields of expertise enough so that we can make the necessary connections and use at least some of the right terms in a way that communication becomes possible.

One way to accomplish this in an organization is to find people who are competent at translating geek. Find people who understand the technology, but who also understand budget, law, records management, supply chain, and other important parts of your business. Either locate or train these folks with excellent communications skills in both public speaking and writing as the liaisons between your IT staff and the rest of your organization.

If yours is a small organization or if this is a need of yours in your personal life, it may be your job to become a competent and skilled translator of geek. If so, read on, and as we end this chapter, we offer some tips on translating geek.

2.5 Translating Geek

So, how does one go about learning to translate geek, or where do you find these folks who might be your organization's all-important translators? In this section, we take a look at those two questions and consider things you can do to create these important liaisons within your organization.

First, think about ways you can understand more about both sides of this language barrier. You already made a good start by virtue of having started this book. The concepts and ideas we discuss in detail will go a long way toward allowing you a better understanding of both the legal side of the issues and the IT side.

Once you begin to get a better idea of the what, where, and how of electronic evidence, you will be well on your way to understanding how to assist your IT and legal staff in working together.

But you can learn even more by paying attention to the sources of information that IT folks count on to keep themselves up to date. At the end of this book, an extensive list of resources is presented in Appendix I. One section is a list of some of the more accessible books, magazines, websites, and online magazines or blogs about IT and information security that you should start spending time with. By reading and checking those on a regular basis, you will begin to pick up the lingo and understand the concepts that IT professionals use every day.

Also listed in the resources you will find references to information about recent legal rulings as well as some good primers on the law and how it works. Again, by spending some time with these resources, you can begin to educate yourself and become the valuable liaison that your organization needs.

However, if you are not motivated to take on this new role yourself, maybe you would rather look for others in your organization who

Figure 2.7   The person who can take on the task of translating geek will be of huge value for an organization.

might have this level of understanding and be able to take on this role (Figure 2.7).

There are a couple of possible sources I would suggest. First, connect with your legal department or outside counsel. Check with them to see if they have people on staff who have a good understanding of IT and electronic evidence issues.

This is definitely an area that is becoming more important and many law firms and legal organizations are beginning to either hire or train staff to take on that role. Often you will find that younger paralegals or lawyers who have been raised in our new world of ubiquitous electronics will be naturals for this role.

The other source is within your IT organization. Here you will be looking for folks who are excellent communicators and enjoy learning. These are the people who are likely to be willing and able to take on the task of learning about the legal side of things and bridge the communications gaps. They may well have already begun to consider these ideas, and in any case, if they are good at speaking and writing, they will have the beginning skills required to take on this role.

Skilled and experienced project managers can fit these criteria as it is often part of their job to create and communicate a plan to a wide variety of stakeholders, so check out those folks in your organization as possibilities.

In any case, it behooves all of us to find or become this liaison for the betterment of our organizations. Translating geek is a specialized but also a very important role that will continue to be of extremely high value.

3

WHERE IS ELECTRONICALLY STORED INFORMATION? IT'S EVERYWHERE!

3.1 Introduction

Electronically stored information (ESI) surrounds us like an ever-deepening fog or an overwhelming flood (Figure 3.1). Look around yourself right now as you sit here reading this book. If you are reading it online, you are immersed in the most obvious world of electronic information, the computer, and the immense worldwide network we call the Internet.

Even if you are reading it on old-fashioned tree fiber, I bet you can find several items within your immediate vicinity that are storing electronic data. Go ahead, I'll wait.

OK, welcome back—how many did you find? Here are a few I can see from here. My cell phone, my desk telephone, my watch, USB thumb drives, CDs, DVDs, and (yes, I still have them) floppy disks. Of course, I also know that in my drawer I have a laptop and an external drive that contain a bunch of data. And that's only talking about the physical locations within my reach.

Now, because of my work, I may be more inundated than you are by these devices. But I can safely say that within reach of my desk I have immediate near-line access to terabytes of electronic information, and that is not counting the Internet, or my organization's network, backup tapes, and so forth. That's just what I can literally touch. When you add in the rest of the online universe, the numbers are staggering and growing exponentially.

As citizens in this electronic universe, we all need to understand where these data live and how to find the data, especially if we are responsible for managing that data or preserving it for legal or compliance reasons.

Figure 3.1   In our current world of ever-expanding electronics, we are all inundated with data.

In this chapter, we look in much greater depth at many of the different locations, both physical and logical, where electronic information resides. We discuss the types of data and how data are created, stored, and accessed. In Chapter 5, we talk about the processes you need to understand to preserve or manage all of the different types and locations of data.

Before we start with that, I think a basic description of what electronic data is and how it works is in order. Now, before you start worrying, I promise to make this relatively simple and to the point. No engineering degree is required. So carry on without trepidation.

3.2 Basics

The first thing to understand about electronic data is that anything stored in a digital device is represented by ones and zeros. Those ones and zeros are created by electronic pulses that are either positive or negative. I promised not to get too geeky, so we do not get into the engineering any further than that, but this is important to understand, so you realize that everything we talk about later is based on nothing more than these electronic pulses of energy that are translated by the computer's processors into ones and zeros.

Each one or zero is called a bit. If you put eight of those bits together into a row, they are called a byte. For some purposes, each byte is divided into two parts of four bits each that are called nibbles.

Are you noting a theme here? It is my theory that the inventors of this system spent way too much time playing with electrical pulses and forgot to order out. In the process, they got very hungry and that caused them to be distracted when they got around to naming these parts.

Computer data are coded in binary language—meaning simply a mathematical language that only uses two (thus the "bi" in binary) symbols—you guessed it, ones and zeros! Each nibble of data can be (and they usually are) translated into hexadecimal or decimal numbers for programming purposes. The hexadecimal mathematical language uses 16 characters—0, 1, 2, 3, 4, 5, 6, 7, 8, 9, A, B, C, D, E, F—and the decimal language or code is the one we are used to which runs from 0 to 9.

Note, however, that the binary code, the hexadecimal, or the decimal do not ever have a two-character number as part of their basic characters. That makes sense if you think about it in terms of the mathematical language we are most familiar with, decimal.

Decimal code is what is known as base-10. You use 10 characters, starting with 0 and going up to 9. Then, to increment further, you start over again with zero but prepend a one, so you have 10. Thus, the first character on the far right of a decimal number equals the number of ones, or that character multiplied by one. The second character will equal the number of tens; the next character will be the number of 100s, and so on.

Binary works the same way, but because you have only two characters to work with (base-2), every increment is a multiple of two. So, the first character on the far right of the number is the number of ones, the second character is the number of twos, the third is the number of fours, the next is the number of eights, the next sixteens, and so forth.

With hexadecimal, you now have 16 possible characters (base-16) so you are operating in multiples of 16. For instance, the first 10 characters, 0 to 9, have a value that matches their number, but the character A is equal to 10 (in decimal notation), B is 11, C is 12, D is 13, E is 14, and F is 15. Then, to increment to the next number, you go back to 0 prepended with a one, but 10 in hexadecimal does not equal 10 in decimal (of course). The first character on the right

Decimal	Hexadecimal	Binary
0	0	0
1	1	01
2	2	10
3	3	11
4	4	100
5	5	101
6	6	110
7	7	111
8	8	1000
9	9	1001
10	A	1010
11	B	1011
12	C	1100
13	D	1101
14	E	1110
15	F	1111
16	10	10000
17	11	10001
18	12	10010
19	13	10011
20	14	10100

Figure 3.2   Decimal to hex to binary conversion table.

is the number of ones as always, but because we are using a base-16 language, the next character to its left will be the number of sixteens. The number to its left will be the number of 256s (16 × 16), the next will be the number of 4096s (16 × 256), and so on. Figure 3.2 compares the three mathematical languages used for recording or coding digital information.

Hopefully, this is beginning to make some logical sense. The reason this is important is because if you are ever in the position to have to actually look at digital data in its most basic form, it will probably be represented in hexadecimal notation. Behind that coding are the basic ones and zeros of binary code that the computer processors work with to create and manipulate the information that you see on your screen or that is used to run your programs.

Now, consider for a moment why those hungry engineers would have chosen to use hexadecimal notation instead of decimal or just the binary code. Think back to the beginning of this section when we were first digging into the culinary ideas of bits and bytes and nibbles. Notice anything about those sets of numbers? Yes, I bet all of you smart people are way ahead of me—eight bits in a byte, four bits in a nibble—a base-16 notation system gives you a nice way to represent those nibbles one at a time, thus shortening the notation you need to use for programming.

Did you notice in Figure 3.2 that the end of the base-16 hexadecimal characters corresponds nicely with the end of the four character strings in the binary code? Guess what that means to those hungry engineers when they need a shorthand for each of their nibbles? You guessed it—they simply translate each nibble into its hexadecimal equivalent, and voila!, they have a nice shorthand. For instance, say they want to code the byte 1011 0001. In hexadecimal, that would be: B1 (you can look that up in Figure 3.2)—B in hex equals 1011 in binary, and 1 in hex equals 0001 (we add the extra padding zeros so it will be a nice four-character nibble).

At this point, you as an astute and thoughtful reader may be saying to yourself, "OK, that's all fine and good, but how does 1011 0001 get translated into words or symbols that I can read on a screen, or that those programmers can use to make applications run?"

I'm glad you asked, because that's an equally interesting part of the puzzle that it is important to understand.

In order for computers to communicate with each other in a language, they needed to have a way to encode letters, numbers, and even some basic communication commands using these binary codes.

Way back in the early days of electronic communications, these types of characters were encoded using dots and dashes over radio or telephone lines—some of you may have even heard of and remember Morse code. There were many different types of electronic communications codes used during the early days of electronic communications, but the one we are interested in was developed in the 1960s and was based on teleprinter coding.*

---

* The history of printing. http://inventors.about.com/od/pstartinventions/a/printing. htm. Retrieved February 12, 2011.

The standards committee that developed it decided that seven bits were the optimal number of units to code everything they needed to code, and that an eighth bit would be allowed for error checking. Thus the codes fit perfectly into the bytes that computers were using.

These codes basically created a standard that used a byte of binary code to correspond to upper- and lowercase letters, numbers, symbols, and communications control codes. The standard is called the American Standard Code for Information Interchange (ASCII).*

So, without getting any deeper into the engineering of computer communications, suffice it to say that everything you see on your computer screen; all the data that will be important if you need to capture, organize, preserve, and produce electronic data; all the coding that runs the applications that allowed you to create that data or locate or look at that data; basically everything that happens inside of a digital device all depend on those bits and bytes of information and the way they are organized.

As you probably figured out by now, data storage on a computer is often referred to with terms that end in the word bytes. Or you may have heard it referred to without the "bytes" part and wondered what megs and gigs were.

Well, think about those bytes of data. As you can imagine, it takes quite a few of those to create a sentence, or a section of code. If you put a thousand of them together, it would be a pretty good number to start with, wouldn't it? Well, there you go—1000 bytes is a kilo of bytes, better known as a kilobyte.

One thing I need to make clear, however, so I do not get in trouble with the geeks out there, is that a kilobyte is not actually 1000 bytes. If we were dealing with decimal notation that would work, but because this is binary, we have to use binary notation and binary math. So, a kilobyte is symbolized by 2 to the 10th power (2^{10}), which adds up to 1,024 bytes. A megabyte would be 2 to the 20th power, which equals 1,048,576 bytes. So, the numbers we talk about are not exact, but they are close enough to give you the idea.

There is a quote that has often been attributed to Bill Gates (but that he vehemently denies ever making) that 640 [kilobytes of storage]

---

* The debut of ASCII. http://edition.cnn.com/TECH/computing/9907/06/1963. idg/index.html. Retrieved February 12, 2011.

should be enough for anybody.* Whether he ever really said such a thing is unlikely, but it is worth recognizing that way back when, this much storage seemed like quite a bit. At one time, 640,000 (or so) pieces of information probably seemed like plenty.

But, it was not long before we started talking in terms of megabytes or one million bytes (actually 2^{20}, as noted above). That might seem like it would be a lot, but these days, if you told someone you had a hard drive with one megabyte of storage, they would laugh in disbelief that such a tiny amount of storage could even exist. It is impossible to find a hard drive with any amount of megabytes of storage these days because we kept running out of room and we had to move up again.

The next step is gigabytes—or 1 billion (plus) bytes. All modern hard drives are listed with capacities of gigabytes. In fact, at the time of this writing, it is nearly impossible to find a hard drive with less than 250 gigabytes of storage. Drives with 500 gigabytes are available for under $80, and in fact my favorite computer store recently had a sale on 1 terabyte (1 trillion [plus] bytes) drives for less than $50 and 3 terabyte drives for less than $130.

Now, I have to admit that I hesitated to emphasize those numbers above because of something called Moore's Law that predicted that the number of transistors that could be placed in a computer (thus the size and capacity of the computer system) would double every 2 years. This has in fact proven to be true and is expected to continue for some years to come. Thus, the numbers that seem pretty amazing right now will no doubt be blasé to folks who might be reading this book in years or even months to come.

But that's as it should be. Understand that way back in the dark ages of 2016, a terabyte hard drive for under $50 was a pretty exciting thing to a geek.

One final idea we need to understand before moving on—and that is the difference between volatile and nonvolatile types of data storage. All these bytes of information are stored in your computing devices in one of two ways (and often both). As you are working on a document or in an application on your computer, data about the application and data you are creating are most often stored in what is referred

---

* Bill Gates: "I never said 640K should be enough." https://groups.google.com/group/
  alt.folklore.computers/msg/99ce4b0555bf35f4?pli=1. Retrieved February 12, 2011.

to as memory. You may have heard it called RAM, which stands for random-access memory. This storage is available much faster than the data stored on your hard drive, so it is used by applications as dynamic or volatile storage. It is faster for the very reason that it is volatile. It is stored electronically in bytes of electronic impulses but not "written" onto media as it is on a hard drive or other storage device. Because I promised not to get too deep into the engineering, let's just use an example.

As I write this sentence, the word processing application that I am using has placed this information into volatile memory so that it is easily shown on the screen and available for me to see and edit. It does so by holding electronic charges that represent those ones and zeros we talked about earlier. However, the electricity that holds those charges and keeps them available on the memory is only available when there is power being provided to the memory "sticks." These so-called sticks are usually sets of computer chips mounted on a rectangular plastic card that slips into slots on the computer's main or "mother" board.

The computer has also placed some application commands and coding into that memory such as processes and services that allow my computer and, more specifically, my word processor application to respond to my requests quickly.

In order to preserve this information so I can use it again after I have finished writing and turned off the word processor, I have to choose to save this document. When I do so, my word processor's programming takes the data that make up this document and makes a copy of that data on my hard drive. It does so by changing the magnetic positive and negative pulses of electricity on the media of my hard drive in patterns of bytes that represent everything on this document. That includes all the words, spaces, symbols, graphics, and so forth. But it also includes something that is very important to understand—metadata.

Metadata are basically data about these data. In the case of this document, that would include information about when it was created and by whom, when it was edited and last saved, the number of characters, where it is saved on the drive (its address), and so forth. Metadata are very important to understand when talking about electronic information, so we return to that later in this book.

Now, if my computer shuts down unexpectedly before I have a chance to save this document to the hard drive, all the work I have done will disappear. That is because it is stored in volatile memory that goes away when you either shut down the computer or close the application. As any one of you who has had that happen to you will attest, that is a very upsetting thing. It has happened to me, even while writing this book, and I was not a very happy person!

We will spend more time talking about memory and hard drives and other types of storage media, but it is enough for now to understand that there is a difference in how the data are kept in those types of storage and that if it is volatile storage, it only lasts as long as the application that created it is running. Within milliseconds of closing down an application or turning off your computer, everything that was stored in memory fades away to nothing because the power that preserved that memory was removed.

So, there you have it—your entire Computer Communications 101 course and all in a few easy-to-digest pages. Probably less than four kilobytes of digital information. With this basic understanding of what is under the hood, you are ready to begin looking at the ways and places that data are stored.

3.3 Database Systems

Databases can be hosted in many different configurations. There are relatively simple databases created with programs like Microsoft Access or FoxPro and more complex ones created within sophisticated database applications such as Oracle or MySQL. You can even create a database in a spreadsheet program such as Microsoft Excel.

But databases are extremely important to understand because nearly every type of application you will interact with on a computer or the Internet will use some type of database to organize and manage your user experience and the data you create (Figure 3.3).

A database is simply defined as any organized collection of datum that has a relationship with each other. An Excel spreadsheet with a table of columns and rows of values could be defined as a very simple "flat" database.

More complex databases are made up of more than one table that are related to each other in some fashion, usually through a common

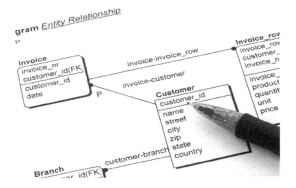

Figure 3.3   Databases are everywhere and it is extremely important to understand how they work.

field such as a record identification number. These can be used to store information about anything imaginable.

Let's look at an example to make this easier to understand.

You might create a relatively simple database of all of the DVDs in your media library. You might have a common identification field that is simply a number that increments as you add new records. So the first DVD you put in your database would have the common identifier of 1, and all the information that relates to that DVD would include a reference to that number.

Next you might create a table in your database that is a list of all the different publishers of DVDs (e.g., Sony, Disney, etc.). Then you might create a table that lists all of the movie themes such as westerns, thrillers, romance, and children's; and another table that refers to all of the actors; and another table for directors.

Now, you create a new record of your first DVD that refers to the Actors table and the Themes table.

The main DVD records table you create would contain the identification number, the name of the DVD, maybe the date and place you bought it, and the price you paid. Then it would also include references to the publisher of the DVD (taken from the Publishers table), the stars on that DVD (taken from the Actors table), and the theme of the DVD (taken from the Themes table). If you refer to Figure 3.4, you get a visual idea of how this all might look.

You might begin to see that these related tables can be used for data that are common to several different records. Without getting too

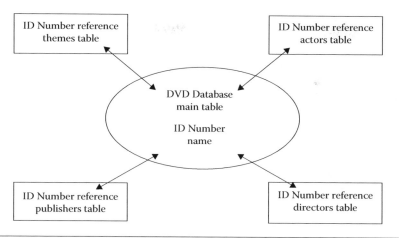

Figure 3.4 Our sample relational database design.

deeply into database theory, this should help you to understand the basics of what is referred to as a relational database.

To add new records to any of those tables, database applications include forms where you fill in the blanks to add and save new records. They also include some kind of query tool that allows you to ask questions (queries) and get answers (reports) from your database.

For instance, you could put in a query that asks your DVD database for every Brad Pitt movie you bought in the last 2 years, and it would create a list of the matching records.

To do this, the database programming would check the Actors table and look for matches to Brad Pitt. It would then compare the reference number(s) from those records that relate to the main table list of DVDs. Then it would go through that list and check the date range you entered against the dates of the entries in that table. Finally, the database front-end application would present a report to you of all the items in the database that matched your query. Depending on what you asked it to show you in your query, it can create a report with all of the details or just a few of them, or even just a single item such as the name of the DVD.

Databases can be stored on desktops, laptops, or servers, depending on their use and the need for access. Your simple DVD database would probably be stored locally on your home computer or laptop. However, a large and complex human resources database for a global organization would need to be stored on a very powerful and large-capacity server or servers.

In most cases, especially with enterprise-level databases, they will be backed up on a regular basis, and sometimes, for disaster recovery or just performance reasons, they may also be "mirrored." Mirroring creates an exact image of the database either on a separate hard drive, a separate part of a large hard drive or set of drives, or even in a physically separate location.

This is important to understand and be aware of if you need to manage, preserve, or analyze data from a database. Any or all of these physical and logical locations might need to be searched or preserved.

On the enterprise scale there are a number of more complex and expensive database applications that are common. These include Oracle, Postgres, Microsoft's SQL, and the open-source version, MySQL or SQLLite.

Access to databases is controlled by authentication rules within the database.

An employee in an enterprise environment should have access to only the part of the database that is required to complete his or her work.

There may be many different front-end applications that access and manage different subsets of data from one large database. These front-ends might consist of separate smaller databases or other applications that use the data from the larger database.

Front-end applications can be located on workstations or run over a network intranet or the Internet via websites. Websites often have databases from which they get data and to which they send data collected on Web forms.

Access to your simple database at home may be comparatively open if you have not secured it with a password, but the database owner or administrator controls that access by his or her design decisions when the database is built or as it is managed going forward.

Data stored in databases are accessible only with the correct level of authentication. In a typical enterprise, this requires a user identification and password.

In larger organizations, usually only system or database administrators have access to all of the data, including the coding within the database that controls how it works and the log information that identifies who accessed the database.

If you are the manager or owner of an organization, the counsel for an organization, the records manager, or a compliance officer, this may be the data you need to preserve, analyze, or manage for legal or compliance reasons. It is important to understand all of the different types and locations of databases in your environment, who owns them, and who has administrative access to them.

A very important first step toward complying with records management regulations or legal rules or just your own auditing ability is to create and maintain documentation of all of the different types of databases you or your organization own, where the databases are stored physically and logically, and who owns, controls, and administers the databases.

To that end it is highly recommended (and even required under some court rules and regulations) that you or your organization makes an effort to create such a reference. Think about all of the databases you or your organization have access to and document the contact information for the custodians and administrators of those databases. I guarantee you will find this an extremely valuable exercise and source of information.

3.4 E-Mail Systems

E-mail is perhaps the largest and most well-known repository of electronic information. Anyone who pays attention to the news knows that it is also one of the most often contentious and litigious information sources. Many examples can be found of organizations and individuals whose finances and reputations suffered because of poor e-mail management practices. For resources that document case law and news items, please refer to Appendix I.

There are many different types of e-mail systems. At home you might use an e-mail system connected to your Internet Service Provider (ISP), such as AOL, Comcast, Frontier, or Sprint. Or you might use one of the popular online e-mail tools, such as Google's Gmail or Microsoft's MSN or Hotmail. These systems are hosted on the provider's servers, and those electronic records are usually available only to you. Some version of those records may also be stored on

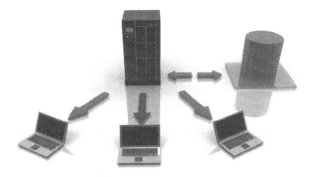

Figure 3.5   The client/server model is used for many different applications.

your local computer. Law enforcement can sometimes get access to those records that your provider keeps, but they should always need a subpoena and that requires (and should) a very sound justification before a judge.

In the work environment, e-mail systems are often much larger and more complex and are generally hosted on servers within the enterprise. Again, there are several well-known programs. The most predominant is Microsoft's Enterprise that uses Outlook as the client. You might have Outlook as your client on your home computer as well, even though your home e-mail is hosted by your Internet provider.

This might be a little confusing, so take a quick look at the client/ server model in Figure 3.5. This is a model that is used for other applications besides e-mail, so it is important to understand.

In an e-mail system, all of the processing, directing, possibly filtering, and storing of messages take place in a database that might be hosted on a server. The database might also be stored separately and simply accessed through a server.

A server is usually a more powerful and higher-capacity computer that "serves" more than one desktop or workstation computer with application features. In the case of an e-mail server, it is responsible for taking input of messages or contacts, calendar items, tasks, and so forth, from the computers it serves and organizing those into the correct storage space (your e-mail box, for instance); directing them to the e-mail system they are addressed to; and possibly archiving them or sending them to a separate e-mail repository. It is also responsible for collecting and properly distributing incoming e-mail and in some cases filtering those e-mails.

The client, however, is the part of the e-mail application that you see on your desktop. It can be Outlook, or a Web-based client like Gmail. This is your interface or connection to that back-end server. It is where you compose your e-mail messages and address them. It can also be where you input addresses and contact information or add calendar items or tasks. But all of these are just forms, exactly the same as the forms we talked about in the section on databases that you should have just finished (if you skipped ahead, now you have to go back). In fact, e-mail systems are a type of database.

So, when you fill in the "To" form field in your e-mail client, and then fill in the "Subject" field, and so on, all of that information is sent from your computer, as data in field records, to the e-mail server. The server then puts all of that information together into packets of data, identifies from your "To" field data where you want the e-mail to go, and directs it out onto the Internet or into the correct tables of the e-mail database and eventually toward that destination.

What happens then and how data packets move around the Internet is a bit beyond the scope of this book. But suffice it to say that your "client" is simply your window into the e-mail server. As such, it also serves as the place where you retrieve e-mail messages that were sent to you.

In effect, you create a query, just like we talked about with databases, every time you open your e-mail client and check to see if there is new mail. The e-mail server looks to see what new, unfiltered e-mail it has in its storage with your name on it and serves you up a nice list of who sent you e-mail with the subject lines and dates received. When you click on one of those, it returns the actual e-mail.

The e-mail server is the key component for us to consider as we think about the location of electronic information.

Even though you can access your own e-mail records from your client, you should not be able to access anyone else's. Again, this is similar to the database model we discussed earlier. Access to the e-mail server is regulated by authentication credentials, usually a user ID and password. Only the person with the correct user ID and password has access to the records in a particular e-mail storage container. The exception, as with all databases and any other information technology storage, will be the administrators of those systems.

The e-mail server contains all of the records of messages, contacts, calendar items, tasks, and so forth, that any of its clients have put into it.

E-mail administrators utilize different retention policies and procedures depending on performance, storage, and regulatory requirements. For instance, in many organizations, it is common to let e-mail be automatically deleted after a certain amount of time or when it reaches a certain capacity unless it was specifically saved or archived.

Online services also have a certain time or space limit that they allow for storage of e-mail. Because storage has not quite become infinite yet, this makes sense from a capacity and resources perspective.

But as noted, there can also be regulatory or records retention reasons that compel longer-term storage of e-mail data, and some organizations also store all their e-mail in off-site or online repositories. Archives of e-mail messages can also be stored on separate servers or on desktops or any other storage media.

Again, if you are the manager or owner of an organization, the counsel for an organization, the records manager, or a compliance officer, this may be the data you need to preserve, analyze, or manage for legal or compliance reasons. You need to recognize all of the different types of e-mail you or the employees of your organization have access to, very possibly including their personal e-mail accounts online, as well as the ones your organization provides. It will be imperative to understand where those systems and their archives reside logically and physically, who owns them, and who has administrative access to them.

3.5 File and Print Servers

In most organizations of any size, all of your file and printer services and systems are stored in a hierarchical format on a server or servers. Data stored on these servers may include

Documents
Spreadsheets
Presentations

Databases
Images (pictures or graphics)
Video
Applications
Logs
System files
A wide variety of other types of information

Archived e-mail records are sometimes stored separately on a file server. It is common practice for organizations to "map" a section of the file server to users for their own data. This is often called their "home" directory or drive. This area of the server is accessible only to the user or to a network administrator.

Some organizations also map a section of the server with a drive for separate divisions or workgroups. This area of the server could be accessible only to the specific group or division or to a network administrator.

It is also possible that other "drives" are designated or mapped to divisions or groups for special purposes. However, all of these are simply areas on the server that are designated with drive letters to help manage data and to ensure that only authorized users have access to that data.

Let's look more closely at the design of a typical file and print server to illustrate this a little more clearly.

As stated earlier, a server is simply a more powerful computer with more storage capacity that serves a group of networked computers. From a physical perspective, this server might look just like any other computer, or in many cases it will be a much smaller unit that fits into racks in a climate-controlled server facility.

In larger enterprises, you will often find data centers with rows and rows of server racks filled with small racked servers with a great deal of power. You may also find the larger storage units in those data centers, called storage area networks (SANS), and large robotic tape backup systems. And of course you will find huge cooling units and power backup systems. If your organization has a data center, I highly recommend taking a tour.

But back to the file server example: While physically a server can be a lot of different shapes and sizes, logically they are usually similar in at least some respects. Logically, they are a centralized location that networked computers can access to use different applications or services such as e-mail and printers, or to store data.

If you look at the file structure on a server, you will find it is similar to that on any computer. It is hierarchical in that there will be a hard drive (or group of hard drives) given a name and which is the base of the server's file system. Within that base there may be volumes separated out for organizational purposes.

For instance, there may be an application volume that contains all of the application programming. There may be a system volume that contains operating system files for the server. There may be an administrative volume with specific tools and access for network administrators and a public volume with storage or tools for everyone to use. Within one of those volumes there may be directories and subdirectories such as you would find on any computer.

Network administrators control the access to these servers through the network operating systems that are installed on them. The most common network operating systems are from Microsoft. But there are also some from IBM, Novell, Linux, and Sun, among others.

All of these operating systems organize users and services on the servers using another type of database called a directory service. For Microsoft operating systems, this directory service is called the Active Directory. This works similarly to most other directory systems, so we will look briefly at how it is administered.

Microsoft network administrators use the Active Directory to create groups of users and assign those groups access to different parts of the server. They can take any one of the directories in the file system and create a pointer to that directory and its subdirectories. This is called "mapping." That pointer can be a drive letter so that, as noted previously, if you have a section of the server dedicated to your personal work, they might map it as the H: drive. Then on your computer, you would find the H: drive that contained all of your personal data. Only you would have access to that part of the server because the network administrator would have separately granted you and only you permission to that directory on the server.

Another person would also see an H: drive on his or her computer, but it would be mapped to a separate directory on the server. This is accomplished by matching your login credentials to the permissions you have in the directory services database.

When you log in with your unique user ID and password, the directory service authenticates you, looks up the directories on the server that you have access to and the pointers or map/drive names that have been assigned to them by the network administrators, and connects you to them, showing you those map names, usually in the form of drive letters such as H: or G: or N:. The directory service also knows what applications and services you have access to from your authentication, so it may also connect you to your mail service, Internet access, printers, or other applications.

As noted, the rights to access any of the data on these drives are managed by network administrators, who are the only people who have access to all parts of the file system. Therefore, any recovery, preservation, or management of existing data on file servers will require the assistance of the network administrator.

If you need to manage, retain, or preserve data from a file server, you need to know who the network administrator is and how to contact him or her. You also need to know who has the supervisory authentication to allow or compel that administrator to grant you the access you might need.

Before we leave the subject of servers, we need to take a moment to touch on virtual servers, or virtual machines, sometimes referred to as VMs. Again, without going too deep into the engineering, you just need to understand that a virtual machine is a way to use the storage space and hardware on a computer or server efficiently to store more than one operating system or more than one server on the same physical device.

By utilizing a programming tool called a hypervisor, separate servers with different functions and connections to a network can all use the same hardware such as the processors, keyboards, sound, video, monitors, and so forth, on one device. This same technology can be used on a desktop or laptop computer to create different "virtual" operating systems or sets of applications on one piece of hardware.

Virtual systems have become quite popular as a way to save energy, space, and resources in our ever-expanding information universe.

Another important feature of virtual machines is that they are stored as a large file on the host machine and they are very easily reset back to their former settings. This has become a popular way to manage computer desktops in environments such as schools. It allows the administrators to simply reset the desktops back to their original base image any time they want or need to. For instance, if the computer has been compromised in some way, this allows a simple return to a pristine instance of the desktop application and data.

Using virtual desktops has another administrative advantage that harkens back to days of yore when all workstations were dumb terminals with no actual applications and minimal memory or storage. All of the applications resided on servers and were "served" to the dumb terminals. This allowed administrators to centrally manage updates, security, and so on, and was less expensive and resource intensive than having each desktop storing its own applications and data. We moved away from that model due to network speed and reliability limitations, but now with virtual machines some organizations are moving back. The way that works now is that administrators have a base, a clean and updated image of the workstation stored on and served up from the server; the desktops are again minimally resourced with little data storage and memory; all applications are run from and stored on servers; all data are stored on servers as well; and the virtual machine base image is refreshed/reloaded every time you start up the computer.

This is all very important to understand when you consider the physical location of information you may need to collect for litigation or compliance or retention reasons. It is possible that the information you need physically exists on a hard drive that also contains information and data that have nothing at all to do with your needs.

Where this can become a problem is when you need to shut down the system in order to acquire the data or do some kind of maintenance. This will directly affect all of the other virtual machines and functions using the same physical hardware device. You will need to carefully consider and document what you need to do and how you will do it in order to maintain the integrity and functionality of all the systems involved.

That should be enough to give you a good idea of file servers and their functions. We included the "print" server label as well in this section heading, but do not let that confuse you. Basically, some servers are specifically set up (or a portion of their services can be set up) to accept print requests and to process them, send them to network printers, and administer the printers on the network. Those can contain a wealth of information, depending on the level of logging and archiving that is set up on them, so you do not want to ignore these print servers when you are considering where relevant data might exist.

3.6 Instant Messaging Services

There are many different vendors that offer instant messaging systems online. Among the best known are AOL (AIM), Microsoft (MS Messaging), Yahoo, Google, ICQ, and Skype. Many of the social media sites, such as Facebook, also offer instant messaging or what they refer to as "chat" or "messenger" session features (Figure 3.6). There are many less well-known versions as well.

There are also messaging systems that can be set up and administered within an enterprise, such as Microsoft's Live Communications Server and GroupWise Messenger, so the servers that host and relay the messages are actually within the enterprise instead of in a separate location on the Internet.

However, all of these work in a similar way. Once the client software is installed on the user's computer (remember our discussion of client/server systems above?), a session begins by activating the

Figure 3.6 Instant message chat sessions can be a large store of electronically stored information.

client. Often the client is set up to activate as soon as the computer is turned on.

When the client is activated, it connects to the vendor's server and that server notes that the user is available for instant messaging. Anyone else who has the same type of client or one that is compatible with that client (some clients are able to access multiple types of instant messaging or chat formats) and who has included that person in their contacts list (called a Buddy List in some cases) will then see the first user's name on their instant messenger client, listed as being available. These can also note that users on their buddy or contact list are offline, busy, out to lunch, and so forth.

Either user can then select any of the names on the list of available "buddies" or contacts and type in a message. This message is relayed through the vendor's server and directed "instantly" to the buddy.

These same clients can also be used to send files (documents, spreadsheets, graphics, etc.) between connected users. Some of these applications also allow you to have chats with groups of people and even share "white boards," where the participants can type and share ideas in a virtual meeting. Some (i.e., Skype, Google Hangouts) have an audio and video function that allows you to see and speak to the person or persons with whom you are communicating.

There are often settings available on the client software that allow a user to choose to save his or her chat sessions. In some cases, these logs will be saved to the user's computer, but in others they are saved to a central server.

In an enterprise-hosted system and in some of the vendor-provided systems, a central IT administrator can set policies that automatically configure the clients to log all messaging sessions. This can be very important when it comes time to access that information due to litigation or some other information recovery need.

There are also various settings that administrators or users can configure that allow or disallow file sharing, Web addresses (URLs) to be included in messages, voice capabilities, contact from people not on your buddy list, and so forth.

Depending on the configuration of these settings and specifically the location of any logs or copies of conversations, important electronic information may be stored in many different locations. It might be kept locally on the person's desktop or laptop or cell/smartphone. It might be located on a central enterprise server, or possibly on a provider's server.

If the configuration is controlled by enterprise administrators, they can treat it the same as database or e-mail information as noted previously. Depending on organizational policy, regulations, and retention laws or policies, they may or may not store logs and archives of the conversations. Users may or may not have the capability to choose to store logs or conversations on their personal computers, and providers such as AOL or Microsoft will have differing policies and regulations that they follow as to their storage and retention of that data.

All this is to recognize that for the responsible attorney, manager, or owner of that data, there are a myriad of possibilities to be aware of. If you need to preserve or manage this type of electronic record, you will need to know

- Who controls the storage of message logs and content
- Who has the authority to access that data
- What process is required to gain that access
- What exactly is saved and for how long

3.7 Mobile Devices

Mobile devices are becoming ubiquitous. At the point at which this is being written, mobile devices are many and varied. And in the years to come, this list will only grow as new ideas and technology allow for more and more mobile electronics (Figure 3.7). A few examples of the current list include

- Smart phones, including the iPhone, Androids, and Windows Mobile
- Tablet computers, such as the Apple iPad, Kindle, Microsoft Surface
- Laptops of every size and shape from tiny, lightweight netbooks, to large-screen work platforms
- A wide variety of special-use devices, such as handheld workflow management devices for utility workers, or ruggedized mobile devices for use by the military or in police or fire vehicles

Figure 3.7   Smart phones and laptops are just two of the many mobile devices in use today.

Every one of these devices is basically a computer. The input mechanism might be by a stylus, or a touch screen, or a keyboard and mouse. But in every case, they store data in similar ways.

When you install, update, or start an application on one of these devices, be it a word processing application, a spreadsheet application, a database, a picture editor, or anything else, a change is made on the storage media within the mobile device.

Data on these mobile devices are held on storage media that can be a hard drive, or some type of small memory storage device, such as a Secure Digital Card (SD Card). In a later section we look more closely at how the data are stored on these media. Some of the newer mobile devices are using these types of nonvolatile memory cards for storage instead of the traditional hard drive because they are faster to access and can be removable or expandable.

Whichever is used for storage on the mobile device, every action you take makes a change that is reflected on that storage medium. Let's look at some examples.

When you install a new application, many things go on behind the scenes. During the installation process, data will be held in the volatile or random-access memory. This is the memory on a computer device that holds data only temporarily. When you turn off the computer, that data will disappear for the most part. However, traces of what took place are stored in certain system files that are accessible only by special tools.

A new application will store some data on those volatile memory devices for use during the installation. Other files needed for the installation will be stored in temporary folders on the nonvolatile memory storage. The installation process will continue by putting the files it will need to operate into different areas of the folder structure, depending on how its programming is configured.

Files needed to run an application can be stored in several different folders. For instance, the main executable file and supporting graphics, dynamic libraries of supporting programming information, and so forth, may be stored in a program file specific to the application. Other files that might be shared between different programs may be stored in a separate shared folder. System files referenced by the application for access to the hardware or input/output systems on the device could be stored in hidden system folders.

Finally, depending on the operating system, referential information about the application such as the location of all those related files, when the application was installed, its version number, and so on, is stored in some type of operating system database or registry.

All of the data are organized and stored in the appropriate places each time you add a new application to your mobile device. This process is the same on any type of computer but will change in some respects depending on the operating system the computer employs. We discuss different operating systems in a future chapter.

Also, at the end of the installation process, the data stored in random-access or volatile memory will be deleted or allowed to be written over by being flagged as no longer necessary. In our earlier discussions of how memory works, we looked at how that happens and exactly when and how the data actually disappear.

Finally, the files that were stored in the temporary folders are sometimes (but not always) deleted at the end of the install process. It is important to note that sometimes data are not deleted. That can create an interesting source of information and it can also create problems if you begin to get short of storage room, just by virtue of clogging up your data system and affecting the efficiency of your device.

When you access an application to use it, several different records are created and data changes or are added.

Most devices have some kind of logging that tracks the activity on the device. Those logs will reflect when an application is accessed or shut down. Any system files that need to run for the application to work will start up and create changes on the device, starting or stopping related services that need to run, such as sound, keyboard, mouse, and monitor.

All of these changes may be recorded in the aforementioned logs and can also be recorded in the registry. The registry often tracks when applications start and keeps a record of recently accessed files and applications.

Finally, several data files also track the activity on the device, some of which specifically track Internet activity, but can also include information on files that were opened on network drives.

Any documents or files that you open with an application will also create a record in the registry and in other tracking files. The document or file will include a record of when it was last accessed or modified.

When an application is updated or patched, similar changes happen as during the installation process. Data are stored temporarily in volatile memory and in temporary folders. Changes are made in the registry, and logs are created or changed to reflect the updates.

In many operating systems there is a process recorded in the registry that creates a copy of all of the data as the data existed before any new applications are added. This is called by several different names such as restore points or shadow copies, but in essence it is a rollback or restore function that allows one to go back to a known good configuration of your computer should the addition or update of a new application cause problems.

This also creates data and records in the registry, in logs, and in specific system restoration files that can contain very useful information.

The point of all this description of what happens during different activities on your mobile device is to illustrate all of the ways data can be added or changed on these types of computing tools. All of this information can become relevant when you need to understand the answer to the questions, "What happened, when did it happen, how did it happen, and who did it?"

Finally, we need to consider what is unique about mobile devices as opposed to their more stable cousins, the desktop computer or workstation or server.

The bottom line is that in the areas we talked about, there is not a lot of difference. Mobile devices will tend to use smaller form-factor storage and will usually be contained in one piece of hardware as opposed to nonmobile devices.

Some mobile devices will have the capacity to attach peripheral hardware such as keyboards, speakers, mice, or external storage drives, but generally they are built to be able to be used without any of those attachments. This makes a difference in the data that might be found on those devices, because peripherals require drivers and create their own set of logs and system files.

Other than the difference in hardware, there will often be different operating systems used on mobile devices. Smart phones especially are likely to be run using specialized operating systems.

Each operating system will store the required files and data needed to run their applications in different ways. We look more closely at that in a future chapter, but suffice it to say here that this can affect your ability to access, acquire, organize, and preserve what may be important information stored on those devices.

3.8 Physical Access Records

Another important electronic record that many people might not consider are the records of your entering and leaving the building where you work, or other facilities where you shop, work, or learn.

Whenever I enter my workspace, I use an identification card that I wave in front of a proximity reader that looks like a little gray box with a red light on it that turns green and unlocks the door if I have the correct authentication to enter. That creates an electronic record of my entrance into the part of the floor where I work (Figure 3.8).

Figure 3.8 Identity cards are often read by proximity card readers to allow access. These create records.

When you take classes or go shopping you may use loyalty, membership, or ID cards to register or to get discounts, student fees, or other privileges for which you need to authenticate your identity. Whenever you use one of those methods of identification, another electronic record is created.

These records, for the most part, are probably saved into a database. Often this will be a proprietary system that was created by someone specifically for the task of tracking ingress and egress or access to a facility, or access to privileges such as special discounts. Or in some cases, it may be something that was developed by someone in the organization to simply keep track of these authentications. In any case, when you swipe your card at the door, or present it to the clerk, electronic data are created that tell the date and time of use.

There are many reasons you or someone else might want to access that data. It could be needed to answer a question regarding litigation, or to prove you were somewhere when you said you were, or perhaps to show that someone was not where he or she purports to have been. In all cases, you will need to know where the data reside, who has control over the data, and what will be required to recover, examine, preserve, and organize the data for whatever need you have.

For example, consider the case where a manager feels that one of her employees is not getting his work done efficiently. As far as she can tell, the employee is showing up for work on time in the mornings because she sees him walk by her desk on his way to his cube. And he seems to be leaving work when he is supposed to because, again, he waves to her as he leaves the office. So, unable to understand what might be going on to keep him from getting his work done, one of the things she does is to ask the facilities manager for a report from the proximity readers on their floor.

She has part of the information we spoke about—she knows someone who knows who has control over the data she needs. She knows that her facilities manager will have access to the person who controls the data and can give her a report. She establishes through her conversation with him that his administrator can create a report in Excel that will show her each time the employee entered the workspace.

She receives the report, and lo and behold, the electronic records show that nearly 10 times a day, the employee enters the workspace through the alternative entrance, back by the smoking area. By looking at the times, she is able to illustrate that her employee is spending an inordinate amount of time outside smoking each day, and that is probably the reason he is not getting his work done on time. (It might also account for all that coughing.)

Here is another example, this time using the access records from a grocery store. Jane goes every week to her local grocery store, where she has a loyalty/discount card. Every week she buys bread, milk, eggs, fruit, vegetables, and meat for her meals. She is a very organized person and pretty much has the same grocery list every week. She clips coupons and uses her discount card religiously to ensure she gets the most benefit from shopping at her favorite store.

One week she gets home and finds that she does not have the milk, bread, and eggs. She assumes that she left a bag behind somewhere and returns to the store. But she also realizes that her receipt must have been in the same bag, because she cannot find it.

Now, of course, the clerks at the store know her pretty well, but they have a new manager, Joe. Joe is strictly a by-the-book kind of guy. He retired from the Marines and started working with his big brother in the grocery business. He is a big, tough, serious guy, but it means a lot to him to do the right thing all the time. He just started at this store, and he wants to make sure he does not mess up anything.

When Jane arrives back in his store and asks about her lost bag of groceries, the clerks are empathetic, but the bag is not there and without the receipt they do not know if they can help her. And they are all a little scared of their new tough-guy manager. But they all like Jane, so they call him to the front anyway.

At first Joe is unmoved and simply tells her that he is sorry, but without a receipt he really cannot help her. But Jane, a little upset but holding it together, tells him, "I've been trading with you folks for 30 years now. I'm a simple woman and I don't change my habits—I just know that I had those groceries and now someone's taken them! I'm on a small income and I can't afford to buy them again. I've had this discount card with your store for so long it's getting frayed and worn out!" and shows him the old, worn card.

At that Joe's serious expression softens a bit and there is a slight twinkle in his eye as he says, "Ma'am, may I take a look at that card? Hold on, ma'am, I'll be right back."

Joe walks back to his office and asks his assistant to call the main offices. Again, Joe recognized that he needed some electronic data, and he knew who could find it for him. The assistant calls the main office and asks them to pull up their records for the card number of Jane's discount card, and fax him a report. They let him know that they will be able to do so and it should arrive at his fax in the next few minutes.

Sure enough, about 3 minutes later a fax comes in with a long table of numbers and dates. These would not mean much to most of us, but to Joe it is recognizably a list of item codes for all of the different grocery items purchased using Jane's discount card. Joe is not only able to establish that she does purchase nearly the same grocery list every week, but that in fact she purchased those same items this morning and has been doing so for as far back as their records show.

The tough old marine looks a lot friendlier as he walks out to Jane with a bag containing her bread, milk, and eggs. (He was able to match the item numbers, of course.) He apologizes for the inconvenience and the time she lost, and tells her how much he appreciates her as a longtime loyal customer. He also brings her a brand-new discount card, along with coupons for a free loaf of the bread she usually purchases next week, just as a gesture of appreciation.

These are just two short examples of how this type of record might be used. Take a minute to imagine some other scenarios. Perhaps an event that happens in a place of business, such as an accident or theft that would require an understanding of who was present at the time, or a dispute between an employee and her coworker about who spent the most time working on a project.

Some people might feel that this type of tracking is invasive to their privacy, and that is something to consider as well, especially in the case of the grocery or other store discount cards. They do, in fact, give the retailers specific information about the items you buy and the frequency of your shopping trips. These might not technically be called physical access records, in that they were not established for the purpose of showing when you physically accessed a facility, but they nevertheless provide that information.

This is an important point to consider when you are thinking about electronic records that illustrate the presence or absence of a person in a building or store. There are many types of identification cards that we all have in our wallets, purses, or on our persons. Most of them allow us privileges that might or might not include access to a building or room. For instance, you may have a library card that allows you to borrow books from your local library.

A library card is a great example of an identification tool that might or might not be usable to establish your whereabouts. If you are able to use your library card to check out books online, the electronic records of the use of that card might not distinguish between which computer you were using to check out a book, or if you were even at a computer instead of at the checkout desk. Yet those records may record your location, including the IP address of the computer you used to check out a book, whether you chose to have it mailed to you, or if you were at the checkout desk or went in to the library to check out your book after ordering it online.

All of that information could be used to pinpoint where you were at any given time. Think about the implications of that in a legal case, whether it is you trying to prove your innocence by establishing you were not where the activity in question took place, or if it is the prosecutor trying to prove the opposite assertion.

Simply by knowing who has those records; how to collect, preserve, analyze, and organize those records; and how to present them, one can put together a very convincing timeline and description of where someone was at any given time.

In the end, electronic records that prove where someone was and when can be extremely important. In order to utilize those records, as with all electronic records we will discuss, you need to understand first that they exist, second that there is someone with access to them, and third that there will be some way of acquiring those records that you will need to put into practice.

3.9 Telecommunications

In March 1876, when Alexander Graham Bell uttered those now-famous words, "Mr. Watson, come here, I want to see you," into the first working telephone, I doubt very much that he had any idea how ubiquitous and important his invention would become. I wonder if he would even recognize today's smart phone as a distant relative of that crude device that transmitted vibrations over a simple circuit to another device that was able to translate those vibrations into intelligible words that Watson heard clearly.

Those first words created records only because as a scientist Mr. Bell bothered to write down what happened. No electronic records were created or stored from those or myriad other electromagnetic telephone conversations that followed for many years after that.

But then something changed.

It is likely that his namesake, Bell Labs, and others like it can be held responsible for at least some of those changes.

Without getting into the history of the invention of the digital computer, suffice it to say that, mostly as a result of wartime efforts to encrypt and decrypt communications, the digital computer was developed during World War II, and nothing has ever been the same.

And that is especially true when we talk about telecommunications. As telecommunications began to take advantage of digital computing and its attendant efficiencies, an entire sea-change occurred in the engineering of the systems that enabled telephonic communications worldwide.

The first digital records that occurred as a result of that change were simply records of the switching of connections within the system. But very soon there were (and are) records created of every connection to every other connection, as well as the time spent and the location of each connected device. As computer technology began to enable different uses of telephonic communications, the attendant records became more and more concise and important.

To get a better understanding of telecommunications as it exists today and all of the resultant electronic records that we need to take into account, let's begin with a basic look at how it all works.*

We begin with what is known in the telecom industry as the POTS, or the Plain Old Telephone System (yes, they really call it that). To those of us old enough to remember this, these are the old "Princess" phones or other plastic devices that might even have dials rather than buttons and that plugged directly into the wall with no need for any other power source.

---

* The history of AT&T. http://www.corp.att.com/history/. Retrieved February 12, 2011.

This relatively simple infrastructure is still the basic internal system that supports our modern telecommunications. It consists of a pair of copper wires that extend from phone jacks in our homes and businesses out to telephone poles, or perhaps buried cable runs, join up with large bundles of other copper cables, and eventually end up at the phone company's switching station, or possibly connect to a box that connects them to a digital concentrator.

But let's start at the beginning. The telephone is a very simple device that contains very few parts, no matter how modern it is. Basically, there is a microphone that picks up your voice and translates those sound waves into different modulated currents of electricity that are transmitted over the copper wires. There is a simple switch of some sort that connects you to or disconnects you from the telephone system. Then there is a speaker, which translates those modulated currents of electricity into sound waves that you recognize as the speech of your grandma in Miami Beach.

There also is some type of mechanism for telling the system who you want to talk to. The POTS systems used "pulse dialing." The dial on the phone would basically click the connection switch as many times as you indicated by the distance you turned the dial. So if you stuck your finger into the ninth hole and turned the dial to the little metal block that stopped your finger (see picture of original black dial phone in Figure 3.9), and then let go, as the dial returned to its starting position, it would click that switch nine times, pulsing that signal nine times, and letting the system know that you just sent the number nine.

Figure 3.9   The original dial telephones were an engineering marvel at the time, and still are.

Somewhat newer phones replaced the dial with a keypad that generated different frequencies down the line that corresponded to the number you wanted to connect to. And, of course, most of us now have telephones with computers in them. Those computers store phone numbers, record messages, keep track of different rings for different callers or different people in our house, keep a contact list that we can look up, block unwanted calls, and much more.

Many modern phones therefore require an outside source of power. And many of them, especially those that are actually radios and allow you to use them remotely by connecting to a base station, will not work at all if you do not have that outside power source. This is important to things we discuss later, so keep this in mind.

There are a few other electronics in modern phones, such as special speakers that create ring tones, and coils that keep you from hearing your own voice or other interference. But in general, that is really all there is to this simple but hugely important piece of technology.

So, you picked up your phone. If you are lucky enough to own one of those wonderful old POTS phones, just by picking up the receiver, you connected to the system, because the switch is in the "hook." You could even dial using pulse dialing by simply tapping the hook switch quickly the number of times you want to input as a number. But instead of doing that, you tap out grandma's number on the keypad.

When you picked up the phone and connected to the system, a switch opened up at the switching station we talked about earlier, and in our day and age, a computer started listening for what you would do next.

But let's not get ahead of ourselves. As noted before, this is best understood if we consider how it was done in the beginning and then work our way up to the way things are done by computers today, because as with nearly all digital systems that evolved over time, they simply do the same things we have always done but faster and more efficiently.

So, when your Grandma Betsy wanted to call her local pharmacist, here is what happened.

Back in the day, the telephone company had a central office in every town. In that office sat the "operator," or many operators. No doubt you have seen a picture or an old movie with a woman sitting in front

Figure 3.10   Adele the operator was always standing by at her switchboard.

of a large switchboard with a lot of wires plugged into it or hanging loose and a headset on her head (Figure 3.10).

When grandma picked up the phone at her house, the hook switch turned on a light over the corresponding socket on the operator's switchboard (let's call her Adele). Adele plugged in a cord to the indicated socket and was able to talk to Betsy, who told her she wanted to talk to Tom, the pharmacist. Adele said, "Why certainly, Betsy, hang on while I connect you." She then unplugged the cable from Betsy's socket and plugged it into the pharmacist's socket and pushed a button that sent a signal down the line to ring the pharmacist's phone.

When Tom heard the ring, he put down his mortar and pestle and reached over and picked up the phone, which switched his hook switch and connected him over the copper wires to Adele's circuit. Adele told him that there was a call from Betsy, and he said, "Thanks, I've been expecting to hear from her!"

Then Adele simply unplugged that cable from her own socket and plugged it into the socket for Betsy's connection and Betsy was connected to Tom and could ask him if he had finished preparing her sleeping powders. After Tom told her they would be ready for her that afternoon, the two of them put down their phone sets and switched the hook switches on their phones to off, disconnecting from the network and consequently turning off the lights over their sockets at the central office. Adele took note of this and pulled the cable out and set it aside for later.

This was a very simple system that worked incredibly well. Of course in a bigger city there would be rows and rows of switchboards and possibly hundreds of operators.

Now that is all very well for calling Tom across town, but how did Betsy get a hold of her old friend Marge out on the west coast? Well, it was still a pretty simple process, but now it included a few more parts.

This time when she got Adele the operator on the line, Betsy said, "Hey Adele, how's it going today? I need to talk to my old friend Marge in Seattle." Adele answered, "Not too bad if it don't rain, Betsy dear. What's your friend's number?" Betsy told her the number including the area code, and Adele then told her to hang on and plugged her line into a special socket that connected her to a long-distance office where another operator (let's call her Louise) saw the light turn on over the socket for Adele's office and plugged in her cable to say, "Long Distance, how may I help you?"

Then Adele told Louise the number she needed to reach, and Louise plugged a cable from Adele's socket into the socket for another long-distance office in the Seattle area code. In that office, yet another operator would politely ask Adele for the number she wanted to reach and then make the connection to the central office that controlled the number. Finally, the operator in Marge's central office would make the final connection to Marge's phone, send a ring signal, and let her know she had a long-distance call from her friend Betsy, then make the final connections so they could finally have some time to complain about their husbands and talk about when they would be seeing each other at Christmas. The long-distance operator recorded when the call started and when it ended, and they billed you accordingly. Records were being created, but they still were not electronic records per se.

This is all really pretty simple when you think about it. Despite it being incredibly slow and inefficient in terms of what we expect today, it basically set up a direct, wired connection between anyone, anywhere, and anyone else as long as the telecommunications infrastructure existed where it was needed. In fact, when transoceanic cables were laid, you could use this same system to reach people across the entire planet.

It did not matter how far away you were; as long as the infrastructure existed and there were connections between them, you could eventually be connected and be able to have a conversation as if you were in the same room. It was, and really still is, revolutionary.

When this all started to change, at first it was just by making those local calls automatic by creating switches that recognized the signals you sent via your pulse dialer and connected you to the corresponding circuit mechanically. You still had to dial 0 to get an operator to make those long-distance connections.

But then came the computer.

Now, both the local connections and the long-distance connections, as well as the records of how long you talked to Marge and how far away you had to call were (and still are) handled by computers. The signal frequencies broadcast by the buttons on your phone are translated by the computer and the connections are automatically switched to the number you request, whether it is local or long distance.

When you dial your call, if you start with a 1, the computer at the local switching station knows you want to dial long distance and it directs your call to a long-distance switch. The area code you dial in directs the switch to the correct long-distance office. The first three digits of the phone number point the switches to the right local office switch that then connects you to the person you are trying to reach. While the original signal frequencies start out as analog, or wave-type electrical currents, they are translated into digital signals when they hit the first switching computer and are transmitted digitally from there until they are translated back into an analog signal to be sent to your friend's phone.

One big difference between the call you make to check in with Grandma Betsy in her retirement condo in Miami Beach, and that call she made to her friend Marge back in the day, is that all of that information is now carried digitally on fiber optic cables that are capable of streaming thousands of conversations at once as optical bytes of data, as opposed to the single conversation going over a copper cable.

Another big difference now is that back then, every call and every connection was handled by one big company, at least in the United States. It was the American Telephone and Telegraph Company (AT&T), a monopoly that many called "Ma Bell" (named after the inventor we started out with, of course). There is a wonderful character named Ernestine, played by Lily Tomlin, an operator with a bad attitude who regularly and rudely cut people off and disconnected important calls. In a skit from a *Saturday Night Live* show she stated "We don't care. We don't have to. We're the phone company."*

---

* Lily Tomlin as Ernestine the obnoxious phone company operator. http://snltranscripts.jt.org/76/76aphonecompany.phtml. Retrieved March 10, 2012.

AT&T owned the entire infrastructure and was pretty much able to do whatever they wanted and charge whatever they chose to charge.

That was all broken up in 1984, when an antitrust case originally brought by the U.S. Justice Department 10 years earlier, and settled 2 years before that, finally went into effect. AT&T agreed to divest their infrastructure and open it up to other companies in return for a chance to get into the computer business.

In January of that year, AT&T split all of their local groups into what became known as the "Baby Bells," although it held onto its entire long-distance infrastructure. Eventually it lost much of that market to competitors as well, so that now when you make that call to grandma, the computer switch also has to check to see which long-distance company you have an account with and connect you via their switching network.

Now that you have a better idea of how all of this works when you pick up your home or office phone and punch in those numbers, let's talk about the digital records that result.

Oh, and do not worry, we are not forgetting about those smart phones. But cell technologies, and especially smart phones, open up a whole different aspect and level of digital records that deserve their own chapter, so stay tuned and we will get to them soon.

Let's go back to the beginning and begin to think about all of the records that are accumulated as you make that call to see how the weather is in Miami before you commit to having Thanksgiving with Grandma Betsy.

You pick up your phone and push the Talk button. A record was just made in several places. First, in many cases there may be a record on your phone, as it may begin storing information on the call so you can use the redial feature. Second, at the computer switch that you just connected to, a record is made of the time and date your phone connected to the network, information that identifies your phone and your ownership of it (account name, number, etc.), information about the circuit you are connecting from and to, and information about your phone provider.

Now you dial a number. Again, a record was created or appended in your phone in many cases. And in the local switching station, the computer there recorded the number you are dialing and information about that number, such as the switch it is connected to, if it is long distance, and if so, which carrier it is using to make the connections.

You are connected nearly instantaneously in most cases, but if there are any glitches in that connection, those may be recorded by the switching computers or other troubleshooting computers owned by the phone service.

Once you make your connection and begin to carry on a conversation, in most cases no digital record is kept of that conversation. Of course there are exceptions to that if there is some reason for recording the conversation, such as law enforcement-initiated wiretaps. Or it might simply be a legally requested and pre-notified recording, "for training and quality control purposes," like you often hear when you are contacting a service provider.

Normally, though, there will not be a digital record of your actual conversation. But when you are done and say, "OK, grandma, we'll be out for Thanksgiving" and hang up the phone, another record is created. That records the time you disconnected the call, the cost of that call, the minutes you used for the call, and possibly other information about the quality of the connection.

Once again, I am sure you can imagine many different scenarios where the information stored in those records could be of great interest and significance. It could be as simple (but important to your bank account) as verifying the number of minutes you spent on long distance, in case there is a mistake on your bill. Or it could be much more significant in a legal dispute when you need to answer the questions, who did this person contact, when, and for how long?

To be able to utilize that information to answer whichever query might arise, you have to know

- Where the data live
- Who has access to the data
- Who has the expertise and the resources to gather, preserve, and deliver the data in a readable format
- How to go about contacting that person or entity in order to retrieve that information

That all may seem pretty basic. After all, it is basically the same set of requirements we discussed when looking at all of the different types of data so far, isn't it?

But I would challenge you to give it a try sometime. Call your telephone provider and ask them to give you records of all the phone connections you made in the last month. This should be pretty simple and I predict you will be relatively successful.

Now, ask them to provide you with the records from the entire last year. That might be possible as well, but you might run into a little more resistance, and very likely some cost.

OK, now it is going to get a little harder. Ask them for records from 10 years ago. I venture to say that at this point you may find that these records are no longer available, at least not without some research and time. The farther back you ask about, the less likely the data will be readily available or even possibly still in existence at all. There are simply too many records, and phone companies, like all of us, have only so many resources and limited storage capacity.

Take it one step further, and you will hit the proverbial wall. Ask them for your grandma's records for any time period at all. Unless you have a legally provable right to those records, it is unlikely that you will be able to obtain them.

Here is where, in a litigation or law enforcement environment, things can get complex. Telecom service providers all have strict rules about what they will release and the requirements for releasing those records to any other than an account owner. And well they should.

For law enforcement or an attorney or court to obtain relevant records for a case, they have to go through legally defensible procedures. This could mean requiring a subpoena, a warrant, or a court order. Different telecommunications companies will have different requirements and different levels of collaboration processes with law enforcement or the courts, but in all cases, there will be a process that has to be followed, and it will usually take some amount of time, resources, and effort to accomplish.

We discuss legal processes in greater detail in later chapters, but for this subject suffice it to say that you may well need to understand at least the rudiments of what is required if you think you might be in a position to need these types of records.

Think about your own situation at work, or at home with your loved ones, and consider when and how a situation might arise where you would need to obtain records from a telecommunications provider that is not part of your account.

For instance, you might have an aging parent whom you can foresee needing to have you deal with their affairs in the future. One of those affairs may well be the control of their phone services and accounts. You may need to consider the legal processes required for you to become their proxy with the phone company.

Or, if you are managing workers at your organization and there might be a question of phone use, what will it require of you to be able to access the phone records of an employee if you are not the person of record on the account?

This could become even more complex if your workforce is able to work remotely, especially if they might be using their own private phone while they are supposed to be conducting work for you. What kind of agreement or contract with the employee would be necessary to allow you access to those records?

These are all questions that you should have legal counsel to answer. And because, as I try to make extremely clear throughout this book, I am not an attorney, and because there is no way for me to know enough about your specific situation to give good advice in any case, I will not attempt to offer solutions or answers here. I simply want to ensure that you are recognizing both the existence and possible importance of these types of electronic records and carefully considering what you will need to be able to acquire them if it becomes necessary.

3.10 Cellular Devices

As noted earlier, cell phones and smart phones, while part of the telecommunications sector, deserve and demand their own section in this book because they open up a whole new level of complexity and data than that we considered in Section 3.9.

All of the basics we discussed in that section are still germane, if you only consider the phone feature of those devices. They still create records both within the devices and the servers of their service providers that enumerate and describe the times and dates of connections, the durations of calls, and the numbers that were connected to, as well as possibly some information about the systems that were utilized and the quality of the service.

However, right away there is one difference, even for this most basic service. In many cases, particularly if these devices are owned by organizations, there will be another administrative server through which the devices connect. Those servers are controlled by the owning organization and are used for setting policy and administering the use of the corporate devices. For instance, with BlackBerry phones in my former organization, we had what was called the BES, or BlackBerry Enterprise Server. This gave our administrative staff a way to set policies on the phones, such as whether they could download applications, whether a password was required, and how strong the password needed to be, as well as how often it had to be reset.

But that server was also another repository of electronic data about the use of the phone, and it kept track of the calls made and the durations and resultant charges. So now there is yet another place where relevant electronic records exist that one should be aware of, and as noted earlier, you need to understand who has access to those records and how you might acquire them if necessary.

Even in the case where you might own a personal smart phone, there is very often a server of this type somewhere in the mix that will hold data that could be important and that might not depend on the service provider, but might be tied to some other level of support or carrier in between you and your provider of phone services. You need to know if that is the case, and if so, again, where the data live and how to access the data.

Yet this is just the tip of the iceberg when we are talking about today's cellular phone system. The days when such a thing as a single-feature device existed are fast disappearing. Though there still exist some cellular telephones that only make phone calls, they are increasingly rare. Even the most basic phones are likely to have a camera in them, and they most always allow for sending SMS (Short Message Service) messages or texting.

Of course, many of them also have the ability to connect to the Internet, play games, shoot video, and more.

To start, let's look at some of those features and how they work in order to begin to understand the types of records that might be created by them.

To begin, let's look at what has become the most ubiquitous and to some folks an absolute necessity—text messaging. In an interesting experiment, my son's high school asked students to volunteer to do without text messaging or any social media for a whole week.

To those high school–aged kids that was an incredible and daunting challenge. Text messaging along with other quick messaging, video, and other social media communications tools, for example, Snapchat, Instagram, and so on, have become some of the primary modes of communication and as such these are also now one of the primary sources of electronic information.

All signals to and from a cell phone work the same way. They are basically radio wave signals that must be picked up and transmitted via cell towers or control channels. These signals are coming and going from your cell phone even when you are not sending a text or making a call. Your phone is continually sending and receiving signals to towers to keep track of which communications channel it is closest to and communicating with. As you move around, your phone sends out signals basically saying, "where am I?" and "which of you towers is the closest or has the strongest signal so I can most efficiently communicate with the cellular channels?" The towers receive those signals and from them can tell which phone is which and what cell phone number corresponds to that phone. That is how the cellular system makes connections between your phone and the phone with which you are communicating.

When you do the flashing thumb trick and type out a text message to your friend, those key taps on your phone are translated into electronic signals. Inside your phone they are channeled to the screen so you can see what you are typing, and they are stored in the phone's memory.

When we spoke earlier about memory, we spoke of it as volatile, meaning that it would lose data once the device was shut down or the application turned off. With phones, however, their memory might be thought of as semi-volatile instead. Because of their size, a phone's memory will be somewhat limited (although, thanks to Moore's law, that limit keeps growing), so data stored in a phone's memory will generally be kept until it needs more room. Then one of two things will occur. It might automatically be purged to make room for more data in what is called FIFO (first in–first out) by computer engineers. This indicates that the oldest stored data will be purged first to make room for more. Or, in some cases, your phone might tell you it is out of memory and prompt you to delete some data such as photos or movies that are taking up room.

In any case, the message you are typing will be stored in the phone's memory. Most often this is the type of data that the phone will automatically purge as it needs more space, so you will not have control of how many messages are stored.

Finally, that data will be sent in a signal to the cell tower that is closest or has the strongest signal. The signal will include information about who sent the message, the type of message body (is it text or pictures, etc.), and the destination of the message, as well as some error checking information to ensure it arrives at its destination the same as when it left your phone. The cellular network will interpret that signal and relay the message signal to the appropriate tower (or towers) to get it to your friend.

Remember when we talked about the POTS, or the Plain Old Telephone System? If you think about it, nothing has really changed here, has it? The only difference is that all of the information that used to be handled by the operator manually has been converted to electronic signals so that the routing and connecting of one person's communication to another can be handled by computers. And, of course, the other big difference is that now we have persistent records of each and every communication that occurs.

One more thing to note about that text message you just sent to your friend telling her about your new boyfriend and how "OMG, he's so hot!": There is a better than likely chance that message is stored somewhere else besides on your phone where it will eventually be purged.

Anyone who owns a cell phone knows that you are paying someone for cellular service. Those organizations are responsible for carrying your electronic signals from point A (you) to point B (your friend). And they charge you for doing so, often by the time spent (minutes) or the amount of data you use. In order to charge you, they have to know what is being sent and received, so they store that data, at least for a little while.

Now, you might imagine how much data that would entail if you begin to think about the amount of data you generate all by yourself and then multiply that by millions of customers for each of those cell service providers. Believe me, it is a lot. And even though they expect that and plan for it and have unbelievably huge storage capacity, there is still a limit to what they can store.

So, this is another place where records of your actual text message might exist, but it will not exist there for long. In general, most cell providers I talked to agree that they keep less than a week's worth of text messaging data at any given time for any given customer, and often it is less than that.

Yet, an article from the online *Wired* zine about a secret memo marked "for law enforcement only" is somewhat sobering in this regard.* The article talks about how long the different telecoms actually do store information and what information they keep.

For instance, only Verizon is said to actually store the contents of text messages, and then only for 5 days. However, all of the providers store information about everyone you texted. At the time of this report that was dated August 2010 (and these policies and procedures definitely change for better or worse over time), T-Mobile was reported to keep that information as long as 5 years! Verizon was the best of the major providers and only stored data about the parties engaged in texts for 1 year.

Perhaps the most sobering and potentially important to all of us when thinking about our privacy or what might come up in a court case is the practice of storing "cell-site" data. This basically keeps track of where your phone was located. Remember we discussed this earlier when I pointed out that your phone is always keeping track of the nearest cell towers so it can efficiently make a call or connection when required.

As usual, that feature has a possibly more sinister use. It can be (and has been) used to track a person's location and establish if that person was where he or she said he or she was, or possibly at or near the scene of a crime. The article mentioned above states that "Verizon keeps that data on a one-year rolling basis; T-Mobile for 'a year or more'; Sprint up to 2 years; and AT&T indefinitely, from July 2008." Here again we note a large repository of specific and important information that you may have a need to access.

But unlike voice data from a cell phone call that is never recorded and stored (outside of the needs of law enforcement and only then

---

* *Wired*, David Kravets, Which telecoms store your data the longest? Secret memo tells all, September 28, 2011. http://www.wired.com/threatlevel/2011/09/cellular-customer-data/. Retrieved October 12, 2011.

with the proper wiretapping protocols), text messaging is stored for at least some period of time on your cell provider's storage media as noted in the article. Even if, as is noted in the article, it is preserved for only a short time, that data certainly exist on your carrier's servers for at least a brief period of time.

It must also be noted that text messages are stored on a smart phone's memory for as long as there is space to do so. I saw a demonstration recently at a mobile forensics conference that showed complete text messages on the presenter's phone going back for more than a year. The bottom line is that those messages take up very little room in memory and so are likely to exist for a very long time.

Before we leave this subject we also have to note the somewhat disturbing recent revelations about both intelligence agencies and private companies' practices. We now all must accept (though many of us in the information security field never doubted) that any and all data about you and/or your communications may well be being collected and stored by government entities (and not necessarily legally), or by companies who want to use your data to sell you more stuff or just study your habits.

You can also browse the Internet on many of these devices. We are going to discuss the records created by Internet browsing in more detail later, and those records will remain the same whether you are using a computer or a smart phone. So all we need to note here is that, again, your phone will store information about where you have been surfing, what you downloaded, what you searched for, and your favorites as long as there is room in its memory.

Finally, modern smart phones allow you to run other applications such as games, news readers, book readers, and even production applications like word processors and spreadsheet programs.

Often, because of the memory limitations on these devices, they will store the actual documents, and so forth, on a provider's site on the Internet. This is often called cloud storage or cloud computing, and that is a separate section (3.12). They may also store that data or back it up on your personal computer when you tether or link your smart phone to the computer via a cable or docking device.

For games or readers, the information is usually stored on the phone, sometimes on removable memory cards that are getting larger and larger in capacity even as they get smaller and smaller in size.

These removable memory cards use flash memory and can be as small as a fingernail. In the section on memory we get into more detail about how they store data. But for now simply recognize that these can be another source of information. They will store not only the books and applications you use, but information about those applications and books—the all-important metadata we referred to before. That might include when you last opened the application, or the page you last read in the book, or any notes or bookmarks you inserted into the book or magazine as you read it. All of that information might become very important when or if you need to answer a question about what you or someone else was doing when.

For instance, imagine if you received a text message from someone you did not know very well saying that that person was out of the country and stranded and needed financial assistance. This is a real example of a common scam.

How might you use the information you just learned to tell if this is a scam? You might be able to contact your cellular provider to find out the source of the message. If you are law enforcement or an attorney, you might consider a subpoena to the provider for all information about the source's device.

Or, as another more likely example, what if your daughter insists that she could not possibly have sent 1000 text messages last week. You can simply take a look at her phone and check the records it stores and in most cases it will tell you exactly how many messages were sent. Your provider will certainly have that information available online and in some detail, including when and to whom your daughter was texting. If you happen to be a forensics expert like me, you can be even more cruel to your daughter by pulling out the records from the phone and having the actual messages to look at (but I would never do that to my daughters, so do not try this at home—it will only cause family strife).

The point to recognize here is that once again we revealed a source of electronic information that you need to be aware of, and that you may need to gain access to.

In order to acquire, preserve, organize, and produce that information, you will need to understand and have access to the sources of the data. That might entail a contractual relationship with your cellular provider. This is something that a business might be able to arrange, but that a private person is unlikely to have. Of course, law enforcement or attorneys have legal procedures that might allow them to gain access to some of these data if the data are located at the provider or on a personal device.

In most cases, a private customer's access to these data is going to be limited to the records a provider keeps for billing on your account, and anything that the device will report on, such as minutes, most recent contacts, and so forth. But that can be important and valuable information, so it behooves you to be aware of it and to understand how to access it.

If you are a legal professional, law enforcement, or an IT staff person who might be providing assistance in this regard, it is important to consider all of the types of data that exist and to become familiar with the resources, tools, and skills required to acquire it. In coming chapters, we discuss those in detail, so stay tuned (or skip ahead if you cannot wait).

3.11 Digital Video

If you look up digital video recording on the Internet, you will find that they want to tell you all about that little black box that some of you television addicts have attached to your TV, such as TiVo or your cable company's DVR. They are basically a large hard drive with a connection to your cable TV provider that allows you to record hours of television offerings and play them back (skipping the commercials if you like) at a later time.

While those devices store a great deal of electronic data that could conceivably be used as evidence (perhaps just to show your tendency toward sappy romances or violent cop shows), they are not the type of digital video we will discuss here.

However, it is still worthwhile to note that there are data there and that because they are basically digital storage, they can hold electronic evidence that might need to be captured and preserved. It is just one more place you should keep in mind as you are considering all of the possible sources of information that surround you.

What I would like to discuss here, however, is digital video that is captured by video surveillance devices (Figure 3.11). You may hear these devices referred to as CCTV, or closed-circuit television. These

Figure 3.11 Video surveillance cameras can be an important source of digital evidence.

devices are simply cameras that can be (and are) mounted anywhere. They have proliferated in these days of more fear around terrorism and crime, and in many cities you will find them peeking at you from every street corner. Most corporations and buildings use these as part of their surveillance for security, and of course most retail service providers have them strategically located to try to prevent or deter theft. Banks have had video surveillance for as long as the technology existed.*

In the past, these devices were, as advertised, simple closed video feeds that sent those signals down the cable to a television screen that was sometimes monitored by a security guard. Other times it was simply recorded to tape for review in case of an event.

But, as with everything else, all of this signaling and recording evolved so that the majority of these devices store their data digitally on hard drives. This increased the capacity for storage, and the quality of the video also increased as the technology evolved and improved over time.

Another big change, besides quality, has been the incorporation of wireless technology to allow for the deployment of these devices in more places and without the need to hide cabling to make them more discreet.

Video surveillance cameras can be a simple fixed device in the corner of a room; a high-end movable, zoom-able device overlooking

---

* The impact of CCTV. http://webarchive.nationalarchives.gov.uk/20110218135832/ http://rds.homeoffice.gov.uk/rds/pdfs05/hors292.pdf. Retrieved February 12, 2011.

a large area; or even tiny, barely noticeable "pinhole" cameras used for gathering intelligence without anyone being able to see them.

In all cases they work in a similar fashion for our purposes. They are controlled either by an automated program or by a human controller (or both), and the data they record are stored for varying amounts of time depending on the storage capacity and the retention laws or regulations for the organization capturing them.

As an example, a bank will have regulations from financial laws as to how long it must keep video records of daily activities. They will also probably have organizational rules that dictate how long those records are preserved. To that end, they will be required to purchase or arrange for enough storage capacity to serve those needs.

Digital video, especially at the higher quality with which it is currently captured, can take up a great deal of storage space. A high-definition video file of approximately 10 minutes length will use approximately 3 gigabytes or more, so imagine how much data storage you would need to preserve a workday's worth of video data. If you do the math, you realize that we are looking at close to 150 gigabytes for an 8-hour day, and because most organizations are likely to record at least 10–12 hours daily, it will be closer to 200 gigabytes a day. If they are recording 24 hours a day, it would be at least twice that.

We said earlier that storage is getting less expensive and larger all the time, but it still is not free. So, even assuming you have a very large data store of say 50 terabytes, if you are storing 24 hours of video, you would be at capacity in about 4 months.

Two things are likely: first, many organizations cannot and will not afford the cost, space, and resources to maintain 50 terabytes of storage; and second, many organizations will require data to be retained for longer than 4 months, especially if they might be under litigation or regulatory constraints.

And therein lies the rub, as the Bard so clearly put it long ago. The data are often very important for legal cases, for understanding traffic patterns, for monitoring efficiency in a workplace, for just knowing what the weather is at your final destination, or for many other uses. So how do we handle this proliferation of data?

Organizations and application developers came up with several ways. There are applications that allow you to define the specific time frames you want to capture. There are others that will discriminate between times of activity and inactivity and only preserve data from the times when something is going on in the video frame. There are even more sophisticated and "smart" applications that are able to discern specific patterns of behavior or types of activities and record those.

Then, there are many tools for compression of those data files as well as storage alternatives that allow organizations to store that data off-site with archival services, either in physical tape storage or as online or cloud services.

Once again, we have arrived at the point where I remind you to think about where any of this data might be located in case you need to access it, preserve it, or look through it for any reason.

For instance, imagine you work in an organization where the physical or facility security staff has CCTV cameras located around your office space. For weeks, people have been complaining that their lunches have been gone through and their apples keep disappearing from the shared kitchen space.

Do you know who is in charge of your security staff? Can you contact that person and ask him or her to begin preserving some of the video from the CCTV cameras closest to the kitchen? This is not only a practical question; it may be a legal question as well. Have you checked with your legal department or outside counsel to see if it would be legal for you to use those video files as evidence to capture the apple thief?

On the practical side, do you know if the video from those cameras is being stored at all, or for how long? Let's assume you answered in the affirmative so far. You know the staff lead for the security guards; you know from checking with her that the cameras store up to 2 days of data before they overwrite the hard drives they are storing information on; you checked with legal counsel, and their opinion is that you can use this information as evidence.

The next part is the interesting part. Now you need to have the time and tools to preserve that evidence in a forensically sound manner (again, we talk a lot more about that later), review it carefully and completely, document everything that was done, and produce it as evidence to whoever will take action. That might be the apple police, the human resources department, or maybe your attorney.

As trivial as this example might seem, it is a good way to begin to recognize all of the parts of the puzzle you need to think about when considering the existence of this type of digital information.

As a business owner or even just a manager, you will absolutely want to have thought about these things ahead of time in order to be sure you have a way to deal with them as needed. If you are an IT staff person, you may well have the responsibility of assisting your management, human resources staff, attorneys, or even law enforcement in the acquisition and preservation of these data. And finally, as a citizen, it is important to realize that digital video data are being collected on you nearly everywhere you go these days. For the most part that is benign, and unless you are criminally inclined it is unlikely that you will ever have reason to access that data. Yet there may be good reasons you might need to do so. You might find yourself in a legal dispute in which digital video evidence is important. Or you might simply have a reason to want to know what is recorded on video equipment that you control or have access to. That could be as simple as looking at a remote Web camera to see what the snow is like at the ski area, or to check the traffic. Or it could be checking your own home surveillance camera records to see if your teenager really got home at midnight like she was supposed to.

Because we now live in the world we do, where digital video is a reality of all of our lives every day, and nearly everywhere we go, it behooves us to recognize its existence and consider carefully the ramifications of this type of stored data.

3.12 Internet or Online Data

Finally, we come to the place where many of us spend most of our time, and where consequently the richest and perhaps most important store of data relevant to our lives and interests and activities resides.

The number of people with access to the Internet has grown exponentially right along with the growth in data storage capacity and computer power. In my former organization, which happened to be public sector, we often discussed the digital divide. This is an ever-shrinking division between those who have access to the Internet and those who do not. It is decreasing to some degree due to the efforts of government and nongovernmental organizations to create opportunities and facilities for more people to have that access.

Worldwide, the infrastructure to bring access to the Web is growing every day. Yurts in the remote steppes of Mongolia have satellite dishes and solar electric panels to power their laptops, free laptops are delivered to remote African villages, and satellite access is connected where the residents live in mud huts.

As this access grows, it also becomes a political issue in some countries where the governments are more restrictive and attempt to limit their citizens' access to the wide open information available on the Internet.

All this shows the immensity and reach of the data that anyone can access on today's Internet infrastructure. And each time someone accesses any of those resources a record is created. This is the focus of this section of the book, so let's begin to explore the what, when, how, why, and where of the data created each time you open up your Internet browser.

The "what" part of that question is almost infinite because of the many uses to which one can put the Internet in its current manifestation. For instance, you can

- Create and access documents
- Read and write and comment on blogs or news articles, or other online messages of varying lengths
- Research nearly anything and contribute to new research
- View, upload, or download photographs and video of any kind
- Search for or disseminate information on any subject
- Make audio or video phone calls
- Connect to friends and develop communities
- Raise money or promote your favorite charities
- Buy or sell anything imaginable (and some things you might prefer not to imagine)
- Offer things or bid on them in auctions
- Listen to lectures and take classes

My son recently introduced me to an online service that I cannot in good conscience recommend. I will not name it as I do not want to promote any specific tools or services here. However, it is a service that takes your input as to what subjects you are interested in and recommends websites you might enjoy from its vast records of the billions of sites available on the Internet. Then it asks you to rate each site it serves up as one you like or do not like, and it learns from that which sites are most likely of interest and continues (for as long as you keep asking) to serve up more and more sites, each of which seems more compelling than the last (because it is learning from your feedback).

It is extremely easy to burn up entire days cruising from one extremely cool website to another on this service. And the problem is exacerbated further if you have friends with similar interests who are using the same tool, because they will send you the cool sites they found. Of course, you will be returning the favor by sending them your finds, and before you know it, no one is getting anything done anymore.

The point of all this is to note that there is so much to do and see on the Internet we all live with today, that the variety, amount, and importance of the stored data on the Internet is absolutely the most important of all the data stores we discussed so far. Of course, the caveat, especially in the more recent "Web 2.0" version, is that anybody can post anything on the Internet whether it has any relation to the truth or not. That raises the obvious problem that even though this is the most important of the data stores, it can also be extremely difficult to establish its veracity or integrity. Keep this in mind as you consider the specifics of this type of data.

The "what" is as impossible to define as any other infinite entity. Suffice it to say that it is unlimited in scope or subject. The "how" is a little easier to define, so let's go there instead.

As with any digital data, the information about what a person accessed on the Internet is stored on his or her computer device in the binary code we discussed at the beginning of this chapter. To access it in its most basic form, a computer forensics expert would open up the data store and read those bits and bytes using a hex editor (a tool that translated the ones and zeros into hexadecimal code). If you know what to look for, you can locate headers (the code that tells you when you have reached the beginning of a particular type of record) that indicate you are looking at the beginning of the data cache or stored information about the user's Internet activity.

Thankfully, for the rest of us there are much simpler ways to at least see the basics of this information that do not require the tools or expertise of a computer forensics investigator.

In order to access the Internet from a computing device, there are a variety of applications called browsers. Most devices that use Microsoft operating systems will have Internet Explorer as their browser by default (or most recently "Edge"), as Microsoft bundles that in with the basic operating system. However, there are many more browser applications available. All of them are free and downloadable from the Internet (so you have to have a browser to start with—it is a good thing most all operating systems include one or another of them).

Some of the most widely recognized and used browsers besides Microsoft's Internet Explorer are Mozilla's Firefox, Apple's Safari, and Google's Chrome. All of these employ different engineering to create storage of everything you access on the Internet.

These stores are usually called a cache file. They can be stored in different folders, or even spread out among different folders on your hard drive depending on the browser application. But in every case, they literally keep track of every data item that you access while on the Internet, record them, and store them for some amount of time.

The length of time those data items are stored depends on the application and often on settings that you control. You can open a menu item in your browser application (usually called "Internet Options" or something similar) that allows you to either set limits on when and for how long cache files are kept, or delete and clear them altogether if you wish.

I said that these browser applications store every data item you access when you are on the Internet, but I am willing to bet that most of you have very little idea of all the types and amounts of data that entails. We look at some examples in a minute to show you, but first let's consider why these applications would bother to store all that data.

There are several reasons, and chief among them is not, in fact, to allow forensics investigators and law enforcement to have a way to catch you if you were bad. In fact, I would venture to say that was not even on the radar of the computer engineers who developed these applications. The main reason these items are stored is to make your experience while browsing more enjoyable and efficient.

When you open a browser and type in an Internet address (also known as a URL, or Uniform Resource Locator), you are taken to a website. As that site loads up, a lot is going on that we look at in greater detail soon. But one of the important things to this part of our conversation is that many different pieces of the website code are being loaded onto your computer so it can show you the site in all its glory.

You know that most sites have pictures, text in different formats, backgrounds, possibly even moving graphics or videos. All of those items are coded into the web page in a specific Internet language—the most common of which is called HTML (Hypertext Markup Language)—and that code language controls what you see on the page. If you click on part of the page or even just move your mouse over part of it, the code might reveal something new or create some other kind of action. All this happens by the design of the page as developed by the HTML code designer.

Remember when we discussed random-access memory, or RAM, on your computer and how data accessed from that memory is more quickly accessed than it is from your hard drive? Well, data that have to be downloaded from the Internet over cables or a wireless connection can take even longer to load up and be displayed or otherwise acted upon during a computer session.

To make your experience with an application more efficient and effective, most applications, including Web browsers, will move parts of what you are experiencing into memory for the fastest recall. So, part of what happens when you are looking at a website using a browser is that some of that data are held in memory during the session.

But all of the data required to make that website work are also stored in the cache file, because it is still much quicker to access the data directly from your computer's hard drive than it might be to download it from the Internet every time you need it. This is especially true of graphic files and movies, but it actually holds true for nearly everything that you see and do on the Internet.

This is the most important reason for the cache file. It allows you to move around on the Internet, and when parts of a page are needed as you are moving around, clicking on links, holding your mouse cursor over a part, or just moving between different areas of the site, they are quickly accessed from the cache file and displayed or acted upon by the browser application, thus enhancing your Internet experience and speeding everything up. Also, when and if you return to that site, the same cached data can be reused to speed up the reloading of that web page.

Let's look at an example of a single page and consider all of the different types of data that might be loaded into cache, as well as their utility or reason for being.

You can try this at home any time you feel the urge. In most every browser there will be an option under the View menu to view the source code or just the source. In recent versions of Internet Explorer, you find this choice at the bottom of the Page menu, for instance. If you do open up the source view, you are treated to pure HTML code. I know—this is terribly exciting, but try to contain your enthusiasm.

At the top of that source page you see header information. As noted previously, a forensics person would be looking for this type of information in hexadecimal code to help him or her recognize the beginning of a piece of HTML code, or the start of a website. This header information will tell what type of document coding is being used and might show the Internet address or URL.

As you move down the page you see a lot of different types of coding that tell the browser application what to show the viewer. We are not going to learn HTML coding here (whew!), but suffice it to note that everything that happens when you view a website is coded in that source view. You may note things like scripts, java, href, and so forth. These are all programming language that results in different actions or links or pictures appearing on the page.

If you were to examine the source page carefully and compare it to what you actually see when you are looking at the website (as only a true geek like myself might attempt—and I have in order to save you the pain), you would notice something interesting, at least to a forensics geek like myself. There are a lot of references to other URLs, to pictures, to actions, to videos, and so forth, that are not showing up as I look at the website in its normal view. Now, why would that be?

Well, it is because of what we talked about earlier. The website developer and browser designers want you to enjoy your experience, so they include everything that you will ever need to access in this source coding. And guess what? The browser loads all of that data into your cache file so it will be easier and quicker to access when you ask for it. Is that not thoughtful of them?

But this brings up some interesting considerations when we discuss the data stored and available on your computer that show your Internet activity. Think about that for a minute using an example page. In Figure 3.12, you see part of a website—the home page for Comcast.net, and in Figure 3.13, you see some of the source code for that same page.

Figure 3.12   A sample of a website view in a browser.

Figure 3.13   The source code for that same website.

What I want you to notice when you look at these two illustrations is the fact that although there is a lot of data showing on the website that you look at, there are many items noted in the source code which you do not see on the page. A very interesting one that you see referenced a lot in this sample graphic are cookies. We spend some more time on cookies later because they are very important, but for now just recognize that there is a lot more being loaded up in your browser from this one website than you see when you look at it.

This brief section that I used as an illustration is a very small part of the actual source code for this one page. In fact, as I scroll through the entire source code page, it is nearly 30 pages long and has almost 1,700 lines of code. And each of those lines of code represents some type of data being stored in the cache file so that the website will quickly and efficiently show you the news items, advertisements, pictures and graphics, and so forth.

If all of those data types are stored in your browser's cache, how much of that data have you actually viewed and acted upon?

In order for all of that data to be stored in my browser, all I had to do was open the Comcast.net site. I did not click on any of the links or read any of the stories or even look at most of the pictures that were stored unless they were at the top part of the first view of the page. There are literally dozens of other pictures and graphics that were stored in my cache that I never laid eyes on. Not to mention links to other sites, text, advertisements, and more that are now stored in my cache, but that I never knew existed.

So, why is that important?

Well, let's consider some extreme cases where it might be very important.

What if a site you went to contained inappropriate content of some type (i.e., pictures, racist propaganda speech, etc.), but the site was designed to look relatively benign on the surface and only reveal those items if you clicked on the right links, or dug deeper into the site. Or what if those items were purposely hidden within the source code as a way to disseminate them discreetly, or as a way to compromise you or your computer? All of the above are not only academic ideas but have happened in real life.

Then consider what might happen if you were suspected of storing such inappropriate data on your computer. An analysis of your

Internet cache files would show that in fact your computer did contain that data. Is it fair or safe to assume that you actually viewed that data or even knew it existed on your computer? Well, we now know the answer is no, but there are many folks out there who would not have any idea that was the case and might jump to the conclusion that if it is on your computer and it got there when you were using your Internet browser, you had to have put it there.

As a computer forensics expert, this is one of the most difficult tasks I face when I am analyzing someone's Internet use and trying to establish the truth regarding their activities. How do you show what actually happens during an Internet browsing session and analyze with some degree of certainty what a user was actually doing online? How do you establish which items that are now stored in the user's cache file were actually viewed or purposely stored there by the user?

It is possible to do so, at least to an acceptable degree of certainty, with some careful and detailed analysis, but it is not in any way apparent at first viewing. And of course that can be incredibly important when you are responsible for establishing beyond a reasonable doubt the activities of a user online.

All this is to help you understand the incredible wealth of information that is captured and retained within an Internet cache file when someone uses his or her browser application to work or play online. But it is also (and equally importantly) meant to be a big caveat about recognizing the limitations of that information and the assumptions you can make from what you find in that data.

I promised to discuss cookies because of their importance on websites, so let's get to that next.

Cookies are, on their surface, very simple text files that seem relatively benign. In most operating systems, there will be a folder within the Internet program folders or storage area that holds these text files. They are created and stored for a certain amount of time based on the website's programming or on actions a user can perform or settings within the browser application that you as a user can configure.

When you land on a website that uses cookies, one of the items it downloads is this little text file. Often it will start by running a program that searches on your computer to see if a cookie matching its parameters already exists. If it does, it will read that cookie and possibly update it or revise it with new information. In its most benign manifestation, a website's cookie will possibly note your username, when you last visited, and possibly some preferences you set up on the site. Again, this is a way to ensure that your experience on the site is easy and efficient. You will see what you saw last time, your username will automatically fill in when you start to type it in, and so on.

A perhaps less benign and more invasive use of cookies are ones that note what you searched for, or maybe the items you clicked on. Those cookies are stored with your computer name or possibly the IP (or Internet Protocol) address from where you are browsing. That information is often sold to data mining companies that work with advertisers.

I am sure many of you will have noticed this when you do some shopping online, using Google or Bing or another search engine. The next time you log in to certain sites on the Internet, advertisements magically appear that are attempting to sell you something similar to what you were searching for. And it does not have to be on the search site you used for your shopping, or even on the shopping sites you ended up on. It can be totally unrelated websites, but the advertisements are uncannily similar to those things you already searched for.

Or perhaps you note that advertisements will be for things in your specific area of town, or for something that your age group would be most interested in.

The bottom line is that marketing has become one of the most important uses of the Internet, and cookies are one of the main ways that marketing is managed. Cookies are used to store information about what you do online. What you search for, what you are interested in, what you follow as far as news, where you physically log in from, and so on. All of that information, along with data collected about your computer's location and the times, durations, and frequencies of your Web browsing are used to establish a profile of who you are and what you are most likely to respond to. This information can be used to simply enhance your Web browsing experience or to target advertising and products to you so you are most likely to respond. And when it works, that adds to your profile and makes it even more targeted and precise.

All of this is not necessarily a bad thing. It is not terrible if your Internet experience is enhanced and your time is saved by having things show up that are of interest to you or having the website configured the way you like it and having it fill in your information for you to save time. But there are some who feel it is an invasion of their privacy to have someone creating such a detailed profile of them and their habits in order to target their advertising.

Some people would argue that it is just a little too close for comfort to a world where a less benign organization could use that information against you. In fact, if you happen to end up on the wrong side of law enforcement or other government entities, the data are absolutely part of what they have available to them as evidence of your character, your whereabouts, your habits, and your personal beliefs, attitudes, or preferences.

Hopefully and thankfully, most of you reading this book are not likely to end up on that side of the law. However, there are many people throughout the world who are accessing and using this same Internet with the same or similar tools and applications for whom their government may not be so benign or restricted by the rule of law and ethics that we are used to here in the Western world. For those people, the ability of Internet cache files and cookies and other Internet storage tools to capture and hold such personal information can be a real threat and a big concern.

When we discuss the Internet and what is stored there, we also need to consider what is stored in that great online cloud of data as well. The data stored locally on your computer are at least to some extent under your control.

You have the ability to delete cache files or restrict their size. You can delete or restrict cookies as well. In fact, there are programs you can purchase or load onto your computer that are designed specifically to make the management and configuration of those types of Internet data stores easier and to give you total control, even to the extent of being able to wipe those files in a way that makes it hard or impossible to recover even with forensics tools.

But when we are talking about the cloud, or all the data created and stored about you online, those controls become much more difficult, and in many cases impossible.

Consider social media sites such as Facebook, Google Plus, LinkedIn, and others. If you do not have an account on one of those sites, you may not realize the quantity and variety of information that one can choose to store there.

These sites and others like them were labeled Web 2.0 because they open up a new way of interacting with the Internet. Instead of simply receiving information from websites that others posted there, in Web 2.0 applications you are actively engaged in creating and posting content of one type or another. The rising use of blogs, or what were originally called Web logs, is another example of a Web 2.0 phenomenon.

On social media sites, people connect with a community of "friends," or colleagues, or people of like interests and share their feelings, ideas, pictures, videos, current status, and much more. This can be of great value in building community and sharing communications. It can be a good way to connect with each other and enhance your ability to learn from each other. Other applications give you quick communications possibilities such as instant messaging (IM) or Short Message Service (SMS) or Multimedia Message Service (MMS), often just called texting.

Twitter is an example of a sort of hybrid of the idea of SMS together with blogging—a sort of short version of a blog in which you can post brief messages of interest to your community (or your "followers" as they are known in Twitter language).

MMS is different from SMS in that it includes the ability to send video and pictures as well as text in a short messaging format or can allow messaging to more than one person at a time.

But with all of the advantages and benefits these types of new Web 2.0 applications bring, we must also consider the other side of the coin.

If you participate in any of these types of Web 2.0 activities, you are sure to have noticed that they are often used in less than advantageous ways. Facebook postings about someone's cat's hairball are just not that important. And receiving a tweet from someone with the profound revelation that they have just woken up from a nap can be disappointing at best and annoying more often than not. Bloggers with little or nothing to say, or with false information to share, nonetheless are often compelled to share that information or spew their meaningless work into the blogosphere.

And then, because Web 2.0 is all about interaction and sharing, there are the comments and commentary that accompany the ability to publish anything you choose. This conversation often seems to bring out the worst in humanity, and I have witnessed many examples of what I could only describe as the de-evolution of our culture and intelligence.

It almost seems as if the discreet nature of a cyber-based personality allows some Internet users to reveal the most bizarre and deeply hidden (and often most distressfully disgusting) parts of their personality.

It has also been noted that the very ability to create a community of any type of belief while hiding behind the anonymity of the Internet has created a place where even the most socially unacceptable behavior can now find empathy and support from a community of like-minded people. This contributed to a new environment where pedophiles, terrorists, and bigots can all find a group of anonymous supporters to validate their perversions and offer them support and encouragement.

That is one dark side of the Web 2.0 revolution that cannot be ignored. Another, less troubling to society but perhaps of equal or greater danger to individuals is the very fact of being able to say or post anything on these forums. The danger lies in the fact that once posted there, the posts are completely out of your control. An innocent wish to poke fun at a friend by posting an embarrassing picture on a social media site could lead inexorably to that friend losing his or her job, being refused admittance to the military or college, or being otherwise harmed.

Your status update saying you had a heck of a party last night and probably will not be over the hangover in time for work could inadvertently end up before your boss, or the HR manager for that job you just applied for. That picture of you at Mardi Gras could become someone else's background that they stare at and fantasize about, or that perhaps is the motivation for them to begin stalking you.

And then there is the use of that data to do that stalking, or to attempt to compromise your computer, or to bully you. The amount of information that can be found about a person posted on their social media sites can be staggering. If someone with ill intent spends enough time searching, he or she is likely to be able to develop a detailed picture of you and who you are, where you live, what you do every day, where you work, what your likes and dislikes are, who your friends and family are, and more. With that information that person can tailor attack e-mails that will draw you in by their familiarity with you. They could stalk you and find you when you are vulnerable to physical attack. They might use that information to embarrass you or bully you or insult you in the forums.

All of this is to recognize, once again, the incredible amount and variety of data that we create, or is created for us, about ourselves in the world we live in today. Online data are particularly compelling to consider because they tend to have a life of their own and to grow with or without our input.

You should also recognize that storage of data for organizations and even individuals is increasingly moving to "the cloud" or to online storage service providers. These can be located anywhere in the world and staffed by anyone. Having a good understanding of how to access and protect that information as well as good contract language to ensure your ability to do so is very important.

And the data are, for the most part, entirely out of our control. Data exist on servers and systems that are physically out of our reach. Even logically, they are often irretrievable and unmanageable by us once the data are collected. There are active and lucrative applications running 24/7/365 to collect, collate, preserve, and use that information whether for good or evil or something less easy to define as one or the other.

Suffice it to say as we end this chapter on the Internet and online data, that this particular cloud of data is growing every day and will continue to grow exponentially.

Your particular piece of that data cloud surrounds you with information that you may or may not want to acknowledge or accept, but it envelops you nonetheless. It is extremely important to consider at least what things you can control and to do your best to both understand what those data items are and to influence their existence and content to the best of your ability. Because if you do not, you can be sure someone else will.

Before we leave this subject, we should at least mention the idea of an intranet as well. An intranet is an online service internal to an organization. Depending on your organization's size and complexity, these can be less daunting to understand and control, as they are limited in scope and are usually isolated from the larger Internet.

However, when we consider the data created for and about us, we cannot leave this data store out.

The information about us in this data store will most often contain the data about the work that we do; the electronic documents or products that we create; our pay scale, taxes, and benefits; our employment history and performance measurements; possibly medical health and insurance information including information about our dependents; and very likely banking information so we can be paid efficiently.

All of this is again a part of the information that exists electronically and can be used both in a beneficial way by beneficent actors such as our employer, or used against us by someone with less beneficent motives. As with all other forms of data, it behooves us to recognize how the data are created, where the data live, and what controls we have over the data creation, maintenance, existence, and acquisition or deletion.

3.13 Storage Media

We referred several times in this chapter to different types of storage media, and these are important to understand as they are the physical components or devices on which all of this important data are actually residing.

Whether we are talking about servers, databases, Internet, or cloud, even phones and digital video, all data that are preserved are stored on some type of media. These could be any of the following (and some data may be stored on more than one type of media even within the same computing device):

- Hard disk drives
- Random-access memory
- Optical storage media (CDs or DVDs)
- Floppy disk drives
- Magnetic tape
- Flash or solid-state memory (USB drives)

Let's begin with hard disk drives. A hard disk drive contains several metal platters stacked up inside itself with a writing arm that swings back and forth across those platters charging and discharging segments of the drive to store all those ones and zeros we spent time talking about. We do not need to get into detail about how that is done. It is enough to understand that all of the data stored on hard drives are stored as magnetic plus and minus spots on those platters. They are microscopic in size, and as the technology has evolved, the platters have become smaller and thinner, the writing arms more delicate, and the drives have shrunk in size while growing in capacity.

Understanding how this works can be important to someone who is depending on gathering data from a hard drive that is separate from its computing device. All those mechanisms can and do sometimes fail, so that there are times when one has to try to acquire data from a drive that no longer functions as it should.

Yet the magnetic ones and zeros still exist on those metal platters, so it is possible with the correct tools and skills to access that information and put it to use again in a court case or for other needs.

We already touched on RAM, or random-access memory, and talked about how and why a computer would store data there. In most cases, these components are made up of computer chips mounted on a plastic "stick."

Each of these computer chips does its part to store all of those ones and zeros as magnetic changes in its internal structure. Again, as the technology has evolved, these chips have become smaller and smaller and are able to store more and more data. However, as we noted earlier, RAM maintains the state of those ones and zeros by virtue of a constant supply of electronic energy. Within a very short time of that energy being removed, all of the data return to a resting state and any information stored there is gone.

Optical storage media uses laser beams to burn pits into special media on disks such as CDs and DVDs. Those bumps burned onto a disk in a spiral form from inside to out represent those same ones and zeros. Some optical storage disks can only be written to once, while others can be reused and have the old data written over or erased.*

These storage media are very portable and can hold a relatively large amount of data, so they are often used to store, archive, and transport information. They are also used for music, movies, and computer game distribution. When these are damaged they can be very difficult to recover data from. However, again, with the right tools and skills, it is sometimes possible to do so.

---

* eHow, Dan Keen, What are optical storage devices? http://www.ehow.com/about_5082834_optical-storage-devices.html. Retrieved February 21, 2011.

Floppy disk drives are not used much anymore, but it is still quite possible that you might find data stored on these media as they were very popular and widely used in the not too distant past. There are a wide variety of types and sizes of floppy disks and other devices that use this basic storage engineering, and we talked about those earlier. But the way they store data is similar to that of the hard drive. The difference is that they most often only use one platter and it is made of a flexible material (thus the term floppy) that is held inside of a solid case.

The biggest problem with recovering or acquiring data from one of these types of media can be the lack of the correct drive or device that will access and read them, especially as you consider the older and rarer varieties of floppy disk media. If you find that you need to gather data from one of these types of media, it will require that you contact someone with the correct drive to access, read, and preserve that information.

Tape drives simply use magnetic tape that is spooled and runs past read–write pads. Those pads pick up or lay down the magnetic pulses representing the ones and zeros of data onto the tape. They can be overwritten and used more than once, though they do suffer from damage and wear and tear more than the other media we discussed so far.

Magnetic tape reels were used as one of the first ways to store large amounts of data long term in the early days of computing. You may even have seen old movies where there were giant computers with spinning tape reels. These can still be found in large data centers, though the more common use of magnetic tape is in small cartridges that are used for backup storage.

These can be hugely important resources for archival data and should definitely be considered when you are thinking about where data might live. But as mentioned earlier, they can be corrupted or worn out, so again they may require specialists to recover data from them.

Finally, we come to the type of storage that is fast becoming the norm: solid-state or flash memory. This type of memory has been around for a long time in places like the BIOS chip on the mother-board of a computer, or in those small SD cards used in cameras.

This technology has evolved as well and many of the new smart phones, tablets, laptops, and so on, are now using this type of storage because it is fast, small, lightweight, and uses less energy and generates less heat than conventional mechanical storage.

Flash or solid-state memory uses a technology known as EEPROM, which stands for electronically erasable programmable read-only memory.* This means that there are no moving parts and it stores data by changing the state of the many electronic transistors to represent either a one or a zero. The data are read-only, but the device can be electronically erased and then reprogrammed with new data.

USB flash drives are perhaps the best-known use of this storage technology today, but as noted earlier, it is used extensively and is becoming very popular.

Forensically gathering data from one of these drives can be a challenge because when they are "erased" there is nothing left behind as there is on a mechanical hard disk or floppy disk drive. There are no telltale traces or pieces of data that can be patched together to try to find deleted or corrupted data. When a flash drive is "flashed," it is completely wiped clean in preparation for more data.

In recent evolutions of this technology it is possible to erase parts of the data and preserve parts without completely wiping the entire device, but the data that are wiped are still unrecoverable unless stored in another location.

That is why many of the newer devices such as smart phones and tablets rely on online or cloud storage as a way to back up and recover their data. Often those archives of data are the only recourse if you have a device using solid-state memory storage that is corrupted or erased. Keep this in mind if you need data from one of these new devices, and be ready to find the backup resource if necessary.

3.14 Internet of Things (IOT) or of Everything (IOE)

There is a growing trend that we need to include in this chapter regarding what is called either the Internet of Things or the Internet of Everything.

Due to changes in the way computer devices are addressed (from IPv4 to IPv6—more on that later), it is now possible to connect billions

---

* howstuffworks, Jeff Tyson, How flash memory works. http://electronics.howstuff-works.com/flash-memory.htm. Retrieved February 21, 2011.

more devices to the Internet. This has been touted and is being used to create conveniences and efficiencies in managing everything from traffic control to smart houses. By installing and connecting computer systems in everything from traffic signal controls to electric meters to refrigerators and toasters, we have created ways to better control our energy use, and enhance our lifestyles.

Imagine a day (and this is actually already being done) when your refrigerator notices that you are getting low on eggs and orders more from the online grocer for you. Or your toaster and coffeemaker and thermostat all automagically wake up and get your morning ready for you.

Smart electric meters have given utility companies ways to be extremely efficient in delivering and managing energy use.

Wearable fitness devices can monitor your health, nutrition, exercise, and so on, and send all that data back to a server in the cloud.

Of course, all of this comes at a price as the security and privacy issues that all of these new exposures create are only beginning to be considered.

There are now new cases that we are seeing where information from these devices has been used in court. For instance, if you are claiming that you have a back injury and can no longer work, but your fitness device shows that you've been running stairs all week, that could affect your case!

Another interesting possibility was raised recently on one of the legal forums I participate in. What is the responsibility of a homeowner with a "smart house" when they sell their house? Should all that data they have collected be required to be divulged in their disclosure agreement on the purchase and sale?

All good and interesting questions whose answers will evolve as we move further into this brave new world.

3.15 Event and System Logs

Another big source of data that must be considered are the logs that are created by all of the devices and systems we have discussed in this chapter.

Each of these devices and systems (including now all of the IoT/IoE devices) probably create some kind of logging that is stored within the system and that can give information on application use, security events, system warnings, and so on. There can be a wealth of data in these logs, however their efficacy is greatly affected by how they are configured, stored, and preserved. Some systems have automatic logging but have limited storage, whereas others are totally configurable and may store little or no usable data dependent upon the administrator's choices.

Collecting, managing, and analyzing these logs can be a challenging task and often requires the tools and skills of an expert.

Once again, it is of utmost importance that you recognize this possible source of important information about what has been happening with any of these devices or systems and know who to call if you need to acquire that data.

3.16 Desktop Computer Facts

In this section we sum it all up by discussing the desktop computer that most of us spend a majority of our time working with.

In our discussion of servers and mobile devices we spent quite a bit of time looking at the engineering and mechanics of how a computer works, so we will try not to be redundant. However, in case you are using this as a reference book and not reading it word for word, one chapter at a time, we will go through the basics once again.

To use that fine old gospel hymn as a guide, we look at this like the story of Ezekiel. The toe bone's connected to the foot bone, the foot bone's connected to the ankle bone, and so on (Figure 3.14).

As I sit here typing these words into my word processor application, a series of things is going on. The toe bone in this case is the action of my fingers on the keyboard. As I strike a spring-loaded key, it presses down and closes a circuit in the keyboard that creates an electrical signal that is sent from the keyboard to a keystroke processor (the "foot bone") inside my desktop computer.

That processor is able to decipher the electrical signals created by my closing that circuit in a particular way and on a particular spot on my keyboard. The signal the processor receives is, as we discussed before, a series of electronic pulses that translate into a series of ones and zeros. Those in turn are translated by the processor into machine code that it "processes" (maybe that is why it is called a processor) and

Figure 3.14 To understand how your desktop works, we work our way up the skeleton.

passes on over the electronic communications system (known as a bus, and consisting of cables or channels of conductive metal on a plastic board) inside the computer—the "ankle bone" as it were.

This processed information, basically saying something along the lines of "he pushed the lowercase 't' key!" arrives at the central processor (yes, the leg bone).

The central processor meanwhile has been processing away and keeping track of everything happening in and on the desktop computer. It knows that I started up a word processing application, and it has been receiving and processing the input and output from that application's programming. It is aware that the input it just received from the keystroke processor belongs to the word processor application that is currently running, so it does several things with that information. And here, I am sure to your everlasting relief, the "dry bones" metaphor becomes less apt, so we abandon it (for now). Try not to be too disappointed.

To me, the most obvious thing that occurs is that it sends more ones and zeros over the communications channels to another processor connected by a cable to my monitor.

That processor interprets those ones and zeros and, having processed the information, sends ones and zeros to the monitor telling it to light up certain pixels on the screen and darken certain other pixels on the screen (pixels are tiny dots of different-colored light on a monitor that create the graphics you see). Those pixels turn on or off in the right part of the screen, depending on the programming and information received from all of the processors along the way and result in the letter "t" showing up on my screen.

Meanwhile, back at the central processor, that information that it received from the keystroke processor was sent to other places as well.

It was loaded into memory or RAM. If you were good enough to read and absorb that section where we discussed random-access or volatile memory, you will remember that data you are working on while your computer is running are stored there because it is much faster to store it there and is easier to access. The ability of all of these things to happen, seemingly without delay, is in large part due to that engineering design that stores that data and much more of what you are doing on your desktop in that very fast input and output storage called RAM.

But wait, that is not all (if I may quote late night advertising). The central processor also sends that information off to more permanent and slower storage on your hard drive, or possibly to other storage devices. Of course, every bit of that happens so quickly, that as I type along at my relatively slow 50 words per minute or so, there does not seem to be any delay between my clicking away on the keyboard and the appearance of the text on my screen. In fact, the delay is miniscule in almost all cases.

But you have probably had it happen as I have, that sometimes this system breaks down. Something going on with your desktop has taken up all the processing power available and suddenly you type and nothing appears. Usually, it is just a matter of time and then everything speeds up again and you are good to go. But sometimes these effects can be long lasting and considerably annoying. We have grown used to the speed of computer life and a delay of even a second can be quite distressing.

If you are as old as I am, you may still remember those bad old days when such delays were not only normal but were considered acceptable as long as they did not slow things down too much.

You had to be careful about what you asked your computer and operating system to handle because you would absolutely see the effects if you pushed too much at it at a time. In fact, it might just give up and die altogether, and unless you were lucky enough to have saved things carefully, all your work would disappear in what we painfully referred to as the "blue screen of death," at least in old Windows operating systems.

This also brings up that while the central processor is capable of doing all those wonderful things, it can only do what you tell it to do. It will not auto-magically back up your work for you unless you told it to do so. Some word processing applications automatically save your work on a regular basis, either defined by you in configuration settings or as part of their own recovery programming. But all of them have a way that you can purposely save your work, and you should do so on a regular basis if you want to be sure it will be there when you need it.

This is another action that you might take that will affect what is stored on your desktop—the "toe bone" from the other foot, if you will. Sorry, I just like that song and that metaphor.

This is the action where you choose a menu item in an application: in this case, the Save option. In most word processors, there will be a File menu that allows you to open a new file, close a file, print a document, and Save or Save As. This is not meant to be an instruction book on how to use applications, so we will not delve into all those options here. But in the Save category you can choose to simply click on Save which will save your document in the same format, with the same name, and in the same location from which you opened it. If it is a new document, you will be prompted to pick a name and place to store it. If you choose Save As, you have the opportunity to give your document a new name, save it to a new place, and even change the format in which it is saved.

As with the other actions that you take on your computer, this starts a series of events. When you select that item from the menu, the application coding sends information to the central processor identifying a data set that might be currently stored in memory or in a temporary folder on the hard drive.

The application then follows that information with the information you give it (or that it has in memory) as to where, how, and under what name that data set should be stored. The central processor processes that information, grabs the data from whichever storage it is currently residing in, and copies it to the next available space on the hard drive. Code is added to the data set that identifies it to the central processor for future access. The identifying data are used to index the data. To do so on a Windows computer, a new record is created in a Master File Table (MFT) at the root of the hard drive's directory structure. This MFT is a flat database file that contains information about every file created on your computer, including when it was created, modified, or accessed; what folder it is in; whether it is still active or not; and other information.

In Apple, Linux, or other operating systems, the indexing and tracking of files are done differently, but we do not have the space or brain capacity to get into all of the different methods here. However, suffice it to say that in any operating system, in any type of computing device, there will always be a method of indexing and referencing the location, format, and status of every file ever created on that device. This is true even if that file was deleted by the user.

The only exception to that rule is if the storage medium has purposely been cleaned, or "wiped." This involves special tools and usually takes some time and effort to accomplish, at least if one is attempting to clean all traces of data from a device of any size.

It is interesting to note that this process of purposely deleting or "wiping" your drive can still leave traces of itself. Those traces or artifacts of that activity have in some cases been considered as evidence of wrongdoing. There have certainly been cases in which law enforcement or the courts made a legitimate and accepted assertion that the very absence of evidence, and the evidence of its having been tampered with by someone with much to gain from its absence, is evidence.

The lesson here is that every tiny action you take on your laptop, desktop, or any other computing device for that matter, has an effect.

This is most important when you consider the implications for the preservation and integrity of electronic data for litigation or any other reason. The action of turning on your computer makes changes to some of the data that reside there. Opening a file in a word processor makes changes to that file, even if you do not change anything in the words or even type in a new comma.

And that brings us neatly to the end of this section with our final discussion on metadata.

3.17 Metadata and Other Nonapparent Data

As the final section of this chapter discussing the location and types of places that data can live, we need to talk about metadata.

Metadata is best described as the data about the data.

In nearly any data set that is created by any application, there will be data included that are not apparent to someone merely viewing that document, spreadsheet, photo, video, and so on. That might typically include information about

- The application that created the data
- When it was created, accessed, modified, or even deleted
- In audio, picture or video files, information about the location (GPS coordinates) and type of device used to record the information
- The author or user information/coding for whomever was logged into the computer or application at the time the data were created or modified
- Coding information identifying the type of code used to create the file
- An unlimited variety of other information inserted by the application, or by the user of the application

In order to view that information, one either has to have tools that will open and interpret the basic hexadecimal coding or the application's code; or use tools within the application that show you that data.

There are also special applications specifically designed to decipher, display, and manage metadata from different applications. These are commonly used in legal matters when metadata are either specifically required or need to be removed.

It is more and more often the case in litigation proceedings that astute counselors and judges recognize the value of metadata and their relevance and are insisting that metadata be included in the evidence discovery process. In fact, there are several recent cases that establish metadata specifically as an integral and important part of ESI that must be included in any electronic discovery and production (see Chapter 1 for case law examples).

If you would like to see a simple example of what we are discussing, and if you use Microsoft Word, you can do so very easily by clicking

Figure 3.15 To see some of the metadata in a Microsoft Word document, open the Properties.

on either "File" and then "Properties" in older versions, or clicking on the Windows button on the top left corner, and selecting "Prepare" and then "Properties" (Figure 3.15).

In other word processors or applications there will be a similar menu item somewhere that is usually called Properties or might be included in a View menu.

In any case, when you open those menus you will be shown the metadata stored about your document. In many instances this menu item will also give you the option of turning on and off certain types of metadata recording and even the option to create and input your own.

All of this becomes part of the data set that is your document, spreadsheet, photograph, video, and so on. And though you will not normally see that data if you print out or simply view the data, the data are definitely there and can have extremely important consequences.

After all, what is the bottom-line reason for having a court case nearly every time? It is to establish what happened, when did it happen, and who did it, right? So, where does that information live in a data set? It lives and is recorded and stored in the metadata.

Before we leave this subject of hidden data, we need to mention something with the odd name of Steganography. Steganography is basically the intentional hiding of data within a data set.

Now, way back at the beginning when we were talking about how a computer creates and stores data, we discussed the basic coding that goes on at the machine level.

We said that coding is represented in hexadecimal notation and that if you examine a computer's hard drive or memory using forensics applications, you can see that hexadecimal code. And if you know what you are looking for, you can find clues in there that indicate that the next thing you will see might be an Adobe PDF file, or a Microsoft Word document. These are indicated by headers—basically a string of hexadecimal code that tells the processors what type of data set follows.

If you then proceed through the hexadecimal code that follows, you will find all of the elements the application that created that data has used to contain the metadata, the actual data, information about status, coding, storage location, and so forth.

But here is where it gets interesting. It is absolutely possible, using a hex editor, to insert new hexadecimal characters into that code that will be included whenever someone saves the document, photo, spreadsheet, and so forth. However, that data need not ever be viewable, printable, or even discoverable by the application that created the original data set, or the users or viewers of that data.

This is an actual method used to hide and transfer data and information. It can be used to send messages and information in secret from one place to another. It has also been used by inserting executable code into a data set, to deliver malware or viruses hidden within a document or graphic.

Once again, this can certainly be important, relevant, and consequential information. The problem, of course, is that because it is purposely hidden, it is unlikely to be found unless you have the correct tools and skills to seek it out and discover it.

So, this is not something you, as an everyday computer user, are likely to run into or be able to find. However, if there are legal or other reasons for considering the possible presence of such data, it behooves you to understand the possibility of its existence and to enlist the assistance of someone who has those skills and tools to check to see if this type of data might be included in the data sets you are considering.

Usually, the methods they will use to find steganographic information will include some type of comparison of the fingerprint or hash of a known good file with the suspect file (we talk more about hashes later in the book). There are also special tools and applications available that can sometimes decipher data hidden within a picture or a document that is not part of the file.

Again, this is very specialized and difficult work that will probably require the skills of a professional, so make sure you have someone with those skills in your contacts list.

3.18 Conclusion

This chapter is basically the core of this book because it lays out the bottom line of our discussion of ESI. It is meant as a guide to anyone who needs to understand the what, where, and how of electronic information in a deeper and more complete way.

The important takeaway from all of this wealth of information should be that electronic information is created in myriad places and is stored in a huge number of ways, but that in the end it is all still just ones and zeros piled up in some designated and agreed-upon format of computer coding.

That coding can be understood, discovered, preserved, and managed with integrity and care if you are familiar with and cognizant of all the possible ways and places it might exist. Only by having that understanding can one hope to be diligent and complete in the management of the data that might be required for litigation, records keeping, regulatory compliance, or just historical archiving.

So, it is in all of our interest to have a good grasp of the information related in this chapter and to be able to follow procedures and actions necessary to maintain the integrity of that data when it is needed.

In the next chapters we delve into those processes and discuss how we maintain that integrity and preserve that data when needed.

4

WHO'S IN CHARGE HERE?
ALLIES, OWNERS, AND
STAKEHOLDERS

4.1 Introduction

In this chapter we consider the question of "who." Who are the people you need to work with to be able to identify, acquire, process, preserve, manage, organize, and produce all this electronic evidence that you have spent your time learning about in this book. This is a huge part of the puzzle because behind every bit of data there are the humans who are the owners, keepers, controllers, and creators of that data. In the legal world, these are most often referred to as the custodians of the electronically stored information (ESI).

We enumerate here the people who you can work with, and discuss how to find them and engage with them to your advantage in your quest to deal with this information tsunami.

4.2 The (Long) List of Stakeholders

When you begin to work with electronic evidence, whether as a part of your organizational business strategies or simply as an individual who is interested in getting a better handle on the data you might need access to, you will need to consider all of the different stakeholders and other participants who will need to be involved (Figure 4.1). Here is a comprehensive list with some explanation of each of their parts in this endeavor:

4.2.1 Information Technology Professionals

There are many different information technology professionals whom you will want to include in your stakeholders list:

Figure 4.1   The list of stakeholders can be a large crowd, but all of them are important and need to be engaged.

- Messaging—These people administer and manage e-mail and other messaging tools such as instant messaging.
- Software developers—these folks can help you to understand the way that your software is designed and what information might be created or stored in different applications.
- Web administrators—They will have access to your Web services and be able to assist you with locating, acquiring, and organizing the data hosted on either your internal network (or intranet) or the external Internet. They may also have access to blogs or social media sites.
- Network operations—These staff members will be able to assist you with locating and acquiring data from networking devices such as firewall logs and data flow information. These logs can be invaluable to understanding the actual data traffic that goes into and out of your network and establishing who did what and when.
- Desktop support staff—These technicians are able to assist with access to and acquisition of data from desktops and laptops and other devices like printers and scanners.
- Telephone systems administrators—They handle the telephone access and records and can provide data on land-line and cell phone use, as well as text messaging information.
- Database administrators—As we discussed in other chapters, every organization uses databases to store and manage information. These folks are able to assist with understanding where data exist and with gathering, storing, managing, and producing that data.

- Data center, backup, and server administrators—In the end, all of these data will be created and stored on servers, backup tapes, or other large-capacity storage systems. The people who manage those devices can be your allies in understanding the physical location of the data you need and in accessing those locations or resources.

- Project managers—The information technology (IT) project managers are often the most able to communicate to a wide variety of people about how systems work. They can be a great resource to understanding what your organization is doing with IT systems, the strategic direction and future IT plans of your organization, and how things are currently set up and organized.

- Administrative staff and human resources—Often these people are the real guts of an organization. They have the historical knowledge and understanding of the internal running of the IT departments. Having them in your court can be a huge advantage when you need to understand who is really in charge.

- Security architects—Many organizations include specific architects or engineers whose job it is to plan for and design secure infrastructure. They will be a great source to understand the strategic direction of an organization as well as its history.

- Response team members and security analysts—These are the folks who are down in the trenches every day watching to ensure the network is not being invaded and responding when it is. They have deep knowledge and expertise into both the current state of the network and any events that have happened and might have affected the state of things. They are also often the folks who are doing ongoing vulnerability testing so they are aware of any issues that might arise or may have contributed to a past situation that might be of interest in a case.

- Management, supervisors, and executives—The overall governance and strategic direction of the IT department are handled and overseen by the management-level people and executives. These people absolutely need to be involved and supportive of your efforts, because they will direct other staff to work with you. They also know better than anyone else the big picture "lay of the land" in the IT department.

Bottom line: Your IT department is full of expertise that will be extremely valuable as you attempt to gather, manage, store, and produce electronic evidence, so this is a great place to begin.

You do not need to invite every single one of these groups to the table every time. But taking the time to meet them and understanding who they are and how to reach them is an important first step in gathering the right people to assist your efforts.

4.2.2 Legal Staff

The legal department or your outside counsel is an obvious and important stakeholder. You will want to understand the level of expertise that each person brings to the table and each person's areas of expertise (Figure 4.2).

The practice of law is complex and extensive, and attorneys should not be expected to understand every aspect of every type of case. There will be specialists in the different types of cases that you might need to be involved in.

So if you are concerned with a contract issue, you will want to find the attorney with expertise in contracts; if it is a tax issue, look

Figure 4.2   You will want to know and work with your legal staff.

for the tax specialist. Most organizations will have legal counsel that specializes in human resources or union issues. Or you might be looking for someone with expertise in records retention laws.

The point is that you need to include the attorney or counsel who is an expert in the field that you are concerned with. To do so, you will need to make an effort to understand what resources are available to you and how to contact those people as needed.

Do not forget the other legal staff. Paralegals and research assistants or other administrative staff in the law department or in the outside counsel's offices are often the people you will have the most contact with. These people will most often be responsible for establishing and managing litigation holds, gathering and organizing evidence, and conducting the research into relevance and precedence for the attorneys.

The paralegals are a great resource that you will want to spend time getting to know and work with. They will be key to your understanding of what electronic evidence is relevant and what needs to be preserved and for how long.

4.2.3 Records Managers

If your organization has people specifically tasked with records retention and management, they can be extremely helpful to have on your team. They will have an understanding of what data retention regulations apply to your organization, as well as the likely location of archives and storage of that data.

They will often be involved with every level of your organization, assisting in the understanding of and compliance with records retention laws. As such, they can be important allies both in assisting with locating data and in establishing policies and practices that will make the task of locating data much easier.

4.2.4 Auditors

Inside or outside auditors are a good resource. They will have information on the financial structures, policy and regulatory compliance, and other issues that can inform your search for important and relevant electronic evidence.

They are also often aware of legal, ethical, and compliance issues that were dealt with in the past or that need to be considered by your organization. They can be a source of very good strategic guidance as you work with your management and legal department on building or preparing for litigation.

4.2.5 Human Resources

It will often be the case that human resources managers or staff will assist you, especially if the data you seek are related to employees of yours or another organization.

Getting to know them and understanding their policies and procedures will be of great value in your efforts.

4.2.6 Department Heads, Vice Presidents, and Executives

You must have the assistance and buy-in from the leaders in your organization if you expect to accomplish any of the goals and tasks required to gather and manage electronic evidence (Figure 4.3).

You need to include these folks from the very beginning. They can assist you with not only understanding where data might exist that they have management responsibility for, but also with gaining the cooperation and assistance from their staff when that is required.

Figure 4.3   Buy-in at the executive level is an absolute necessity.

4.2.7 Physical and Information Security Personnel

Even though information security professionals are sometimes within the IT organization, I separate them in this list because they can be one of your most important allies.

The people who manage physical and information security in your organization understand better than most how important it is to protect the data that you all depend upon. It is their job to ensure that the organization's assets are safe and available at all times.

Physical security staff can assist with access to security camera data and physical access information when that is needed.

Information security professionals especially will be involved in the protection of electronic data. They can be of great assistance in your understanding of where and how data are stored and preserved, how to ensure the integrity of that data, and how to keep that data confidential as appropriate.

They will often include computer forensics experts who will be able to gather data from computer systems, even if the data were deleted, and in a manner that ensures its integrity in case it needs to be presented in court.

They are also quite often a natural liaison between the IT staff and other parts of the organization, as their jobs require a full understanding of the business environment in order to effectively manage risks around data assets.

All of the different people listed above will be important to your process of gathering, managing, and producing electronic evidence. Some of them should be full-time allies, while others may need to assist only in specific instances. However, if it is your job or your intention or need to access electronic data, you will want to consider who all of these people are in your organization or in the organization from which you need to acquire data.

Taking the time to create a list with contact information for each of these resources and keeping it up to date will pay off in a big way for you and your organization.

4.3 Ownership of Data

The next thing to consider when looking at the "who" of digital data is the ownership of that data. In order to gather that data, we need to understand who owns the data and how to contact them.

Figure 4.4 Everywhere you go in your community there are owners of data.

Of course, in some cases you are the owner of the data and thereby have the control and access necessary to acquire it. However, this is not always the case. For instance, think about the organizations you work for or work with. There are community and spiritual organizations, retail stores where you purchase things, either online or in the physical "brick-and-mortar" buildings. There are all the other virtual locations that you access on the Internet. There are entertainment venues and restaurants and, of course, your workplace (Figure 4.4).

In all of those locations, data about you are created and stored that might be needed for the many reasons we discussed earlier. If you have a need to access that data, you will have to understand who owns the data in order to do so.

Let's consider some of these examples.

Start with your workplace, as that is where most of us spend the majority of our time. When you walk in you create a record if you need to go through some type of security access or punch a time clock or simply log in to your computer. All of those could be relevant and important records. If you need to access the record of your entering the office through a secured door, who would you contact?

What about if you wanted to know what time you logged in each day or look at your punch in time records?

In my former organization, the facilities department kept records of all of the ingress and egress through secured doors. If I wanted to know when I or someone else had come into the building, I would contact the administrator of those access systems and ask for a report. In some cases, that might just require me to know the name and contact information of that person. But in other organizational structures there might be a formal process for requesting and receiving that information.

If I wanted to see time card information, I would contact someone in the human resources department, as they were the keepers of that data. For logon/logoff activities I would need to connect with someone in the desktop support division.

In almost all of these cases, because I would be asking them to create reports, I would need to go through their supervisors as that creates new work for them.

In effect, I am tapping into the ownership of the data in each of these cases. I have to understand not only where the ownership lies in the organization, but who controls the access to that data.

It is important to make one point clear, however. In the case of computer data managed by the desktop technicians such as logon/logoff data or Internet search information, and so forth, the actual "ownership" might be more correctly assigned to the company. And if I were an outside counsel or auditor or even someone in an adversarial position in a legal matter, that level of ownership would be the first consideration. It would be important to establish the legal ownership of relevant data in order to establish who has the right to allow for its release.

Yet, inside of that organization, some entity, possibly a department, division, or person, will control and manage that data. This entity owns the access to that data, or is the custodian, with whom we will need to communicate if we hope to acquire the information we need.

As we talk about the ownership in this section, it is important to understand that both types of ownership must be considered, but the custodian who controls access to the data in question is whom we most need to be concerned with.

If we look at the examples given earlier, it should be clear that throughout our lives we create data that are controlled by many different entities. In the quest to gain control over our digital data, it behooves us to consider and enumerate as many of those sources of data as possible.

Take the time to consider all of the places that possibly relevant electronic evidence might reside and who would have ownership of and access to that data. If you are creating an electronic discovery process for an organization, or even simply thinking about your own processes should they become necessary, you should create lists of the owners, custodians, and managers of data and their contact information.

For an organization, there is great value in creating such a list and keeping it up to date.

In the revised Federal Rules of Civil Procedure (court rules that we went over in depth in Chapter 1), there is one section that requires organizations to provide "a copy—or a description by category and location—of all documents, electronically stored information, and tangible things that the disclosing party has in its possession, custody, or control and may use to support its claims or defenses, unless the use would be solely for impeachment."[*]

Now that would seem like a large order and a difficult one for most organizations to manage. I would venture to guess that most of you reading this could not point to such a document in your organization.

However, the intention (and in most court cases what seems to be expected) was that organizations should be able to locate and document the existence of any electronic data. In order to do so, one needs to understand where the data live, as we discussed elsewhere, and who controls it, as we discuss here.

A good place to begin will be to complete a thorough inventory of the databases, storage, and management of all data your organization creates. This is often called a "data map."

Document which department or division controls that data. Create a dynamic data map of contact information for the custodians, managers, and administrators of the different data sets in question.

Most importantly, recognizing that this is a dynamic document and a moving target, you need to ensure someone has ownership and maintenance responsibilities for the directory. A role needs to be established (with the all-important executive buy-in) in your organization that will manage and update this directory on a regular basis. If it is done once and then becomes "shelf art," it will quickly become useless.

Figure 4.5 presents an example of what such a data map might look like. This is a simple example, and your data map might contain

---

[*] Rule 26(a)(1)(A)(ii), Federal rules of civil procedure, as amended December 1, 2010.

Data name	Department	Manager	Contact information	Administrator	Contact information
Human resources	Personnel	Jane Jones	jjones@dd.com	Jill Smith	jsmith@dd.com
Building access	Facilities	Bill Carter	bcarter@dd.com	Corey Lewis	clewis@dd.com
Computer access	InfoTech	Drew Thompson	dthomp@dd.com	Mary Styles	mstyles@dd.com
Records management	Archives	Melinda Simpson	msimpso@dd.com	Joseph Minor	jminor@dd.com

Figure 4.5   Sample data map.

a lot more information about the specific type(s) of data, the physical and logical locations of the data, and other methods of contacting the individuals named.

4.4 Data Control Considerations

As noted earlier, the ownership of the data is only part of what you need to consider. The other important consideration is who controls the data and how it is controlled.

In the data map example in the previous section, both a manager and an administrator are listed as contacts. This is important because in order to access and acquire the important or relevant data, you will probably have to enlist the assistance of the person with actual access to the data. To do so, you may need to go through several layers of authority (Figure 4.6).

In a government, military, or paramilitary (police) organization, there are likely to be relatively formal lines of authority to which you will need to make your case should you need access to their data. If you are working within your own organization, it is important to understand those lines of authority and procedures up front in order to expedite your acquisition of data as needed.

Figure 4.6   It is always important to find your way to the leader of the organization.

As an example, begin with that somewhat simpler scenario of working within your own organization. Start by considering the data map (whether or not you actually completed one). Where does the data reside that you will need access to in the future or possibly need right now? Who are the custodians of that data and how do you get in contact with them? What procedures will your organization require if you need their assistance acquiring the data in question?

Assume that you need information about when a person began working for your department and their position and pay rate. That information would obviously be in the care of the personnel department or your human resources (HR) staff.

The process to get that information would probably involve first contacting the manager or supervisor of the personnel department to find out if he or she has access to that information and what restrictions there might be to the release of it. If you find there are no restrictions or that you can meet the requirements to be eligible to receive the data, your next step might be a formal request form with some signatures accepting responsibility for keeping the information confidential.

Now, if you met all the requirements to be allowed to access that data, you will need to get in contact with the administrator of the repository of that information. The manager or supervisor might require that you go through him or her to assign a person and allow that person to spend time working on your task.

Once you clear those hurdles and have actual connection with the person who can access the data, you will need to give that person specific instructions about what you need. In our example, that person would probably need the name and employee number of the individual in question in order to gather the information you need.

Finally, you will want to work with that individual to acquire the needed information in a manner that ensures and documents its integrity. We look more specifically at those methods in a later chapter.

As I hope it will be apparent from this example, the actual control of the information that you require is an important consideration that will need to be dealt with in nearly every case.

Let's look at a more difficult example.

As noted, working with a military or paramilitary organization can require going through very strict lines of authority and

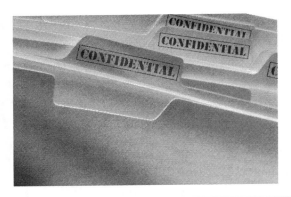

Figure 4.7 Dealing with classified information can be especially challenging.

quite possibly levels of security classification in order to access data (Figure 4.7).

Consider if you need to access information from your local police department about recent arrests during a protest. Perhaps you are a student writing about free speech rights and want to understand the command structure that resulted in those arrests.

The ownership and control of the information you are seeking is going to be within the police command structure. Because you are trying to understand specific command procedures, there will be documentation of their standard operating procedures and specific records of the events in question. These might well reside in different repositories, and it might be difficult to get any assistance or cooperation from the police in discovering those details.

In order for you to acquire the data you desire access to, you might need to do research on your own to attempt to discover where that data would most likely reside. You might be required to go through legal channels to request that information via a Freedom of Information Act (FOIA) request.

If you discover that the information about standard operating procedures resides in a specific department or division of the police organization, there will probably be a public relations or liaison officer to whom you might address your request. That person will no doubt report to a captain, who might report to an assistant chief, and on up the chain of command. Before they are allowed to respond to your request, they may well be required to go up that chain of command authority for permission.

Sometimes knowing or having access to the top of that chain of command might expedite your request for information. Because of the way these organizations work (and in truth the same might be said for any organization), starting at the top of the chain can make things happen more efficiently.

However, that is not always possible and in fact might be counterproductive if your actions are construed as unethical or even simply as not following correct procedures. In those cases, you may end up losing more time than you might have gained because you have to go back and follow procedures and now the people you went around are unhappy and less likely to be cooperative.

These are considerations to weigh as you think about who has control of the data you need and how to gain their cooperation and assistance.

In any case and no matter the organization you are working with, it should now be more obvious that you need to understand and deal with the actual custodians of data. Further, understanding how that control is established and the most efficient way to work with it can be paramount to your actually being able to gather relevant electronic information.

Once again, establishing those procedures up front and documenting and practicing them on a regular basis can be a great advantage to you and the organization you are a part of.

4.5 Required Skill Sets and Tools

The procedures and practices suggested in this chapter will require some important skill sets and tools to accomplish. As with everything in this book, your choice can be to develop those skills and acquire those tools yourself, or find a trusted ally within your organization or community who already has them (Figure 4.8).

The first and most important skill in this as in most endeavors will be the ability to communicate effectively with a wide variety of people at different levels of responsibility and authority. To do so requires both self-confidence (which comes from knowing what you need and why you need it) and an understanding of their business and their position in the hierarchy.

Consider the examples we used above. If you are going to request the assistance of someone in the HR department to gather information

Figure 4.8   You must have good communications tools and skills.

on an employee, you first need to be sure you have a legitimate reason for asking. You can enhance your self-confidence and your ability to make a good case by being well prepared ahead of time with the justification for your request.

Understanding the position and business requirements that determine how the other person will respond will also go a long way to expediting your request. For instance, the HR personnel have a responsibility to protect private and personal information about the employees in their organization. They also bear a responsibility toward their management and organization to keep some data confidential.

So, when you make a request to the manager of the HR department for information about an employee, you should be prepared to justify that request in such a way that it will make sense and not contradict any of their overarching responsibilities. You should understand the proper protocols and authorities and follow them carefully. You may also need to be able to show your ability and willingness to maintain confidentiality of the information and to only use it for the stated and agreed-upon purposes.

We look more carefully at the specific tools you might use when we talk about the actual gathering of the data in Chapter 5. But you will need specific tools to be able to prove your ability to keep data confidential and ensure the integrity of data that you are acquiring and storing.

Those tools might include hardware that allows you to copy data from a device without accidently writing to or changing the data in any way. These are called write blockers, and they can be specific hardware devices that connect between a computer or other storage and the storage to which you are copying.

There are also software applications that facilitate the copying of data in a way that ensures the integrity of the data, and can in some cases prevent writing to the copied device as well. To do so, the software can use mathematical algorithms called hashes to create a digital "fingerprint" of the data before and after the copying in order to show that nothing was changed.

Because, as we discussed in earlier chapters, digital data are all based on binary mathematical constructs, these algorithms are basically formulas that when run against any set of digital data will result in a long hexadecimal string of numbers and letters (hexadecimal math includes the letters a through f; see Chapter 1 for a more in-depth discussion of digital data and the binary and hexadecimal notation). If you remove a space from between letters, or add a period to the end of a sentence in a digitally saved document, the resulting hash will be completely different when that algorithmic formula is run against the storage media again. This results in the perfect way (well, nearly perfect, as some hash systems are more reliable than others) to ensure that the data you copied is the same when you need to use it as it was when you acquired it.

Because this provable integrity of the data may be very important to the owners and custodians of the information you require, your ability to show that you understand the requirements and have the tools to ensure that integrity will be paramount.

Another important consideration will be the necessity to understand the business requirements of the organization or entity from which you are requesting data. That will require that you take the time and do your research in order to truly understand their business model.

In the second more difficult example above, we were looking at the possible complications involved in requesting information from a police department. In order to develop this skill set, there are several things you should take the time to understand

- The command structure of the organization
- What societal and regulatory obligations and restrictions they will be working with
- The business model and methodology that they work under
- How all of these will affect their willingness and ability to assist you

This will be time well spent, and in nearly every case it will increase your ability to acquire the information you require more effectively and efficiently.

5

THE HUNT

Recovery and Acquisition

5.1 Introduction

In this chapter, we begin looking at the recovery and acquisition procedures you should think about in your organization or even as an individual. These processes and ideas can assist anyone who needs to better understand the "where" and "how" of electronic evidence (Figure 5.1).

We consider the "hunt" and all of the different ways that all important electronic data may elude capture. We also discuss the classification of data as "privileged" or "sensitive" or "unreasonably accessible," and all the requirements you need to meet to prove those classifications. We give you the means to recognize, organize, and document those classifications in a way that will hold up in court, or for an audit, or simply for your own organization and protection of said data.

We also talk about nonrepudiation versus plausible deniability, the very basis of evidentiary law, and in many cases, the facts on which a court will depend to decide if evidence is admissible.

A big part of that nonrepudiation or integrity of electronic evidence for admissibility is often based on time stamps, so we look at how time stamps work, how they can be corrupted or compromised, and how they can be used for or against your case to prove the efficacy, integrity, and reliability of your data.

Finally, we lay out some suggested procedures for the gathering of the relevant electronic data in a way that the courts will respect and understand as forensically sound. In other words, we offer you tools and processes to allow you to collect, organize, and preserve electronic evidence in a way that you can ensure no alterations were made to the data and that the integrity of the data was maintained in its pristine and original state. Let's get started.

Figure 5.1   The hunt begins.

5.2 Where, Oh Where, Has My Data Gone?

The first thing you need to consider when you begin the hunt for relevant data is the big question of where is it hiding? Like any good hunter, you need to first be familiar with your prey and its habits. In Chapter 3 we spent a lot of time considering all the different types of electronic data and the myriad ways in which it is created and stored. For details on the question of where data could be, I refer you back to that chapter.

But even if you memorized every word of that chapter and completely considered all of the possible places the data you need might be located both physically and virtually, you might still have a problem finding it. How could that be, you ask?

As we noted before, computers and other digital devices that store electronic data can and do lose data sometimes or possibly store it in ways that are inaccessible to the normal user. And in many cases, data are stored in a way that can only be accessed, manipulated, or recovered using a specific front-end application or interface. We look at each of these with examples to make this clearer.

5.2.1 Applications as a Vital User Interface

For our first example, we look at the most popular electronic evidence item in most court cases: e-mail (Figure 5.2).

Figure 5.2 E-mail is the most often requested electronic evidence.

Nearly all e-mail applications that reside on a computer have a database of some sort behind them that is responsible for storing and organizing all of the items you receive or input. When you get an e-mail message from your sister in Roxbury, the database stores it in the database in such a way that when you open your e-mail application and go to your Inbox, you will see the new message from your sister.

Usually, that message, being new, will have some formatting attached to it to indicate that it is new and that you have not opened it yet. That might be a closed envelope icon, or something similar. That message also contains a considerable amount of metadata or data about itself, as we discussed in detail in Chapter 3. It will contain information about who the original sender was, what time it was posted, the e-mail servers it started from and went through to get to yours, the types of e-mail applications that were used, what time it arrived, and more. The message may also contain attachments such as pictures and documents that your sister sent to you. And each of those items will also contain metadata that contain information about when they were created or modified, by whom, and so forth.

However, as soon as you open that message, its properties are changed and the back-end database will add new attributes to that data and possibly store it in a different way when you close your e-mail application or shut down your computer. If you open and save the attachments, that will be recorded in the e-mail application database. You might choose to move the message to a folder to keep yourself organized, such as perhaps a Family Stuff folder or, depending on your relationship with your sister, maybe to the Junk Mail folder.

Those actions will have an effect on the way the database behind your e-mail application treats that message. The message may be stored in a different way to indicate it can be found in the Family Stuff folder. It might have special attributes or rules attached to it as a result of being stored in the Junk Mail folder.

Some e-mail applications will make the assumption that when you store things in Junk Mail you would prefer that any further correspondence from that same e-mail address be stored therein as well. So, it is possible that future e-mails from your sister will then be automatically relegated to the Junk Mail folder.

Of course, in most modern e-mail applications, you are also able to create and store a task list, contacts information, and calendar items. Again, each of those pieces of information is stored in the database in a particular way so that when you use your e-mail application to look them up, they are revealed to you in the place you expect them to be and in the correct format to indicate whether you have read them or completed them yet.

Sometimes in the case of calendar items, they can be formatted to indicate if they are family related, work related, birthdays, holidays, and so on. All of this information is stored and managed by a back-end database.

In many cases, those databases are based on what is known as proprietary programming. This means that the organization that created the e-mail application and its back-end database chose to use a database programming language that can only be read by that application and is specific to that application. In other words, there is no way to locate that database and find the information you stored in it, other than by using the e-mail application for which it was created.

And here is one way that you might know perfectly well where your data live, but be unable to access the data. Any application can fail, go out of date, or be accidently deleted. So if what is lost is an application that used proprietary programming to store data, it might be impossible to access that information without recovering and reinstalling the original application.

Here is an example of that problem from my own experience.

As the family geek and official tech support guy, I cannot say I was terribly surprised one day when my Mom called to say that their computer was no longer working. When I began my troubleshooting process, I again was not too surprised to hear that my Dad had been doing some "cleanup" on the hard drive because it was getting too full.

This was back in the day when a huge hard drive might have as much as 500 megabytes of storage, and theirs was an old computer with considerably less than that. As they added pictures, documents, and applications with little understanding but a great deal of enthusiasm for their brand-new computer, they began to run out of space.

If they had come to me first, I would have spent some time cleaning things up and could probably have gained back plenty of space by deleting temporary files, and moving some things off to CDs. But Dad thought he had it figured out and simply went through the C: drive directory deleting things that he figured were not important.

When he deleted sol.exe, Mom was a little bummed out that she could not play solitaire anymore, but she let that pass with her typical stoicism. But when he went back and decided that win.exe looked like an unnecessary file, things went south in a hurry. Of course, many of you are probably giggling right now, at least those geeks among you, because you recognize that once upon a time, win.exe was the application that started up Windows.

Microsoft has since become a little more human savvy, and they now hide that and other all-important system files so you cannot mess with them. That, of course, brings up another way that data can be made hard to locate, but we get to that soon.

The end of the story with my Dad and Mom's computer was that I needed to go to their home and reinstall Windows for them before they could use their computer again. And the point of that story, besides entertaining all of you, was to help you understand how important and indeed vital data might become impossible to access simply by virtue of a vital application being deleted, corrupted, or lost in some way.

In my parents' case, they could no longer access anything on their computer even though everything still existed on the hard drive.

If we go back to our example, they could in no way have accessed their e-mail because the application that ran their e-mail depended on Windows to run and to give them the interface they needed to open, review, store, or manipulate their messages, calendars, tasks, and contacts. All of that important data was as good as lost to them.

Even if they had not deleted win.exe, but had simply deleted outlook.exe, or whatever other e-mail application file they might have been using, the results would have been the same. There is simply no way for a normal computer user to access those back-end databases of information, even though they exist and are perfectly sound on the hard drive, unless they have the front-end application that creates the interface with the database.

Now, all of this e-mail, contact information, task lists, and calendaring items might be the most important things you need or want to produce for a trial or an audit, or simply for your own records or mementos. So, if something happened to the front-end application that gives you access to that data, what can you do?

There are several different possible solutions to that dilemma.

The first and most obvious one would be to acquire and reinstall the front-end application to access your data. However, this can be tricky. You will need to have the exact same version and type of application that you created the database with in the first place if you have any hope of it still being compatible and accessible.

You may also need to do some manipulating of the reinstalled application to allow it to find and open the back-end database that was left over from your original application. This can be a difficult task, requiring some technical expertise to accomplish, depending on the application. In many cases, you may be well advised to ask for help, either from your family geek or from a real expert like that 13-year-old who lives across the street.

Another possibility will be to find a separate tool or application that is made to open and access the back-end database for your particular application. In the case of Microsoft Outlook, for instance, that back-end database file can be stored as what is known as the PST file. It is a hidden file that contains all of the information from your e-mail application, stored in a proprietary programming language that Outlook is designed to access and interface with.

However, there are other programs available that allow a user to access and open up a PST file and search for e-mail, calendar, contacts, or task items. These are specialized tools that are probably most often used by forensics or other investigative organizations. Some law firms are also likely to have tools to open these and other back-end e-mail databases because it is not uncommon for a discovery request for e-mail data to be produced as the back-end PST file.

Other applications might have a SQL database, or an Oracle or other database system backing them up. This is especially often the case with Internet-based applications.

If that is the case, there are many tools and applications available that will allow you to open and query those databases to find the relevant evidence. Of course, the efficient use of those tools will require expertise and experience that not all of us can claim. Once again you are well advised to consult with an expert or the kid across the street.

5.2.2 Hidden or Restricted Access Data

Another place that important information can be stored is in log files or data files that your computer's operating system might hide from view. As noted in my example of my parents' mistaken "cleanup," there can be very good reasons for hiding these files from the normal computer user.

These types of files and folders are called *hidden* or *system* files, and most operating systems have some special storage space just for them that is inaccessible to users without the correct privileges on the device. Yet they may have information that could be important to you in a court case, or just in the general understanding of what might have occurred when on your computer.

There are several different types of files on Windows devices that are hidden from normal view. These include files that contain data for what is known as the registry.

On a Windows system, the registry is yet another database that keeps track of all of the different software and hardware your computer uses, the paths and interdependencies to those applications, and connections between the operating system, applications, and the hardware. It is a very complex and technical database of connections that is the heart and soul of how your computer and its applications interact with the Windows operating system.

There is no reason or need to get into details of the design or even the contents of this vast database in this book. However, it is important to recognize that the registry contains electronic records of actions taken on your computer that may be relevant in a court case.

Here are some examples of the data that can be found in the registry and that might be of interest to someone trying to understand what has taken place on a computer, for whatever reason:

- A record of every USB device that was ever plugged into your computer—the serial number, model, and date it was first plugged in as well as the date it was last accessed
- Records of all of the last websites you typed into your browser
- Records of all of the most recently accessed files (depending on the version of Windows, these can be records of hundreds of files back into the past)
- Records containing data about all users of the computer, including encoded passwords (that with the right tools can be un-encoded)
- Records of all network and other drive connections that have been made
- Records of what applications have been installed, when and where they are located in the directory system
- Records of when applications were last accessed
- Records of who logged in when as well as what networks or shared directories they were connected to when they logged in
- And much more that can be of great interest to someone with the tools and expertise to winnow that data from the registry in order to understand who has done what on that computer

Other files that are hidden are the files that contain information about your Internet browsing. These are stored in small flat database files with a .dat extension on some Windows operating system computers. For Internet Explorer, these files are most often called index.dat and are stored in various hidden folders depending on their specific purpose.

One folder is for your Internet history, and with Internet Explorer the index.dat file in that folder contains the information you see when you select History from your Internet browser's menu.

Other browsers use different storage mechanisms, but in every case these are not files that you can simply find and open on your own. Some of them are made available through the interface of your browser. History is one, and another common one would be the cookies file.

Cookies are small text files created by websites. They contain information about your access to the websites with the purpose of speeding up your access when you visit the same site later. They can, however, be less benevolent and store information about your browsing history with the intent to know what you purchase and target advertising toward those favorite items.

So cookies, though generally benign, can be used in more malevolent ways, and there are reasons sometimes for you to check them and possibly remove them. Many modern antivirus programs will look for the malevolent versions of cookies (sometimes called *tracking cookies*) and delete them for you.

However, in order to see and manage cookies, you most often have to access them through the interface of your browser. There are other tools and applications that will also allow you to manage cookies, but in every case they are referencing one of these hidden data files to which we are referring here.

There are other hidden data files like these as well that keep track of every single item that you access either on the Internet or even just on a network. I think it is pretty easy to see how those could contain vast amounts of interesting information about the activities on a computer, especially Internet browsing activities.

Another hidden folder in Windows operating systems contains data on all the files you accessed in a given period of time. It is called the 'Recent' folder, and similarly to the registry items we noted above, it can give a lot of good information to an investigator about what files a computer user accessed recently. Included in that database will be the name of the file, the path where it was located, the creation date, and the last accessed date. All of this might be extremely interesting information.

Other hidden files and folders contain information on all of the applications you installed and any error messages or logs that were created by those applications. Others contain data on security alerts or system issues, such as every time you logged into or out of your computer, or when the time clock was changed. Again, these can be extremely important sets of information to someone trying to establish use patterns or general usage of a device.

There is one hidden system file in Windows computers called $MFT. MFT stands for master file table, and that is exactly what it is. Again, it is a flat database created the first time your computer starts up, and it keeps track from then on of every single file created on your computer. The MFT of a brand-new computer already has tens of thousands of entries, and that number can grow into hundreds of thousands as you add new applications, create documents, surf the Internet, and so on.

Almost every action you take on your computer will result in files being created. Sometimes it is log files that an application keeps in the background for the purpose of troubleshooting, or simply as a means of evolving and making your experience more efficient.

As we noted before, every trip you take on the Web creates literally hundreds of new files as it opens up the various pictures, text, movies, and so forth, that make up a website.

Every one of those file creations, modifications, last access times, deletions, archiving, or anything else that the operating system needs to track about those files is recorded in the MFT. This can be a wealth of information for someone who needs to know what happened on a computer. In fact, it can be far too much information.

As a computer forensics practitioner, I use the $MFT file on a regular basis to try to understand when malware infected a computer and what type of malware it is. Yet, even if I have a pretty good idea of when the device was infected, it can be like searching for a needle in a haystack to look through the thousands of files created every day on a computer.

One more type of hidden file that can be of great value in understanding the actions of a computer user is called the "*Restore*" file or "Shadow Copy" in some Windows operating systems. The Restore file contains records that the Windows operating system keeps of the state of your computer at a given time and date. Every time you add a new application, a restore file is created. Windows also creates these whenever it does an update, or just on a regular schedule.

These are created for the purpose of restoring your computer to a known good state in case something goes bad. Sometimes a new application will cause conflicts with existing applications, or will not work correctly with your device for some reason; perhaps it has bad hardware drivers or some incompatibility with your system.

If that happens and you recognize that the problems started when you installed that software, you can use the system restore points to roll back your computer to the state of things before the problem started. Now Windows keeps these restore points for a long time, going back many years sometimes. Think about the value that might have to understanding what happened on that computer sometime in the past.

If someone was purposely trying to hide his or her actions by deleting applications, Internet browsing activities, documents they created, and so forth, the restore points give an investigator a way to go back into the past to see how things looked before.

Finally, as mentioned earlier, most applications will keep log files that track how they are being used and any problems that come up. Most often these are hidden files that are only reachable through the application interface and sometimes only by knowing advanced options in the application that will allow you to view and manage those files.

There are many more hidden and system files on your computer, and we only touched on some of them and only talked about Windows computers. Other operating systems such as Linux and Macintosh also have system files that are not generally available to a casual user.

Yet in every case, these can contain vital information when you need to understand what has been taking place on a computer. They can hold data that will assist you in locating other relevant information and possibly point you to other sources of information, such as those USB drives that were connected to the computer, or the list of most recently accessed files, or the information in one of the restore points.

If you want to see some of these files, or at least their folders and their file names, on a Windows computer you can select, "show hidden and system files" in your folder settings. However, being able to see them will do you no good whatsoever if you actually hope to gather some information out of them. They are all encoded in such a way as to only be accessible and readable either by an application interface or by the system.

There are special tools that computer forensics experts use to parse and access these files for analysis. So, if access to any of that type of information might be important to a court case or audit or simply record keeping that you are doing, you will need to either gain that expertise yourself or hire someone with those skills and tools. In the understanding of where data live, do not neglect this rich source of information. In many cases, it contains some of the most important facts and clues to understand what really happened on a computer and when and by whose hand.

5.2.3 Encrypted Data

Yet another way that data might be made hard or impossible to access is through encryption (Figure 5.3). There are many ways to encrypt data on a computer, from the relatively simple act of assigning a password to a file, to the incredibly complex process and management of digital certificates that automatically encrypt data in e-mails, or specific folders, or even entire hard drives.

On some newer Windows operating systems, they include a tool called BitLocker. This allows you to create specific encrypted folders such that any data that you want to protect can simply be stored in those folders and a pass phrase is required to access the data.

Other encryption tools work as noted earlier with a certificate system. In those cases, an individual or a device is given an electronic certificate that is basically an encoded file that contains the necessary information to prove the individual's identity. Again, these will use a

Figure 5.3 Encrypted data can present extreme challenges to access or even be impossible at times.

pass phrase of some complexity and length to ensure you are authenticated to open files.

Any in-depth conversation about encryption is far beyond the scope of this book, but it can be a fascinating and mind-challenging study if you lean toward the mathematical geek edge of things. But for those of us normal and mortal humans, we simply need to recognize how this can affect our ability to gather and access data from our computing devices.

If you have a need to access data from a device, drive, folder, e-mail, or file that was encrypted, there is really only one sure-fire solution. That is to find out what the authentication mechanism is and learn the pass phrase or password. Failing that, even if you have a way to locate and try to open the encrypted information, the data in its encrypted form will look like long strings of bizarre characters and will mean absolutely nothing and be completely worthless.

How does one obtain those passwords and phrases? That will often depend on the circumstances.

In an ideal situation that is not confrontational, you may be able to simply ask. Even sometimes in a more combative situation such as a court case, you might be able to convince the person with access to supply his or her passwords if there is a compelling reason to do so. Each case will be different, but this is obviously the first and easiest solution and the one you should always strive and hope for.

Barring that easy solution, there are other possibilities depending on the level of encryption and the technical astuteness of the person or persons who encrypted the data in the first place. With the relatively simple encryption that is done when you password protect a file, such as an Excel spreadsheet, for instance, there are quite a few readily available tools available that will allow you to crack those passwords or sometimes bypass them.

More complex encryption schemes can be extremely difficult or even impossible to break through. Again, there are tools that your friendly neighborhood computer forensics expert will have that will make the cracking of difficult passwords possible. But even they can fail at times, and often it can be a very long and complicated process.

Encrypted data can be a real problem if the data are relevant to a case or necessary for some project you are working on. If you have no way to gain access to that data, you might have to declare it not reasonably accessible and look for other ways and places to gather the electronic evidence you require.

5.2.4 Deleted or Corrupted Data

Of course, any data can be deleted by accident, or in some cases simply corrupted so that it is no longer accessible by the applications or computer operating system.

Whenever someone deletes a file on a computer, the operating system makes a small change to the data that makes up that file, basically placing a flag consisting of a couple of bits of information at the beginning of the bits and bytes that make up that file. That flag tells the operating system (and any application that interfaces with it) that this storage space is available and that the information stored here can be written over with new data whenever the space it is using on the electronic storage device is needed.

Sometimes, due to a problem with the operating system, a virus, or something wrong in an application, some of those bits and bytes that make up a file or other piece of information can be destroyed, changed, or moved out of sync with the rest of the file. This can make that data unreadable or inaccessible by the application that created it. This is called corruption of the file.

In both of those cases, what is important to understand is that most often a large part of the data is still intact and still available if you have the tools and skills to find it. The bits and bytes that make up the files still exist, all except for the corrupted ones. Or they might all still exist but simply have that "deleted" flag prepended to them. If these have not yet been overwritten or are not too seriously corrupted, it can be relatively simple to recover them, given the right tools and skills.

The best example I can give to illustrate this is one that happens to me fairly often in my role as the community forensics dude.

I will hear someone bemoaning the fact that he or she just uploaded all their pictures from their vacation to their computer, then pressed the wrong buttons and deleted all of them from both the camera and their computer.

Or, someone will tell me that their computer was infected with a virus and he or she can no longer get it to start up and all of their important documents were never backed up—forensics dude to the rescue.

With tools at my disposal, I can often gain access to a corrupted hard drive, or find all those deleted files on a camera memory card or computer. Those tools basically take a look at the hexadecimal code that makes up all those files. Then it goes through and recognizes the pieces of different file types and puts them back together again in a form that I can then export to recover the data.

In computer forensics terms this is called *data carving* because the tools look through the lines of data stored on whatever medium we are searching through and carve out the pieces that make up different file types.

The way it recognizes those files is by standard file headers or bytes of data that tell the operating system the type of file that is stored, its length, date and time information, and possibly information about where on the disk different parts of the file are stored.

All of this information is part of something we discussed in other chapters called metadata or data about the data. The operating system, applications, and my forensics tools read that information and use it to access the data that make up all the different types of files.

Once again, we have another type of data that though it might be incredibly important to your case or your project, might also be difficult to gain access to without the right tools and skills.

What is important to recognize here is that deleted or corrupted or lost data might still be accessible. Depending on the circumstances, such as how important that information is to your case and how available and costly the resources to recover it might be, you will need to make decisions as to whether you consider it reasonably accessible. And be aware that while you might deem it not reasonably accessible due to high costs or difficulty in obtaining the data in question, the courts or other parties may disagree with you.

This makes it important to understand what data might be there and to do your best to preserve it by not continuing to use a device that might result in that data being overwritten or further corrupted.

5.2.5 Proprietary Data or Data Stored on Obsolete Media

We already talked a little about proprietary data when we discussed the need for a front-end application in the first section of this chapter. However, another way that proprietary methods of creating and storing data can result in your being unable to access that data is by virtue of its having been created by an application that no longer exists. It could also have been stored in a format or on hardware that is no longer available. Let's look at some real-life examples.

Some of you, like me, have some miles on you and have been around long enough to remember those halcyon days when computers were a new and exciting invention that only a few geeks in research universities could afford to own.

Over those many years there have been many types of storage devices. We discussed some of the more common and modern ones in Chapter 3 on where data can be stored. But if you happen to have old data kept on some of these older types of media, you will be facing different challenges.

Data have been stored on many different types of media (Figure 5.4). Here is a list of some of them:

- Punch cards and paper tape that used holes punched in the paper to code those ones and zeros we discussed before

Figure 5.4   Storage devices have been many and varied over time.

- Magnetic tape on reels the diameter of an automobile tire, to smaller reels and audio tape–sized cassettes, down to mini tape cassettes you could hide in your fist
- Floppy disks in sizes from 8 inches to 3.5 inches
- Hard drives of various capacities and interfaces
- Various magnetic disk drives such as the Jaz and Zip disks
- Other outliers such as the SuperDisk and the MiniDisk
- Solid-state drives such as SanDisk, and so forth
- Optical drives—CDs and DVDs
- And even one hybrid optical/magnetic drive

If data that you need for a case, or an audit, or just for your own historical records are stored on any of these types of older media, you could face some unique challenges.

Consider first those floppy disks.* Floppy disks were first invented and used in the 1970s, and as noted previously, they came in 8 inch, 5.25 inch, and 3.5 inch sizes. It is rare to find an 8 inch floppy these days, but you might still find some 5.25 inch disks laying around getting dusty in a closet, and the 3.5 inch floppy drives were still pretty popular up until just recently, so you can still purchase them and some computers still have a floppy disk drive for reading them.

A floppy disk is made up of a flexible (floppy) magnetic disk contained within a square or rectangular plastic sleeve that protects it from dust and damage. They could hold relatively small amounts of data by today's standards, but they were still used extensively to store information.

If you have one of these disks and need to gain access to it for any reason, you are faced with some challenges. The first is the very real possibility of damage or corruption of the data. As with any magnetic media, these are vulnerable to magnetic fields. There has also been some research indicating that they may lose some of their magnetic charge over time, thus making them impossible to read.† Basically, the ones and zeros are maintained by different levels of positive or

---

* The chronology of disk storage. http://www-03.ibm.com/ibm/history/exhibits/storage/storage_chrono20.html. Retrieved June 17, 2011.

† June Jamrich Parsons and Dan Oja, *New Perspectives on Computer Concepts 2012: Introductory*, Florence, KY: Cengage Learning, p. 78. Retrieved June 17, 2011.

negative charge, and if that faded, there is no code for a drive to read and interpret.

Second, unless you are a true geek and saved every computer you ever owned back into the computer stone age, you probably do not have a running computer with an 8 inch or even a 5.25 inch floppy disk drive installed. If you have the need to acquire data from one of these older types of media, it may require a trip to your friendly neighborhood computer antique store or a search online for someone willing to sell (or loan) that hardware to you.

The same thing applies to any of the other older or rare devices we mentioned above. I imagine that many of the readers of this book never even heard of a Zip or Jaz drive, though for a little while they were a pretty popular choice for storing more data. The Jaz drive could store up to 2 GB of data, which at the time was a huge storage device.

Some of the interfaces of older hard drives (SCSI for instance) are rarely used anymore and may also be hard to find or connect.

If your task is to gather some important information from one of these types of devices, I recommend an online search as your first step. You will find that there are still organizations out there that will sell you the proper hardware to access the data on those media. However, if you know or fear that the data were corrupted or the media was damaged, you will probably have to turn to a reputable and experienced computer forensics organization for assistance.

Another way that data can be made inaccessible is through its having been created in a proprietary format. Again, some of you oldsters will remember word processing applications such as Word Perfect and spreadsheet tools like Lotus 123. Some of these are still in existence and use today, yet they have faded into the background with the ubiquity of Microsoft Word, Excel, and so on.

When applications are used to create and store data, those applications use different types of coding mechanisms and architectures to do so, and in many cases you cannot open or view data created by those applications without using the original applications.

Say your mother spent a lot of time 15 years ago documenting your family history and lineage using Word Perfect version 1.2. She carefully saved all of that important information on her 5.25 inch floppy disks and stored them in a shoebox in the closet.

You went to a family reunion and started talking with her and your aunts about your ancestors, and she remembered that work she did. You decide it would be a great time to gather up that information and update it with recent events like the birth of your children and your nieces and nephews. Well, we already discussed the problems with the floppy disks, but you are in luck. Your mom actually saved her old Commodore computer with a 5.25 inch drive.

You plug it in and fire it up, but it only boots up to a DOS prompt. There are no windows, there is no mouse, and there is no "user interface." Just a black screen with C: at the top waiting for you to do something. (This is what is known as the DOS prompt, or the computer's way of telling you in the old digital operating system that it is ready.)

If you are old or geeky enough to remember what to do next, you might manage to plug that floppy into the drive and even navigate over to it to see what is on it. There is a command for that. You can type it in after the DOS prompt (if you are interested, it would be DIR D: assuming the computer was recognizing your floppy drive as D:).

Let's assume you got this far either because you are old and geeky like me, or because you found some help somewhere. You can actually see file names that end with the extension .wp for Word Perfect. Excellent. Now you just double click on them. Oh wait, there is no mouse and no cursor.

OK, so you do some more research or call that old guy back and you figure out the command that you need to type to open those files in Word Perfect. You try that out, but it does not work. Unfortunately, the way those old systems worked, you had to have the floppy disk with the Word Perfect application on it and load it up first. Once you loaded it on the computer, you could then open those files. Do you have that old application floppy disk? No? Oops, game over.

Again, this is all meant as an illustration of one of the many ways important data might be difficult or in fact impossible to gain access to when needed. In the example just given or in a similar situation, your choices would be to find someone or an organization with the correct software to open and recover those files in a meaningful way.

Now, a computer forensics expert, even without the correct software, might be able to gather enough of the raw text in a text-based document to at least give you something to work with. However, if it is something with formulas, or graphics, or pictures that were saved in some proprietary format, it is unlikely that even the best experts will be able to decode and restore that to anything usable.

The bottom line is that data stored on obsolete or rare media, or stored by an application in a proprietary code, may be considered unreasonably accessible or may be impossible to recover.

If you have to deal with any such information, keep this in mind and consider the resources and time that you will need to be prepared to expend if you choose to attempt the acquisition, restoration, or production of such data.

5.3 Privileged, Sensitive, and Inaccessible Data Management

In order to manage and understand the implications of privileged, sensitive, or inaccessible data, we have to begin by defining and documenting what we mean when we use those terms. In this section we consider each of these carefully and give you some things to consider as you strive to define and document your understanding, procedures, and management of these types of data.

In the courts, it has pretty much always been the case that if you wanted to assert that evidence could not or would not be produced for a case, you needed to prove that it was privileged.

We begin by looking at what the courts consider privileged data and how that can be established, documented, and managed. If you are in the legal profession, this should be old news to you, but for the rest of us mere mortals, this is important to understand.

Anyone, at any time, can be embroiled in legal issues such that they must understand what parts of the information they have access to will be produced. All of us therefore will benefit from understanding that some information that is exchanged or stored in certain proscribed ways might be exempt from being produced in court because it is considered "privileged."

Let's begin with the legal definition of privileged information:

> n. statements and conversations made under circumstances of assured confidentiality which must not be disclosed in court. These include communications between husband and wife, attorney and client, physician

or therapist and patient, and minister or priest with anyone seeing them in their religious status. In some states the privilege is extended to reporters and informants. Thus, such people cannot be forced to testify or reveal the conversations to law enforcement or courts, even under threat of contempt of court, and if one should break the confidentiality, he/she can be sued by the person who had confidence in him/her. The reason for the privilege is to allow people to speak with candor to a spouse or professional counselor, even though it may hinder a criminal prosecution. The extreme case is when a priest hears an admission of murder or other serious crime in the confessional and can do nothing about it. The privilege may be lost if the one who made the admission waives the privilege, or, in the case of an attorney, if the client sues the attorney claiming negligence in conduct of the case.*

This definition does a good job of summing up the legal understanding of privileged communications. This can also be called attorney–client privilege if it is specifically addressing your communications with your lawyers about a case.

How would this affect you as someone engaged in a legal issue? For one, you should understand that if you e-mail or text or otherwise communicate anything to your attorney, or your wife, physician, therapist, or a religious counselor/minister of some kind with some assurance of confidentiality, those communications are out of bounds for that issue and should not be allowed as evidence.

However, what is important to recognize is that, as with all things in the legal arena, the idea of privilege can and will be challenged. There are many ways that these types of communications might in fact end up as part of the case, and most of them come down to good and careful practices by you and your legal or personal counselors.

In order to assert privilege and avoid confidential communications from becoming public or part of a court case, an attorney is required to document all of these types of communications and keep a privilege log. Further, the attorneys are required to note in all such correspondence that the information contained therein is privileged. Other counselors are similarly charged with the duty to manage confidential

---

* law.com, Legal terms and definitions, "privileged communication". http://dictionary.law.com/Default.aspx?selected=1615. Retrieved June 17, 2011.

communications in such a way as to be able to prove to a court or to the opposing party that information is privileged and not available for discovery or production.

To you as an individual, this means that if you think you are communicating to one of the entities noted in the definition above on a confidential basis, you should look for and require that they are maintaining the proper management of those conversations.

For instance, in an e-mail correspondence with your attorney, you should see something in the subject line saying "Attorney–Client Privileged." If you are ever concerned about a professional's management of your confidential information, you should ask and require a sufficient answer and explanation of how they are managing privileged information.

In most all court cases where there is any question of privilege, an attorney is required to keep and produce a privilege log that documents privileged communications and proves that those communications should be privileged and kept out of evidence. That privilege can be lost, however, if data are inadvertently produced through the error or oversight of an attorney or their staff. This has happened in some cases, and it can result in bad outcomes for the interested parties.

On the other hand, I read a case where very competent paralegals who had to go through literal mountains of data inadvertently produced a small number of documents that should have been privileged. When those documents were referred to by the opposing counsel in deposition, the attorneys for the privileged party objected and asked the court to remove them from evidence based on their privileged status. In that case, the court agreed based on the huge volume of data that the paralegals had been working with, their general competence, and the fact that the information should in fact have been considered privileged.

As usual, this can go both ways. In the end, it is always a matter of careful practice and oversight. You can assist with this by being very clear with your attorneys or other professionals when you think something should be confidential and ensuring the proper handling and documentation are being maintained.

Another type of communication that a court will consider unavailable as evidence is what is known as work product. Again, if we go back to the law dictionary, we find the definition is as follows:

n. the writings, notes, memoranda, reports on conversations with the client or witness, research and confidential materials which an attorney has developed while representing a client, particularly in preparation for trial. A "work product" may not be demanded or subpoenaed by the opposing party, as are documents, letters by and from third parties and other evidence, since the work product reflects the confidential strategy, tactics and theories to be employed by the attorney.[*]

In legal terms, you will hear this referred to as the work product doctrine. This doctrine is basically the practice of ensuring that any of the work done by an attorney or his consultants or agents[†] is protected from discovery in a court case.

This can be hugely important for an attorney or anyone working for an attorney to understand because, again, this protection can be lost by mismanagement of the information.

For instance, if you are consulting as a forensics examiner with an attorney, all of the reports and findings, even including the "mental impressions, conclusions, opinions, or legal theories of a party's attorney or other representative concerning the litigation"[‡] (as specifically stated in the Federal Rules of Civil Procedure), are considered work product. Therefore, they are not producible as evidence in court. That makes it extremely important that you as an examiner or agent for the attorney take the necessary precautions to protect that information and not inadvertently deliver it to the court or opposing counsel.

A big caveat for anyone working in this capacity is to understand that unless you are working as the attorney's agent, this work product doctrine will not apply. In other words, if you are hired by the actual plaintiff or defendant, your work is not protected and could be discoverable for a court case.

---

[*] law.com, Legal terms and definitions, "work product". http://dictionary.law.com/Default.aspx?selected=2261. Retrieved June 18, 2011.

[†] Forensic focus: Articles/papers, barristerharri, is your client an attorney? Be aware of possible constraints on your investigation (Part 1 of a multi-part series), September 24, 2011. http://articles.forensicfocus.com/2011/09/24/is-your-client-an-attorney-be-aware-of-possible-constraints-on-your-investigation-part-1-of-a-multi-part-series/. Retrieved June 18, 2011.

[‡] Fed. R. Civ. P. 26 (b)(3)(B). Retrieved June 18, 2011.

It is also quite often the case that experts or consultants are hired by the courts as third-party neutrals or special masters. In that case, he or she is working for the courts, and all evidence, including reports, findings, and opinions, can be considered relevant evidence to be admitted for the case. This can be advantageous to the finding of fact by virtue of the objectivity of the expert who was not hired by either side in a dispute.

Next we need to consider the issues around information that might be confidential or sensitive.

Whether information is considered confidential, sensitive, or public only matters if someone is maintaining some type of classification of that data. Unless and until data are classified and that classification is documented, there is no way to give it the proper protections. Confidential data might include information such as that we discussed with privileged communications. This type of data might also be personally identifiable information (you might hear this called PII) which if revealed could result in harm to a person or his or her financial well-being. This would include data such as

- Credit or debit card or social security card numbers
- Driver's license or other license information, especially if combined with other personal information such as full name and data and place of birth
- Information about your health such as medications or diagnoses (this is sometimes referred to as PHI, or personal health information)

These types of information are considered confidential and private in the United States. In Europe, privacy rules are even more proscribed and include information about where you live or work, what you purchased, and so forth.

Confidential information can be difficult to define precisely. But again, it is in your interest to understand and carefully manage your own exposure of confidential information, or the exposure of your organization or family's data. Find out what the privacy laws in your jurisdiction cover and protect that information carefully.

As an owner or manager of an organization, you may be responsible for another large portion of private or confidential data, such as your employees' personal information, health and insurance data, banking information, and so forth.

Your company may also have its own banking information that requires special protection and management. If you sell or purchase anything, you may also be holding confidential information for your clients or suppliers. And if you accept transactions using credit cards, all of that credit card information must be protected as confidential. All of these data can be and most often are stored electronically and thus require a level of diligence and care to maintain security. This is not a book about information security so we will not go far down that path.

However, it is important to understand that as an owner or manager of an organization, a legal professional, or even just a citizen, we control confidential data that must be protected both for legal reasons and just for the sake of privacy and the security of our assets.

Everyone should have management practices in place to ensure that this type of data is held in a safe and secure method and with good security practices. Some of the most basic of these practices would include

- Strong passwords and authentication policies
- Encryption
- Good monitoring and incident response
- Security-minded development of new applications

Now there are other data that might be considered sensitive and, depending on the importance of the data, might even be treated as confidential. For example, information about critical infrastructure such as the physical or logical location of control systems for electric or other power grids, or water/sewer pumping stations.

By logical I am referring to their location on a network or on the Internet, if they are available over those medium. More and more of these types of systems are moving to Internet access because of the convenience and efficiency that type of access brings with it.

Yet that type of information in the wrong hands could be very dangerous. That data would be considered at least sensitive and possibly should be guarded and secured at least as carefully as other confidential information.

If such information was requested or required for a court case or an audit or other reasons, it would be the responsibility of the producing party to justify its refusal to produce that information by proving the data's classification is based on real and justifiable concerns. The courts or auditors might still decide the data are of enough importance or relevance to require their production. If that is the case, the responsibility for the security and integrity of that data then passes to the court or the opposing side or other parties who will receive that data.

Finally, there will always be data that are simply inaccessible. In this chapter we showed various reasons that might be the case.

In a legal case, it is often true that attorneys will assert inaccessibility as a reason for failing to produce certain discoverable and relevant information. The legal acronym you will hear is NRA, which has nothing to do with the National Rifle Association, though they may have some NRA data. NRA in this case stands for not reasonably accessible. There is ample and various case law that sets precedent for what can and cannot be considered not reasonably accessible. And as with all case law, it often depends on the circumstances of the case at hand.

In some cases, the fact that important data would result in extremely high costs both in finances and resources required, was enough to convince the courts that it should be legitimately considered out of bounds and not entered as evidence. However, in other cases, the courts felt that the information was so important that the costs were immaterial or justified and the data must be produced.

Sometimes the courts would do what is known as cost shifting and require the party with either the most resources or the most at stake to pay for the acquisition of data that were deemed NRA.

In at least one case, the court decided that the information was important and that the party asserting its lack of accessibility had contributed to that lack by virtue of extremely poor records management practices or outright spoliation (a legal term meaning destruction or corruption of evidence). In that case, the courts basically slapped the offending party by requiring that they spend the money and time to acquire and produce that evidence no matter how long and expensive it was, because it was through their own fault that the data had become inaccessible.

In many cases now, the courts are requiring an accessibility log, just as they are requiring a privilege log. This means that they will want clear documentation that justifies the assertion of inaccessibility.

They will want to know about your records management policies and even more important your actual practices around management of your data.

This is a great lesson and a good way to end this section. In the end, it all comes down to good practices and careful management of your data. Whether you are the responsible party in an organization, a legal professional, or just a citizen in our digital world, you are the owner of digital data that may be needed in the future. You have a responsibility to understand and document that data in such a way that it is properly classified, indexed, and protected against corruption or loss. If it is confidential data, it should be classified as such and treated with the correct practices that ensure it is safe from exposure.

Whatever type or classification of data is within your realm of responsibility, you are well advised to manage it carefully and understand where it exists and how to access it if needed. A large part of that management is knowing what parts of that data need to be treated differently due to their classification as privileged, confidential, or sensitive, or for some reason inaccessible.

5.4 Proving Ownership and Integrity

One of the biggest issues that can get in the way of electronic evidence being accepted in a court of law or any other venue is the ability (or lack thereof) to prove who actually created that piece of evidence.

This can create a situation that is referred to as plausible deniability, meaning that it is possible for a party to deny having created a piece of electronic evidence based on the inability to prove that he or she ever had access to it.

Creating and managing data in a way that maintains its integrity, documents its access, and monitors any changes allows a party to ensure nonrepudiation. Nonrepudiation is simply the ability to prove, based on carefully controlled records management practices, who actually had access and made changes to or saved a piece of electronic evidence.

Similarly, by the very nature of electronic data, it can be relatively easy, whether by mistake or intentionally, to corrupt the integrity of a document. By this I am referring to the idea that it can be difficult to prove that the electronic record in question is in fact the same record you started with. You need to somehow be able to document that the record has no changes of any kind from the one that is required for the case at hand.

In this section, we consider all of the steps you as an individual or an organization can take to ensure the integrity of data such that the possibility of plausible deniability is minimized and nonrepudiation is maximized. We use some examples to illustrate these concepts.

As we discussed earlier, a digital record, whether a document, a picture, a spreadsheet, or anything else, is created using some kind of user interface application. Even if you are using the most basic text editor, there is coding going on in the background both by that application and by the computer operating system. These metadata (or data about the data) are extremely important to our conversation about integrity and ownership.

When one is attempting to establish the ownership of an electronic record, understanding when and where it was created is going to be your best clue. The data are contained in the metadata of every electronic record, or in some cases the data are collected by the operating system and stored in some type of log.

On Windows computers there is a hidden system file called the MFT that we talked about earlier. This is a flat database containing information about every file and folder ever created on the device since it was built and fired up for the first time. Other operating systems use similar methods of tracking files and their creation, modification, and access times, as well as their locations within the folder hierarchy.

How does this work in the real world? Imagine a case where the plaintiff alleged that the defendant stole patented information. These kinds of cases go on all the time.

In our imaginary case, the facts as we know them are that the plaintiff worked for the defendant for many years and was a model employee. She was an engineer who developed many different products that the defendant company developed, patented, and eventually sold. Everyone was happy. However, some of her ideas either were not that great, or at least the company found they did not have the potential of others, so they told her they were not interested. Please go on to your next great idea. Toward the end of her employment with them, one of these rejected ideas seemed to her to be an extremely excellent and wonderful invention that she was very excited about.

Now, as an employee with this company, she agreed that anything she invented belonged to them and was theirs to patent if they wished. When they turned down this idea, she was disappointed and sent an e-mail to her boss asking if she could consider this rejected idea exempt from their agreement and take it up on her own. She received several e-mails from management that eventually agreed to release this invention from their agreement and allow her to pursue it on her own if she wished. Shortly after this, she tendered her resignation from this company and went out on her own to develop her great idea.

As it turned out, she was right to be so excited about her invention. It became a huge success and she and her new product began to become extremely valuable. Everything was looking pretty rosy until suddenly her old company came out with an extremely familiar looking product and started competing with her. Because they were a much larger and more established company, they had a considerable advantage in marketing and brand recognition, and her company began to quickly lose market share for her wonderful invention.

At this point she sued her old company, the defendants, alleging that they had stolen the patent for which they had given up their rights while she was in their employ. She had electronic documentation to prove her assertions including the previously mentioned e-mails and an actual document that was attached to one of the e-mails stating that they released their interest.

It seemed like a cut-and-dried case until in the first days of discovery the defendants produced e-mails and electronic documents from an earlier date than the ones she had, showing that they had not in fact released their interest and that they asserted their ownership of the patent rights. They threatened a countersuit if she did not drop her case.

Now, as was noted, these folks had an established company, and along with that came powerful and experienced legal counsel who felt pretty assured that they could bully our friend the plaintiff into giving up her lucrative patent and bowing to their superior might. However, this is a good illustration of one part of the electronic evidence revolution that we have not really dwelt on too much.

In some cases, at least, it can enhance the justice system by creating a more level playing field. In this case, because they were dealing with electronic evidence and the need to prove or disprove its integrity, both sides had an equally good chance of prevailing if they had the capacity and expertise available to prove their assertions.

Now enter the forensics experts.

The truth of this matter rests squarely on proving the integrity and ownership of the two sets of documents being presented with opposing conclusions. If our plaintiff can prove that her electronic evidence was in fact created when and where and by whom she is asserting, she is one step closer to prevailing in this case. However, she also needs to prove the contrary—that the defendant's evidence is false and was not created when, where, and by whom they are asserting.

In our imaginary case (which I admit has its basis in several different cases I have read), the forensics experts for the plaintiff ask for and receive complete sets of records from the defendants' computers and begin creating a timeline of events to try to understand the discrepancy between the assertions of their client the plaintiff and those of the defendants.

They are looking through the manager's computer, and they are noting regular and expected activities on a daily basis. They can see when he logged in for the day, when he went online and checked his e-mail and his stocks, when he did some Google searches, when he worked on some documents, when he created and sent e-mail, and so on.

The timeline goes along pretty normally, but for some reason on the day that the alleged e-mails and the contrary document were supposed to have been created and sent, they are not finding any evidence of that activity. So, they go into the MFT looking for the creation time and date of the document in question, and there it is with approximately the right time and date. Now this is a puzzle and an anomaly, and experts do not like those.

They next take a look at some event logs for the day in question, and again there does not seem to be any evidence of the application that was supposed to have created the document having been opened at that time and date. Being the careful sleuths that they are, they look further and deeper and suddenly they find something of extreme interest.

On a day several weeks after the supposed day of creation of the document in question, the event logs show an odd thing. The time clock on the computer is set back to a day 2 weeks earlier for a short time and, lo and behold, the application that created the document is fired up during that window as is the e-mail program. After some time goes by those applications are closed again and the time goes back to normal and proceeds in a regular way.

The next day in court the plaintiff's attorney asks the court to allow him to depose (deposing means to question in a special meeting called a deposition), the defendant's IT manager. The court allows this and the deposition is scheduled and occurs some days later. In deposition, the IT manager for the defendant admits that he was asked by management to set the computer time clock back on the manager's computer and did so on the date noted by our heroes, the forensic sleuths.

At that point the defendants for some odd reason agree to settle the case, cease and desist from marketing the product in question, and pay all court costs as well as a substantial award to the plaintiff. Case closed.

This example illustrates many of the ways that the integrity and ownership of electronic evidence can be manipulated and used to either obfuscate or prove the integrity of that data.

We look a little closer at the issue of date and time stamps in the next section, but in the end, the ability to prove who did what and when is often the entire crux of any assertion in court or otherwise.

To establish the "who" is often difficult, especially in situations where more than one person uses a computer or other electronic device. There have also been cases where defendants have used the "virus" defense and insisted that they were not guilty of whatever crime was shown to have taken place from their computer because they had a virus and the "virus made them do it."

This defense might have some merit, but there will need to be some evidence to show this is the case, such as actual virus evidence on the device.

In establishing ownership, one can sometimes find evidence in the metadata. Some applications will record the user name either from something a user typed into the application itself or from the person logged in at the time. However, that can be relatively easy to dispute as without an actual camera taking pictures of who is typing on the computer at the time the document is created, there is no sure way to tell if someone else had control of the computer. The logged-in person may have left it running and went to lunch, or that person might not have specific and controlled login credentials for everyone, so anyone in the family or the office can log onto anyone else's computer.

Given that those metadata may be difficult to prove or at least easy to refute, what other methods can be applied to prove who did what and when? One method often employed is the one we mentioned in our example. Experts will create a timeline of events on a computer that establishes what was taking place when. For instance, they can show that at 8:37 A.M. on Thursday, December 2, the computer was logged into by someone with the user name of Vjohnson. At 8:42 A.M., an Internet browser was started up and the Facebook account for Violet Johnson was logged into. A session of the game Farmville was played for the next hour or so under the user ID of VJ. At 9:56 A.M., a Google search occurred that looked up information on how to poison your husband. Then at 10:23 A.M., another search was typed in with the search term strychnine. Finally, at 10:54 A.M., a Google mail session was opened up under the user name JohnsV1@gmail.com and that session shows evidence of lasting for approximately an hour. Traces of e-mails to and from that address are found with date and time stamps that correspond to that time frame, and all of the ones from that e-mail address have ample evidence of having been authored by the same Johnson.

Now while the above does not establish perfect evidence that Johnson was planning to kill her husband with strychnine poison, if he should show up with that condition in the future, this could certainly be important electronic evidence of her culpability. Even without using metadata that might be difficult to prove, the forensic experts can show, using this methodology, what in this case would be pretty compelling evidence of who was actually on the computer when the actions that establish culpability for a crime took place.

The other part of proving integrity is somehow establishing that a piece of electronic evidence was not tampered with in any way. Because it is electronic, this type of data is susceptible to many different types of changes, often simply by turning on a computer or starting up an application.

In order to use evidence in a trial or for other uses and be sure it was not changed in any way, processes, tools, and protocols have to be carefully followed that ensure against these types of changes.

One often-used tool is what is known as hashing. A hash is a mathematical process run on all of those ones and zeros that make up a file. Because all electronic data are represented by the bits and bytes of numbers that we discussed in other chapters, these numbers can be mathematically manipulated through a known hash algorithm that will result in a very long set of numbers and letters in a hexadecimal format. This long hexadecimal number is called the hash, and it can be made of a file or folder, a group of files or folders, or even an entire hard drive or other storage medium (Figure 5.5). That large and unique number is like a fingerprint of what is contained in the data at that moment. If someone changes even the period at the end of a sentence and you run that same hash algorithm against the file again, the resultant number will have changed.

To guard and maintain the integrity of electronic evidence and to be able to prove that what you are producing for a court or audit is the same evidence as was requested or was created originally, experts will often begin by creating a hash value of that evidence before it is moved or copied. They use special tools that do not manipulate or write any data to the device they are copying from, and they carefully document the chain of custody or any changes that might have occurred and what and why they occurred.

Then, at the other end of things, when they are producing that evidence, they can use the hash values that were recorded, along with their chain of custody documentation to prove that the evidence in

Figure 5.5   A hash of a file, folder, drive, or any piece of digital data is like a fingerprint.

question is the same as when it was created. Or if that is not the case, they can show why it is not and establish whether it is still legitimate and relevant evidence that should be admitted.

That last part probably needs an example to make more sense. Assume you were asked to bring to court a set of e-mails that were created on a certain computer. Those e-mails were copied into a Word document by someone with less expertise in these issues and then deleted from the original e-mail application. Those e-mails saved into a Word document, though they lost the integrity of the original documents, might still be admissible as evidence if

- You carefully documented when and by whom the e-mails were copied.
- You can demonstrate how that Word document was protected from any changes (perhaps by creating a hash of the document).
- You did everything in your power to attempt to recover whatever you could from the e-mail application.

If the courts feel they are important enough and there is good documentation establishing that the core text was not changed, the e-mails might be admitted.

In an interesting example of the importance of maintaining the integrity of electronic documents, the U.S. Congress in 2011 was considering a new law called the Uniform Electronic Legal Material Act. This would encourage all of the states to adopt methods of authentication for any of their official government records. In an article from the Library of Congress,* it is noted that this process can be complicated and expensive, but that states should be considering the best ways to accomplish this for obvious reasons.

Depending on the sensitivity of the documents in question, they might have a simple mechanism that compares a downloaded document to an original, or they might have something more complex that compares hash values.

---

* Library of Congress, Butch Lazorchak, UELMA: A law we all can love. http://blogs.loc.gov/digitalpreservation/2011/11/uelma-a-law-we-all-can-love/?doing_wp_cron. Retrieved 2011-07-09.

All of this will require states and other government entities that come under the purview of this law to create methods of authentication up front when they create and store documents. In other words, each new official document will probably need to have a hash value or some other type of authenticating metadata attached to it that can be referenced in the future.

Establishing and maintaining the ownership and integrity of electronic evidence can be paramount in any type of case. It is always going to be an important role that an organization should create policies and procedures around in order to ensure they have the means to prove that integrity. These procedures should include the following:

- Careful records management and documentation
- Log management
- Good practices around the handling of potential electronic evidence

Those good practices will require an organization to have policy and established processes for litigation holds that ensure all affected people in the organization understand their responsibilities for preserving the integrity of any potentially relevant electronic evidence should there be any indication of a possible court action. We discuss litigation holds in more detail in Chapter 6.

5.5 Marking Time: How Time Is Recorded and Ensuring Integrity

As noted in the last section, the time and date information included in or about an important piece of electronic data can often be the crux of a matter when trying to establish what happened when and to whom. In this section, we spend a little more time considering time (Figure 5.6).

Modern computing devices operate in cycles of time that are tiny compared to what we are normally aware of. They operate in and record those operations in milliseconds (one thousandth of a second). This was not always the case. Some of the first computers did not bother tracking or recording the time of day, but they still operated in timed cycles that they did track.

Figure 5.6   Time is of the essence: The question of when something happened can be one of the most important facts to establish.

Tracking the time is done in different ways by different operating systems. Microsoft operating systems track time on the basis of how many 100 nanosecond periods have passed since January 1, 1601, while UNIX systems track seconds since January 1, 1970.

These are arbitrary choices made by geeks with not enough to keep them challenged in my humble opinion, but in any case that is how these operating systems keep track of the time and record it internally. However, as with everything in our electronic world, those geeks knew better than to expect us normal humans to be able to decode their schemes. All modern electronic devices decode and represent these system time data to users as a time and date we recognize, such as October 15, 1978, at 12:01:06:13, which actually does take us down to the millisecond level if we care to know it (in this case 06 is the hundredths of seconds and 13 is the milliseconds). But the important thing to understand is where the computer gets that time from in the first place. Does it come out of midair? I guess in some cases you might say that it does.

The bottom line is that the time a computer records and stores is entirely dependent on input it gets from outside. There is no magic time finder hiding inside of each computer.

Computers and all of the devices that use computing systems (phones, cameras, toasters, VCRs, televisions, etc.) will contain a chip that keeps track of milliseconds and in many cases will have a backup battery that keeps it running so it does not lose track when you turn off the power. Some of these devices, as noted above, will get their information out of midair by picking up radio signals from the atomic clock at the U.S. Naval Observatory or other sources. These are accepted standard keepers for the "real" time worldwide.

Other devices get their time reference from a network time server that they are connected to via a wired or wireless network. That server has in turn gotten its time from some other source, perhaps the atomic clocks noted above.

Because this is so important to the smooth running of our society, standards have been established and are adhered to pretty much worldwide. The base time standard originally came from the Royal Greenwich Observatory in Greenwich, England, where they carefully monitored the rotation of the planet and calculated the exact agreed-upon "mean" time or what is known as Greenwich Mean Time.[*]

More recently, this was replaced by something called Universal Time that is calculated by comparing many different atomic clocks around the world and adjusting for anomalies to come up with a time standard that is as accurate as possible. This is the base time upon which other time zones around the world are based. Greenwich is still considered the "prime" or base meridian of time calculations, and Universal Time, or what you will hear referred to as UTC (Universal Coordinated Time), is still the time you will find on all the clocks in England.

Depending on the distance from Greenwich and sometimes some arbitrary and even politically motivated lines, the time in a certain zone will differ from Greenwich time, usually (but not always) in hourly increments somewhat corresponding to the movement of the planet around the Sun and its approximate 24-hour spin.

Now you might be wondering how all this is related to understanding the time of an activity on a computer—good question. The reason we are delving into this fascinating discussion on time standards and time zones is that most all computers will record creation, access, and modification times of the activities that occur on them in UTC.

If you are producing records and hope to prove or disprove a point with those records based on the time they happened, you may need to

---

[*] History of legal time in Britain. http://www.polyomino.org.uk/british-time/. Retrieved June 17, 2011.

understand and translate between UTC and the time zone in which the activity took place.

That last part of the sentence above is very important to note. To establish what time an activity took place, you need to consider where it took place and the date it took place as well.

As an example, think about a case where you are tasked with establishing exactly when a document was created and last saved. According to the evidence you have, the document was saved on a computer in Florida on December 16. You are examining the computer 6 months later in Colorado. The time recorded for that document's creation and last access are recorded as noted above in UTC. Your job will be to consider what the time zone difference would be for Florida during December. That would be Eastern Standard time (note that between November and March we have to adjust for daylight savings time) which is −5 hours' difference from UTC. Your time stamps have to be adjusted to reflect the actual local time where the activity took place.

Now, think about how this might be complicated if the activity took place in one of the oddball places like Indiana, where they do not observe daylight savings time, or other time zones like some of the Caribbean Islands that choose to adjust their time by only a half hour instead of an hour. And of course, all of this assumes that the time on the computer in question was accurately set to begin with and was not tampered with or simply lost time due to malfunction of the time chip or power loss in the battery.

Because this can be so important, it is imperative that some type of auditing or other means of verification of the accuracy and integrity of the time be established. If you are in the position of needing to prove the integrity of the time, you may need to gather corroborating evidence such as other devices that show the same time for the activity in question, or perhaps some type of documentation of the time having been audited and monitored for accuracy on a regular basis.

As an organization that might have to prove the integrity of time information recorded on its electronic data, it is important to maintain that type of auditable documentation to show that you have some type of time server or standard that is monitored regularly and carefully maintained.

5.6 Legal and Forensically Sound Acquisition

This chapter has focused on the idea of how to locate and recognize data and the challenges and issues that can arise. Once you have accomplished that task and worked through all of those challenges, you are ready to acquire that information in order to organize it and produce it, either for a court proceeding, some administrative or audit review, or just as a part of your own archival records management.

No matter what the reason for gathering that data, doing so in a forensically sound manner is a good practice as it will ensure that the data you produce can be proven to be the same data as you started with and have not been manipulated or changed in any way from the original.

We talked a little earlier about some of the tools that professionals use to accomplish this maintenance of integrity, but in this final section we will delve into those more deeply and give you some practical policy rules that you can incorporate into your organization's practices.

As noted before, the number one priority is to maintain information in its original state and be able to show that you have done so. To accomplish that, you should begin with good documentation around your records management policies. Much more important than the policies, however, are the actual practices to which you or your organization adhere. In every case, a court is going to want to know and understand what you actually do, not so much what you suggest you or your staff should be doing in policy documents.

So, let's begin with records management policy basics. Of course this could be a book all by itself, so we just hit some main points that you can put into practice, and I encourage you to learn more and apply that knowledge to your specific needs and requirements.

Records management policy should first include classification of data. You and your colleagues and staff must have a good understanding of the types of data you are producing and the legal and archival ramifications and requirements for each of those types.

For instance, there will most always be some records retention rules that attach to certain types of information such as contracts, invoices, and human resource records. These are usually determined as regulations either for your industry or for the particular jurisdiction of which you or your organization are a part.

Spend some time learning about and understanding which pieces of information your organization creates that are subject to these regulations. Ensure that everyone who creates, accesses, or in any way handles that data is aware of the regulations that apply. Create written policies that are available to all employees that explain those regulatory obligations. If you are smart, you will also insist that anyone who has access to this type of data has read, understood, and signed off on these policies. This will go a long way in a court case toward showing that your practices follow your policies.

Another good way to prove that those practices are adhered to is to do a regular audit of your employees and of the regulated information and their record retention practices to ensure they are being handled according to policy.

Once you deal with the regulated information, you still may have other data that are important to your organization and should be managed carefully. This might include e-mail in general or intellectual property, or perhaps log information from your network or a specific application. Again, your task is to have a thorough understanding of the importance of that information as well as considering its possible importance either to your organization or yourself, or as possibly relevant information in a court case.

If you are doing this for yourself as an individual, it is mostly a matter of considering all of the types of information that you store electronically and its possible value in the future. Make good choices about how the data are preserved, organized, and maintained so the data will be available when needed.

If records management practices and policies need to be developed for an organization, I would recommend gathering a group of stakeholders including top-level management, auditors, legal counsel, and IT managers and staff if those positions exist. If any of those positions are outsourced or contracted for, it would be useful to have them in the meeting as well.

Start, as noted above, by understanding the records retention regulations that apply, and then carefully consider all of the other data that you produce. Use the information you learned in this book as a guide to ensure you are considering all of the different places data can be stored and all of the issues and challenges around being able to access that data.

Come up with a set of policies and guidelines that takes all this information into account. Your auditors and legal counsel can assist you with the regulatory requirements, and your IT folks can help you to understand where the data live, who owns and controls the data, and how you will be able to access and manage the data. Management will be able to help you understand all of the different types of information created and preserved within your organization.

Top-level management or executives need to be included in this work as well, because it is extremely important that they understand and buy off on the policies. They will ensure these policies are adhered to throughout the organization if they believe in the importance of these practices.

Document those understandings in policy and guidelines, and when you feel they are as complete as possible (with the understanding that such policies need to be dynamic and flexible as your organization expands or contracts and as technology changes), arrange for regular and ongoing training on those policies for everyone in your organization who will have access to those types of records.

Good records management practices are the most important foundation for ensuring the integrity and availability of records. With those in place and well documented, you have taken the important first steps.

When it is time to gather that data for whatever reason, you now have the information readily available to know who owns it and how to gain access to it. The next important step is to acquire that data in a forensically sound manner. To do that, start with some type of tool that allows you to make one of those fingerprints we spoke of earlier called a hash. Run that application and create a hash value for every piece of information that you will be preserving.

Many computer forensics applications have this capacity built into them. If you or your computer forensics specialist are using those tools to create an exact copy (sometimes called an image or a snapshot) of a set of data, those applications will automatically verify the integrity of the data by creating a hash value before and after the data are copied. In many cases, they will use two or more types of hash algorithms to add even more surety to the integrity of the copied data. They will sometimes store those hash values in a text file that you can save with the copied data, or sometimes these applications actually attach those hash values as metadata to the copied data.

However, you do not have to have these specialized tools. Some operating systems will do what is known as a verified copy. This is usually done from the command line with special switches in the command that you type.

An example of this in a Windows operating system would be to open up the command window by selecting Start, Run, and typing cmd to get the command window (a window will pop up with a black screen and usually a DOS prompt, C:). Then you can type in "Copy [source—path and name of the file you want to copy] [destination—where you want to copy it] and/V" (without the quotes). An example of this type of command line might look like "C:Copy c:myfilessample.doc d:evidencesample.doc/V" (again without the quotes).

The/V option at the end tells Windows to verify that the copied file is the same and was copied successfully. To do this, Windows hashes the file in the background using a relatively simple hash algorithm called a checksum before and after and checks to ensure the hashes are the same.

There is another command in Windows that you can use. (These are all actually old DOS commands as this is the basic structure that Windows was built on, and it is still backwards compatible with these commands.) You would use this instead if you wanted to copy both folders and files. The syntax of the command is the same, but you use XCOPY instead of COPY. Again, use the/V for verify, to ensure everything you copied is the same on both ends.

On a Linux operating system you can use a command line that compares the copied files to ensure their integrity: cp "$file" "$dest" && cmp "$file" "$dest" || echo "failed." In this case, you would substitute the name of the file for "$file" and the path to that file for "$dest." You would insert the two files and paths for the files you want to compare on either side of the && cmp in the command line. The echo at the end of the command will respond on your screen with the word "failed" if the two files do not match.

Unix and Linux operating systems have several ways that you can copy different quantities of data and ensure they are the same on both ends, but this example will work for smaller groups of files. To copy directories, you add the -r switch into the command line right after the cp. If you choose to use this more basic approach, you simply need to document carefully that this is what you did so you can show that you have done your best to maintain the integrity of the copied information.

If you need to preserve larger volumes of data, such as entire hard drives, you can use forensic imaging tools to do so. Some of these are actual hardware and some use software to accomplish this. In either case, you connect the hard drive or the computer containing the hard drive to software or hardware that includes what is called a write blocker.

As noted, every time a computing device accesses information it can potentially change that information subtly by changing the access time, or making other changes to the metadata. A write blocker, whether it is hardware or software based, does not allow any data to be written to the files or data storage to which it is connected.

Once your device is connected to a write blocker, you next make a connection to a storage device. Then you use either an application or possibly command lines to initiate a byte-by-byte copy of the hard drive or other large portions of data.

This is sometimes also called a mirror image, though I do not like that term because in a mirror everything is backwards, and in a successful forensic image everything is the same as in the original. These images become a file with an extension of .dd, or .e01, or other types of recognized image files.

Of course, if this is an image of a hard disk, they can be very large files. In some cases, the forensic imaging applications that create them will automatically divide them up into pieces the right size to fit onto CDs or DVDs so that you can transport them on those media. The forensic imaging software will also sometimes allow you to compress the resultant image files by keeping track of but not actually copying empty sections of the hard drive. When it sees empty parts of the drive, it tracks and records where those are so that if you need to reproduce the exact hard drive it can put those empty sections back where they were on the original.

If you prefer using command lines to create your image, the dd command will work in both Windows and UNIX operating systems. This command syntax is a little different from most UNIX commands and can be used for many different tasks. The basic UNIX command line for copying one drive to another might look like: "dd if=/dev/ad0 of=/dev/ad1" (without the quotes) where/dev/ad0 refers to one drive partition and/dev/ad1 another. The "if" and "of" in this command refer to the input file (if) and output file (of).

The Windows version of that command would be: "dd.exeif=.Physic alDrive0of=d:imagesPhysicalDrive0.img" (again without the quotes) to which you could add some hash commands to verify that it copied correctly, such as: "--md5sum --verifymd5 --md5out=d:imagesPhysicalDrive0. img.md5" (again without the quotes).

Now this is not meant to be a technical how-to book, and there are many different tools and applications that assist in accomplishing the creation of a forensically sound image of a digital storage device. So we will not get any more detailed about how to make all the connections and transfer all of the data. It is only important for you to understand that there are procedures and tasks that must be accomplished in order to ensure the integrity of data on either end of an acquisition process.

If you are going to do this work yourself, you need to take the time to become familiar with these methods and comfortable with these tools. You will also need to purchase and license the tools you want to use. All of that will take time and money, but it is important to both you and your organization that it be done and done well.

If you do not feel the urge to become a forensics investigator or expert, your job will be to ensure that you have access to someone with those skills and tools.

No matter what method you choose to create and preserve the forensically sound copies of data, the important thing to understand is the necessity to ensure the integrity of the data so that you can prove the data are the same after being copied as they were before.

As noted, there are many good tools out there that will allow you to do this using an application interface if you are not comfortable with command lines. One of these tools is free from AccessData and is called FTK Imager. Of course all of the command lines are free to use as long as you have that type of operating system and the comfort level to work with them.

We have reached the end of this chapter, so remember the most important points when you consider the where and how of electronically stored information. Those are as follows:

- ESI can be made difficult to acquire in many ways, whether due to corruption, loss, deletion, encryption, or loss of the application or device that created it in the first place.
- The most important thing you and your organization can do to ensure your ESI is accessible is to have good records management policies and, most important of all, good practices that follow those policies.
- Maintaining and documenting the integrity of data will be paramount in the data being legally admissible as evidence, or usable for audits or simply valid records.

If you are able to use this chapter, along with the information from other chapters to begin to address these important issues, you will be well on your way toward better management of the ESI that surrounds us all.

6
KEEPING YOUR TREASURES
Preservation and Management

6.1 Introduction

One of the most important tasks an organization or individual will face when dealing with electronic evidence is the preservation of that data in a way that ensures the integrity (guaranteeing that nothing about the data changes as you move and manage the data) and availability (ensuring the data are easily and efficiently accessible) of the data. In this chapter, we look at all of the aspects of that task and discuss the tools and requirements that you should be considering.

6.2 Securing the Data

Once you have gone through the process of acquiring electronic information for whatever purpose you might have, you will need to consider how you can secure that data (Figure 6.1). The first thing to consider is the actual classification of the data in question. Thinking about how you would classify the data you are trying to secure will inform you as to the degree to which you need to secure it. For instance, if the data you are working with are publicly available, easily recreated, and not subject to any question of legitimacy (either because the data contain well-established information or because they are simply not very important to the case at hand), you might classify the data as nonsensitive, low-security data.

On the other hand, if the data contain private information about an individual, protected information about intellectual property or critical infrastructure, or simply information that could be used by your adversary to your disadvantage, the data might be classified as

Figure 6.1   Maintaining the integrity of electronic evidence will require securing the data.

sensitive or confidential. Information considered work product or privileged in a legal definition would also be classified as confidential. Of course, if you are working for or with the military or an intelligence organization, there will be other levels of classification that determine exactly who has the right or ability to see that data. These can include, among others depending on the organization:

- For official use only (FOUO)
- Law enforcement sensitive (LES)
- Secret
- Top secret
- For your eyes only

Whatever the requirements of your organization or entity, the first step in deciding the level and processes of securing data is classification of that data.

Making decisions about how to secure information will always be a classical risk management exercise. You will weigh the risk in terms of what vulnerabilities or threats there are to the data storage, the likelihood of those vulnerabilities being exploited, the impact of that exploit if it should occur, and the cost of mitigating the risk to reduce the likelihood of an exploit resulting in the loss or compromise of the data.

In the first instance, when data are publicly available and well established as fact, there is little reason to protect the data. In risk management language, the vulnerability to loss or compromise will be higher if the data are not protected, but the impact is minimal to none. Therefore, there is no motivation to spend resources protecting that data.

In a real-world example, if you have acquired information from an electronic version of *The New York Times* about specific features of a new version of smart phone that you will be using to establish some facts in your case, that information is publicly available and well established as fact. There will be other sources of the same information, again publicly available and easily accessible, which will corroborate your data. There is no reason or motivation for you or your organization to spend the time or resources to secure that information.

However, in the other instances you will not only have the motivation, but in many cases a legal and ethical responsibility to secure the data that you have acquired. Let's look again at an example. If your company has intellectual property in the form of a patent for the technology that enables one of the features of that new smart phone and that could give competitors an advantage, the risk picture changes.

In this case, the vulnerabilities that might threaten the compromise or loss of your intellectual property (IP) might be the same as in our first example, but the potential impact is huge. Some of the possible threats to the loss of your IP might include

- Industrial espionage in the form of an attack on your computer systems
- An insider threat from a disgruntled employee
- An accidental loss of the information through the loss of a laptop, smart phone, or other digital device
- The compromise of your network or computing systems via a bad website or e-mail that installs malware
- The loss of data due to a natural or man-made disaster

The loss or compromise of that data could result in lost profits or business or might have a deleterious effect on a court case if you were arguing for your patent rights.

Here we see that your organizational risk analysis will indicate a greater need to expend resources and time as necessary to secure the data and mitigate the risks. Deciding whether to secure the data therefore becomes the first thing you need to consider before deciding how to do so. To accomplish that first step you will need to do the following:

- Take the time and expend the effort to understand the classification of your data and appropriately apply those classifications.
- Separate the different classes of data into unique groups for storage and/or management.
- Conduct realistic and thorough risk assessments of the data classes.
- Make decisions about the level of resources you will dedicate to the security of the data in their different classifications.

Once you have completed that first all-important risk management assessment, you are ready to consider the procedures and protocols for actually protecting the data.

6.3 Access Control and Management

The actual storage media for data is of relatively little consequence to the preservation considerations we address in this chapter.

As long as the media is reliable, physically robust, and accessible, it does not really make a lot of difference if your data are stored on magnetic backup tapes, optical storage such as CDs or DVDs, solid-state drives such as USB devices, hard disks on a server, in a virtual server environment, or even on the Internet in some type of online infrastructure service (aka, the "cloud").

When you consider the security and integrity of data, what really matters are the controls around who can access the data and how those controls are managed.

In this section, we look at various methods you should consider for managing access to your data. These can include

- Authentication
- Encryption
- Identity management
- Logical compartmentalization
- Physical separation and access control

Figure 6.2   You need to understand and manage authentication standards and procedures.

We begin with authentication mechanisms as these are the most recognizable and common ways to control access to data (Figure 6.2). In nearly every organization, in order to gain access to your network, you use an authentication mechanism. In the world of IT we speak of factors of authentication. These include:

- Something you know—your user name or ID and a password, PIN, or a pass phrase that only you know
- Something you have—a smart card, token, or other identification device
- Something you are—biometrics such as your thumbprint, iris scan, facial characteristics, or even the speed and pressure with which you type on a keyboard

In most cases, only the single factor of "something you know," consisting of the two pieces of information, your ID and password, is all that is required to gain access to your company's network, your e-mail application, or even your home computer or smart phone (if you have bothered to enable that access control on your own devices).

However, when the classification of the data justifies a higher level of authentication, you will see two- or even three-factor authentication come into play. In those cases, you might carry a device around with you that you have to swipe through an installed reader on your computer, laptop, or other device before accessing information and then follow up with your ID and password. Or the device might be designed to give you a onetime password or access number that you have to key in before putting in your regular ID and password. Or you might have to use the third level of authentication to prove who you are and that you have a right to access the data in question. You might have to scan your thumb, hand, face, or eyes or type with the correct and recognized patterns and pressures.

A more commonly used type of two-factor authentication that has become popular with some on-line applications (e.g., Gmail, Facebook, some banking sites) is the sending of a security code via text message to your phone before allowing you to login.

As noted above, all of these different types of authentication mechanisms will depend on the relative risk assessed for the data you are protecting. As you can imagine, the levels and costs of management and logistics for each of these types of controls increase substantially the more factors you introduce.

The next type of control to consider is encryption. Encryption can be the most secure way to protect your data. However, as with any type of control, there are trade-offs in efficiency and convenience. There are also many levels of encryption that can be used. A complete discussion of how encryption works and all of the different possible means to encrypt data is beyond the scope of this book, not to mention being beyond the mind capacity of most normal humans. Suffice it to say that you have choices if you decide that data are important enough to protect with encryption.

There are relatively simple means of encryption, such as password protecting a document or spreadsheet. This is accomplished simply by choosing the right menu item in your document software and typing in a password. The application will then encrypt the data in that document, so that anyone trying to view it without the password would not be able to open it in the first place. Even if they managed to open it with some type of plain text reader, it would be gibberish. However, this is relatively simple encryption and thereby relatively trivial to crack. Easily accessible tools that most anyone can find and install will be able to discover the password and allow someone to access that data.

Encryption types gain in complexity and therefore in levels of accessibility depending on your desires and needs. If you are protecting state secrets, you can use encryption, the keys to which are huge and would take thousands of computers thousands of years to crack. And there are many levels in between.

Enabling encryption requires the management of those keys or passwords. In simple encryption models you only need to manage the passwords. But in more complex models there will be keys of different lengths and complexity that will need to be shared or protected in order to allow encrypted data to be shared and transported safely. Again, the complexities of key management are beyond our scope, but the point should be recognized: Encryption can be a logistical and management challenge.

New research into "quantum" encryption uses features of quantum mechanics and physics to create keys that will be impossible to recreate. Again, this is well beyond the scope of this book, but it presents new and very interesting possibilities for the protection of very sensitive data.

Encrypting data while in storage is only part of the process. If you need to transport or share that data with someone, you have to consider the ways and means of maintaining that encryption during transport.

If you are physically delivering the data, the data can remain encrypted on your storage device and you can provide the key to the recipient. If you are sending it via encrypted e-mail, you will need to have a method to share a key securely with the recipient.

If you intend to provide access to the data over the Internet or a network, you will need to provide the recipient with an encrypted "tunnel" (such as VPN, virtual private network) or an encrypted Web protocol (such as SSL, Secure Sockets Layer, or what you would see as an HTTPS web page; or SFTP, Secure File Transfer Protocol).

Again, the management, development, and logistics of creating and maintaining these controls exact a price in resources and time. The need to use these encryption controls will have to be weighed against the actual risk model that fits with the data you are protecting.

All of these systems and controls depend on being able to authenticate the identity of the person requesting access to data and to determine whether that person actually has the right to access the data. This is known as "identity management," and there are a whole set of tools and protocols set up to facilitate this process. These tools and protocols rely on databases of information that store identifying information and authentication credentials as well as the rights each identified entity has to certain stores of information.

Some of these identity management tools facilitate what is known as "single sign-on," allowing a user to log in once to an organization and be authenticated via the identity management system to gain access to disparate sets of data or applications. This can increase efficiency and even security if the system is well designed and maintained. However, the adverse of that should be a caveat to anyone considering a single sign-on system. If not well designed and maintained, this type of identity management creates security issues that must be thought about carefully.

For instance, if you have a single sign-on system in place, your attack surface becomes less complex and now only depends on one failure to compromise all of the data that a user has access to.

That being said, single sign-on is often most appropriate when access is being granted to similarly classified sets of data. To allow single sign-on with access to nonsensitive data as well as highly confidential data would not be a good risk management decision.

Allowing access to your basic work files, e-mail, Internet connection, and desktop applications through a single sign-on would make sense, but access to a personnel database with confidential information might still require another level of authentication.

In the absence of this type of overall system, identity management is simply the connecting, via authentication credentials, of users or entities to the data or application to which they have rights. It will also manage different levels of rights such as read-only access (so you can view but not change data), write access (you can write new data), or change, delete, move, and so forth, rights that allow you to manipulate data depending on your authenticated permissions.

Another method of controlling access to data is to logically compartmentalize the data within a network or other storage medium. At the micro level, you can create profiles on one area of a computer or network drive or you can create partitions on a hard drive and assign different rights or access privileges to those profiles or partitions.

You can see an example of this on most any Windows-based computer by looking at the Documents and Settings folder. Within that folder will be different names of the users on a computer. If there is only one user and if that user has administrative rights, then all of the subfolders will be accessible. However, if there are different users, they will only have rights to read or access or change the files in their own profile folder.

With different partitions on a drive, access can be created and managed through rights assignments or in some cases through the actual applications that control the startup or movement within the operating system. Different partitions can actually have different operating systems on them to which you must separately log in at the computer startup.

You can also use virtual machine software to create a computer within your computer. This type of software basically will allow you to set up a separate operating system with its own programs and data, all using your same hardware (such as the keyboard, mouse, monitor, DVD/CD drives, network connections, and USB or other connections), but existing as a file within your computer. Access to that system can be controlled via a password as well, and this can be used to store applications and data that are only accessible to those with the right authentication.

Virtual machines are becoming a common way to share space on servers in data centers and each of those virtual servers can have different authentication protocols for access to their data. This practice is becoming very popular because it saves resources in both physical space and in energy consumption by using one physical server device to host many different virtual server instances.

Within a network you can also create partitions or virtual networks. Similarly, these will only be accessible to those with the right credentials or sometimes even the necessary physical access. These can be divided using networking devices such as firewalls, switches, and routers that only allow certain traffic to access those segments of the network.

A final control that you can put in place with relatively little cost is simply to physically separate the data storage. This could be in the form of a limited access data center, locked server racks, or simply locked storage space where you keep tapes or hard drives.

As long as you maintain access control to those places and chain of custody documentation so you can document who has had access and when, you will have a relatively reliable proof of the integrity and safety of the data in question.

6.4 Organization and File Management Techniques

To ensure the efficient availability of your electronic data, you need to consider the management of that data and how the data are best organized (Figure 6.3). In this section we consider different use cases that will suggest differing solutions to managing data. These include

- Simple day-to-day organization of data for business or personal use
- Management of information resources over time
- Organization and management of data in response to an audit or legal matter

6.4.1 Day-to-Day Organization

In the normal course of business or just your personal day-to-day life, organization of the ever-growing amounts of data that we create can be a daunting task. As we have noticed in our reviews of case law, courts and government entities such as tax collection agencies will require knowledge of your data and of its ownership and means of

Figure 6.3   Managing your files carefully is one of the main foundations of data control.

access. In order to ensure that we have the requisite knowledge and access, there are several practices I recommend here.

First, as stated earlier, it is very important to classify your data. That classification process will be the first step in creating the logical and physical containers for your information.

Next, you or your organization should consider the different types of information you are creating and managing and make decisions about where and how the data should be stored.

This includes appropriate separation between an individual's personal works while at the same time considering what data should be shared. To that end, you might create separated folders or network areas, some of which belong to individuals and are only accessible by them, while others are accessible only to certain groups of people.

There may be other storage areas that are accessible to everyone in the organization, such as an internal Web presence on which announcements are created and shared, or virtual bulletin boards or mailing lists. As we discussed previously, correct access to these different areas by the appropriate users will be managed by identity management and authentication tools.

One example of this might be a system of network drive letters that you see when you log in to your work computer. There might be one drive letter that accesses only your personal information. Only you and the system administrators will be able to access or change information on that drive or folder.

There might be a different drive letter pointing to a network storage area on which your organizational division or department shares data specific to your tasks. Finally, there might be drive letters that point to storage for organization-wide data, or possibly administrative or system data.

Managing the data within each of those storage areas is equally important. As an organization, it can be extremely valuable to take the time to create a logical file system that meets and reflects the business protocols and strategies. As an individual, this can be an equally valuable exercise. In most cases, this is rarely done sufficiently if at all. And in those cases, it is often an afterthought or something that you are forced to do at some point in order to find important or relevant data, or an audit or other regulatory compliance issue might require this type of organization.

Taking the time to consider the best way to organize your data is a worthwhile exercise whether it is at the beginning of setting up a system or after it has already been developed ad hoc.

Start by thinking about the good old-fashioned file cabinet. Many of you probably still use these for storage of paper documents. I suggest having the business managers for your organization (or possibly just your division if yours is a large organization) get together and do a little brainstorming about what are the important aspects of your business. You can also do a similar exercise on a personal level.

Outline the different important things you will need to keep track of and the subcategories underneath them and any categories that might fit beneath those. Consider the example of a small, family-owned gift shop. Some of the aspects of their business will include

- Facilities
  - Rental or mortgage payments
  - Insurance
    - Liability
    - Inventory loss
    - Structural loss or damage
  - Maintenance and janitorial
- Inventory
  - Purchasing
  - Supply chain
  - Shipping
  - Resupply and auditing
- Employees
  - Compensation
  - Insurance
  - Taxes—withholding
  - Health care
  - Vacation and sick leave
  - Other benefits
- Management
  - Compensation
  - Benefits
- Taxes and fees

- Local
  - Business licensing
  - Fees and dates of renewal
  - Other taxes, dates due, audits
- State
  - Licensing
  - Taxes
  - Other fees
- Federal taxes
- Marketing
  - Advertising
    - Internet
    - Magazines, newspapers
    - Yellow pages
  - Web presence
    - Company website
    - Social media
    - Specialized gift-shop sites
- Financial
  - Auditing
  - Accounting
  - Procurement
  - Payment methods
    - Credit card online or point of sale
    - Cash
    - Checks

As becomes obvious in this exercise, even a very small organization has a great deal of complexity and areas of concern that are best considered and managed carefully beforehand.

However, there is no reason such an organizational exercise cannot take place later in the process as well. It will always be valuable.

Once you create this outline, consider how you would organize those files in a file cabinet.

You might have different drawers for each year of your organization's life as a way to start organizing. Then you would take each of the above major categories and create a divider alphabetically within the drawer for the current year.

Within each of those dividers could be hanging file containers labeled with the subcategories. Finally, within those containers could be file folders containing the actual documentation of the sub-subcategories.

Of course, the blessing and curse of the electronic version of this system is that you can keep going deeper and deeper with sub-sub-sub-subcategories ad infinitum. That is harder to do in a physical file cabinet as you soon run out of room to stuff more folders.

The blessing can be that you are able to more precisely and specifically organize all of the intricate and complex parts of a business system. However, it is quite often the case that these categories and sub-sub-subfolders are not well considered and become redundant, unnecessary, and extremely difficult to manage.

If you are able to carefully consider the actual needs of your organization and carefully manage the way the data are stored, you could take our example above and create a logical electronic file system in which each aspect of your business is logically segregated and easily managed. As long as it is a part of your accepted business practices to maintain a regularly monitored and carefully managed file system such as is outlined in our example, you are likely to have achieved the goal of efficient and easily accessible data.

If that has not been the case, it is never too late to spend the time considering how things should look and reorganizing your data into the properly labeled and segregated file system.

In one organization I worked with, we had a quarterly meeting wherein we would gather and look through our file systems together, clean out the redundant or unnecessary files, and move or reorganize files as appropriate. It was often the case that we would find a series of files or folders labeled with a similar date or title and realize they could all be consolidated into a single folder with that name. That exercise was both a great team builder and a wonderful way to better manage our file systems. I highly recommend it.

6.4.2 *Management of Data over Time*

When we consider the management of data over time, we are most often concerned with records retention rules and regulations. Depending on the organization you work with, or your personal business practices, there will be differing rules that apply to you for how long you are required to store electronic information. Each state and some local governments will also have specific records retention laws that relate to records held by government entities. The federal government also has records regulations specific to government and to some types of businesses such as the financial sector.

Actually outlining all of the specific rules, laws, and regulations would require an encyclopedia collection, and by the time you finished you would have to start over again because it would have all changed. So, we will not even try to do so here. However, it is a very important business requirement for any organization, or even for you as an individual, to take the time to understand those rules and develop a system to ensure you are complying with them.

For instance, in the local government organization for which I once worked, we had state-mandated records retention laws that stated the specific number of years we were required to keep documents such as contracts for purchases, legislative analyses or decisions, financial records, network logs, and so forth. Our records management team worked diligently and endlessly

- Interpreting the different laws and regulations that applied to each part of our organization
- Training staff and management on those requirements
- Assisting departments with records management systems and designs
- Consulting on the development of organization-wide systems and tools for the efficient management of data

Through their efforts we created e-mail–based archival tools that allowed us to select which e-mail and attachments needed to be saved for a specific amount of time based on their classification and the retention rules that applied.

We also had systems in place for storing and archiving other documents and electronic records based on their designated records retention categories. We were not a huge organization, but this was still a pretty difficult challenge at times. It took a long time and a great deal of effort on their part and a commitment on the part of our management and executives for us to be able to begin to get a handle on these requirements. It was and is made harder by the general tendency toward entropy and disorganization that is inherent in a large, dynamic, and diverse organization.

I want to be clear that I am by no means implying this is a simple or trivial exercise to complete. But I will state with confidence that to whatever degree you can manage your file systems up front or as you continue your business or personal management processes, you will be greatly enhancing your ability to comply with records retention requirements. This may only become important when the auditor or tax authorities come to visit, but it behooves all of us to be ready for that before it happens.

6.4.3 Response to Litigation or Audits

When we are considering the organization and management of our electronic data, one of the most compelling reasons for careful and consistent management is the inevitable need to produce those records for a legal action or audit. Whether you are working with an organization or simply thinking about your own records, the chances are very high that you will at some point be responsible for locating and acquiring those records and managing them appropriately for production to a court or auditor.

All of the methodology we outlined above is the basic foundation of this process. We will discuss in more detail in the following pages the different types of systems that you may need to put in place.

First, though, we look briefly at the different parts of a good production process. If you think about the whole of the data that either you or your organization has accumulated as a large pie chart, in the end there is a very small subset of that whole pie chart that will be relevant and required for litigation or an audit. To get to that slice of the pie you will need to go through several steps.

First is acquisition of the data. To do this efficiently will depend a great deal on your having done your due diligence and created a well-designed and managed file system. You will need a good understanding of all of the places that relevant electronic data exist as we discussed in great detail in Chapter 3. It will be equally important to be able to locate the people who own and control the data as we discussed in Chapter 4.

When you have located all of the relevant data and contacted the custodians to gain access to that data, you will need to carefully acquire the data in a forensically sound manner that preserves its integrity as we discussed in Chapter 5. Now you understand better how all of this works together (and why you need to read all of those chapters!).

Acquisition is the first part of the production process and should result in a smaller part of the pie. In this first step, you will be painting with a broad brush and acquiring anything that might possibly be relevant. As we saw in our look at case law and the rules of court procedures in Chapter 1, the courts require that you preserve anything and everything that might be relevant.

If you have done a good job of organizing and have followed your records retention rules, you should have a pretty good handle on what that subset will consist of and how to gather and preserve it.

An important point that we made earlier needs to be restated here. Your ability to preserve the required data is often predetermined by your or your organization's actual records management practices. A court or auditor will be looking at those practices and not at any written policies or procedures.

The fact that you have well-documented records management rules means nothing if your employees either do not know about them or have not been following them. A great example of this is a case where an organization claimed that their e-mail destruction policies were the reason that certain important and relevant e-mails were deleted before they could be preserved. In deposition, an administrator testified that the organization had never followed those destruction policies until the day after they were served with notice of litigation. Needless to say, that did not fly well with the court, and the organization (and their counsel) was slapped with heavy sanctions for spoliation of evidence.

Once you have carefully acquired and preserved the evidence, the next step will be the review of the evidence. This is often done by paralegals if it is a legal matter. Their job is to sift through all of the preserved data with the facts of the case in mind and winnow out the actual relevant evidence. One way this can be done is by searching through the preserved evidence for keywords. Often the people tasked with reviewing and producing the relevant data will begin by establishing a set of words or phrases related to the case at hand. Automated systems or applications or even command lines can be used to search through large sets of electronic data for "hits" on these keywords. Those hits offer the worker a first hint as to which of the data in question might actually contain relevant information. However, keyword searches do not always do a thorough job of finding all relevant data. Words in documents might have been spelled incorrectly or somehow corrupted so that those relevant pieces of information are missed. Or the keywords you are using might simply not be sufficient to find all of the important data.

Keyword searches can be an important first step, but they are not the be-all and end-all that some organizations consider them to be, and courts and auditors may demand a more thorough review of preserved electronic information to find all possibly relevant evidence.

In fact, in a recent case opinion by Magistrate Judge Andrew Peck of the South District of New York, he approves the use of "computer-assisted" review of evidence and discusses the benefits that can be derived from these relatively new artificial intelligence technologies.* These tools allow legal professionals to train the application to search for and discover relevant electronic evidence much more efficiently than a simple keyword search.

The searchers will also need to look for and categorize any evidence that would be considered privileged or attorney work product and remove that from the producible information.

Once all of that has been accomplished, the paralegals or attorneys will organize the producible data into categories and groups based on the facts and issues in the case, or possibly any agreed-upon production criteria of data for the opposing party.

For instance, the parties may have agreed to produce e-mail records for certain date ranges and regarding certain subjects or keywords. They may also have agreed that those e-mail records could be produced as TIFF files or images with or without copies of the metadata that revealed the source, destination, path, and date/time stamps of the e-mails. They might have required that they be produced in their original format which is quite often the case as that can do a better job of preserving metadata. In this instance, the legal team, after

---

* Judge Peck's opinion regarding computer assisted review. http://www.ediscovery-law.com/2012/02/articles/case-summaries/magistrate-judge-peck-issues-written-opinion-addressing-computerassisted-review/. Retrieved March 18, 2012.

removing non-relevant or privileged e-mails, would preserve the rest of the e-mail data in the fashion that was agreed upon.

At this point we have reached that small section of the pie that is producible, relevant electronic evidence. As you might imagine, this process can be extremely time consuming and resource intensive. But the degree to which your organization has developed and managed its records will make a huge difference in how onerous or simple this process is for you.

6.5 Safe Storage Issues and Considerations

Keeping your data physically and logically safe is one important component of establishing and ensuring the integrity of the data.

In Section 6.3, where we discussed authentication, we discussed the idea of securing your data logically by virtue of good identity management systems, encryption, and segregation of different systems. Those means of securing the access to your data are your first line of defense in ensuring the safe storage of your information.

A second consideration is the actual physical storage and your disaster recovery and business continuity planning. These should include backup and restore procedures as well as emergency readiness and resilience considerations (Figure 6.4).

The physical space where you store your data will need to be secured with access controls. If you are an individual, that could be as simple as locking your laptop or desktop to your desk with a cable lock. A small organization might simply have a locking closet or small

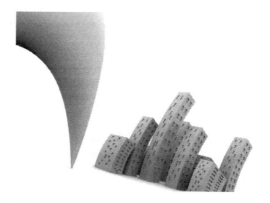

Figure 6.4   Having a disaster recovery plan is important.

room where you store your servers and other networking equipment. However, keep in mind that part of your secure storage responsibility will be ensuring that the devices in those storage areas are not subject to overheating or power outages.

You will need to ensure that there is sufficient cooling capacity and some type of redundant power supply or battery backup for those storage devices. Computer systems can be destroyed by overheating, and if they shut down unexpectedly due to a power outage, data can be destroyed.

In a larger organization there will most often be a special data center. It will have robust physical security including guards, cameras, fences, and often several layers of secured access using authentication mechanisms such as card or fingerprint or other biological scanners, all of which are carefully monitored and recorded.

There will also be redundant systems for cooling, heating, and power backup systems. If you have never visited a large data center, I recommend arranging a tour. They can be quite impressive and complex. One very large center that I toured had multiple large diesel generators and huge reservoirs of diesel fuel. They also had a system that recycles all of the heat generated by the servers to heat the building, and they have managed to cut their energy consumption way down with some amazing and efficient systems.

Whatever your physical storage medium, you should ensure it is safe from intruders and disasters to whatever extent is possible and makes sense from a risk management perspective.

It will also be important to test those systems on a regular basis to ensure that the redundant cooling and power procedures work in an emergency and to consider how you would respond if they failed.

You also need to consider a robust and consistent backup procedure whether you are an organization or simply dealing with your personal data. There are many different backup systems available depending on your specific needs. For a personal system, you can either back up your data on a regular basis to an online storage system or back up to a connected device such as an external USB drive or a separate part of your hard drive.

Online or cloud services are becoming quite ubiquitous and can be relatively inexpensive or even free depending on the amount of data you need to store there. You need to be cognizant of some caveats, however, if this is your choice of backup medium. When choosing to store your data on an Internet site, you are basically extending your network or data set to a physical and logical location that is no longer in your immediate control. In fact, by the very nature of Internet or cloud storage, your data could be residing on a server in another country thousands of miles away. It could be administered by poorly paid and poorly vetted employees of an outsourced contractor for the organization to which you thought you were committing your data. The organization might even be a couple of guys in a garage with a small server center. They might have little or no physical or logical security in place, no backups, and no recovery plan in case their garage catches fire or floods or some authorities come in and confiscate their (your) servers.

On the other hand, the organization might be very well established, only hire employees who have been extensively background-checked, regularly back up their (your!) data, and have well-established and regularly exercised security and recovery plans and procedures in place.

The point is that unless you are very cautious and do your homework, storing your data on an Internet-based service can bring a whole new set of risks to consider.

All of the regulations and requirements we have discussed as your responsibilities for the management and production of your data are still yours even though you have contracted with another organization for the storage and backup of your information. As such, it is inherently your responsibility to ensure you know how your data are being protected and secured as well as how you can gain access to your data at any time.

The best way to do this with an online or cloud service provider is to ensure that you have strong and comprehensive contract language that covers all of the issues we outlined above. Make sure that you have a signed agreement with the provider that you both agree to regarding

- Day-to-day security of your data—ask for a copy of their security policy
- Vetting of their employees
- Backup procedures and timing

- Patch and configuration management of their infrastructure
- Disaster recovery and business continuity plans for recovery and reestablishment of your data
- Notification procedures if any data are compromised, destroyed, or lost for any reason
- Up-time guarantees—should be as close to 100% as possible
- Support procedures and contact numbers, including hours of support and backup support options
- e-Discovery or data production procedures—how do you access and acquire your data if the data are needed, in an efficacious manner

The most important thing you can do once you have such a contract in place and feel satisfied that all of your concerns are addressed will be to test! Ask your provider to demonstrate that their security can stand up to a third-party penetration test or that they have an auditor buy off such as a SAS 70 certification.* Ask them to do an exercise with you where they and/or you have had a disaster or some other need to recover your data and ensure that those procedures work as advertised. A good contract agreement is the first step and an important one, but testing to ensure all of the processes actually work is equally important and should be done on a regular basis.

You can also choose to back up your data via a physical device such as a USB external drive or onto CDs or DVDs or onto backup tape systems. This can be a good choice, but again it will require you to have established, well-documented, and carefully followed procedures in place.

You should have a scheduled and if possible automated backup date and time. It should include full backups on a regular basis and incremental backups (where you only back up data that has changed or been added) more frequently.

Consider where the backed-up data will be stored and whether you will want to have more than one copy. This is again a risk management decision that should be based on the classification and importance of the data.

---

* Overview of SAS (Statement on auditing standards) 70. http://sas70.com/sas70_overview.html. Retrieved December 02, 2015.

It does not make sense to spend the time and money to create an extensive tape library, keep multiple redundant copies, and have both on- and off-site storage if the data you are storing are readily available and nonsensitive information. On the other hand, if the data are proprietary or confidential and difficult or impossible to re-create, you might be justified in expending the time, money, and resources to ensure the data are extremely well protected.

Finally, an often overlooked part of backup systems is the actual restoration procedure. Creating and carefully storing backups of your important data is all very well, but if you do not have or have never tested your restoration procedures, those backups are worth very little.

Backup systems can be complex and subject to failure. Maybe you are an organization whose disaster recovery plan relies on restoring all of your critical data from off-site backup tapes, or simply an individual who wants to be able to rebuild your computer if you have a hard drive crash. In either case, taking the time to test your restoration procedures on a regular basis is extremely important.

If you are a large organization, you should first ensure that you have a disaster recovery/business continuity plan in place and that all of your employees and managers are aware of it. Then you should schedule regular exercises to test that the procedures outlined in the plan actually work in real life.

For instance, do a simulated live-fire test of your processes. Make sure that you have the contact information for your off-site storage provider and your data center recovery staff members. Find out what it would take in time, money, and resources to actually re-create your business after a flood or earthquake or bombing event.

As an individual, take the time to regularly test the recover process of your backup system. Usually that simply means firing up the backup application and selecting "restore." It is a great idea to try this just to understand what it will take and to ensure that your backups have not been corrupted.

I also recommend off-site storage for both individuals and organizations. If you are a victim of physical theft or damage, on-site storage of your backup data might suffer that same damage or be stolen along with everything else.

Organizations should contract for secure off-site data storage. Individuals can simply take their external hard drives or CD/DVD backups and store them away from their premises, somewhere safe and easily accessible.

The bottom line is that backups and off-line storage can be a final and extremely important resource for controlling access to your electronically stored information. Think carefully about the most effective way you or your organization can manage these procedures and ensure they are done correctly, practiced religiously by everyone involved, and tested regularly.

6.6 Litigation Hold

One important process to be aware of and ensure is well established, especially in an organization, is the litigation hold.

In any legal matter in the United States, you are required (as we illustrated in Chapter 1 on rules of procedure and case law) to carefully preserve any and all relevant evidence as soon as you have reason to believe there might be litigation (Figure 6.5). That is a relatively

Figure 6.5   Creating a good litigation hold process will help protect your organization from liability.

vague and anomalous definition of when you should actually trigger that preservation process, and it is subject to interpretation. However, in most of the cases I have studied, it was clear that courts expect you to begin preserving data as soon as you would reasonably expect that there might be a legal matter arising from your actions or from some event.

There have been cases where the courts ruled that data should have been preserved because someone received a phone call from a known litigious company regarding their patent rights. They did not specifically say "we plan to sue you" or serve any kind of legal notice. However, the courts basically said, "You should have known this would become a legal matter and started preserving data immediately—and since you didn't, you are liable for the loss of that data."

As an organization, you should spend time with your legal counsel discussing your policy about what constitutes a trigger for preserving evidence. Again, as always, this is a risk management decision about how much time, money, and resources you feel are appropriate to spend on the preservation, management, and secure storage of data that might possibly become relevant electronic evidence.

Once you have established and documented your decisions around what should trigger that preservation, you should create a litigation hold policy and procedures. This policy should include the following details:

- Who will be the responsible party for notifying any and all owners of relevant data that they are required to preserve and produce that data (this will usually fall to the legal counsel)
- A process for establishing where all of the relevant data reside and all of the different sources and devices that might hold that data
- A record of who the owners of that data are and their contact information
- A process for ensuring the security and integrity of the data
- Who will be responsible for the acquisition and secure storage of the data
- A system of auditing and verifying that all relevant data were preserved (in my former organization we had data custodians sign an affidavit that they had searched for and produced any

and all relevant evidence that they were aware of and that was in their control)

- An ongoing monitoring and maintenance of the hold and preservation of any new data

In my former organization, our law department was the responsible party (and most case law puts the responsibility for litigation holds squarely on the backs of legal counsel). At the trigger event, whether that be an employee being let go or threatening some action, or some event that creates liability, or any other event that they consider a trigger, the attorney or their paralegal would set up a litigation hold meeting. In that meeting we invited the owners of the data, their managers, their IT staff members, and the legal personnel to all get together and discuss all of the places that relevant information might reside.

The legal folks outlined the parameters such as dates and subjects that were in scope. The IT staff was there to assist with understanding the logistics and procedures necessary to acquire, store, and secure the information. We also sometimes included an electronic discovery expert to assist with ensuring that all possible areas of evidence had been considered. All custodians of the data were given affidavits that they were to sign and return to the legal staff when they believed they had preserved all relevant data that they controlled.

After that initial meeting, the legal department was responsible for sending out formal notifications to all affected employees and managers that outlined exactly what they were responsible for preserving, how they should preserve it, and for how long. They were also responsible for following up and ensuring that any new data were preserved and all data were kept until no longer needed.

This type of system and policy will go a long way in complying with what the courts and auditors expect of you and your organization. It will be of value to you to create such a system and put it to use when appropriate.

6.7 Spoliation: The Loss of Relevant Data

We discussed spoliation in Chapter 1 when we looked at the rules of civil procedure and other rules that apply to litigation. An example

Figure 6.6   Destroying or losing relevant electronic information (spoliation) can get you in trouble.

of spoliation is best shown in *West v. The Goodyear Tire and Rubber Company* in 1999, which found that spoliation is "the destruction or significant alteration of evidence, or the failure to preserve property for another's use as evidence in pending or reasonably foreseeable litigation" (Figure 6.6).*

As we consider this in light of the subject of this chapter, keeping our data safe and preserving its integrity, it should be obvious that the procedures and policies we discussed earlier are the most important ways that you as an individual or an organization can avoid spoliation of relevant evidence.

Spoliation sanctions can be administered in cases whether or not the loss of data was inadvertent. If you have good data retention policies and practices in place and can prove to a court or jury that you have followed those policies, it will go a long way toward limiting your liability for lost relevant electronic evidence.

On the other hand, if you have not put those policies and procedures in place or have failed to practice them consistently, the courts are much more likely to administer more severe sanctions for the spoliation of evidence.

---

* *West v. The Goodyear Tire & Rubber Co.*, 167 F.3d 776, 779 (2d Cir. 1999) (citing *Black's Law Dictionary* 1401, 6th edn., 1990), http://www.gwblawfirm.com/ap-spoliation-a-trap-for-the-unwary.php. Retrieved March 18, 2012.

Sanctions for spoliation are common in litigation involving electronic evidence. This is because these types of cases often involve large amounts of complex information and because many organizations and individuals have not made the effort to understand all of the issues and ramifications of our new world of electronic data.

By virtue of your having taken the time to read this book and take other steps to both understand and begin to manage your electronic information, you gain a great advantage. If you carefully create the foundation of a good records retention policy, understand and manage your electronic data inventory, and create and maintain a well-considered and monitored litigation hold process, you will have a much better handle on where your data live, who owns that data, and how to retrieve and preserve that data and the integrity of the data. The chances that you might inadvertently lose or compromise electronic evidence that is relevant to a case or an audit will decrease immensely.

Being aware of and preparing to avoid spoliation will save you and your organization money, time, and resources. The threat of spoliation sanctions is simply another good reason to take the time and effort to develop the policies, procedures, and practices outlined in this chapter.

6.8 Automated Technical Solutions

In this final section, we discuss some of the ways that automated solutions have been designed to assist in the procedures we suggested above.

It is not the place of this book to specifically advocate for one solution over another. And in fact, as with anything involving technology, these solutions are forever evolving, and any that we might recommend would very likely be out of date in the very near future. We will, however, list some of the current solutions that are available in Appendix III (Figure 6.7). Here I will give you some guidelines to what some of the best solutions can provide and what you or your organization should be looking for if you decide to either purchase or develop such a solution.

The primary consideration for any solution is whether it can address all of the goals we discussed in this chapter, such as:

Figure 6.7 Using automated solutions for electronic evidence management is often worthwhile.

- Ensuring the integrity and security of the data
- Creating a methodology to expedite and enhance your ability to locate data
- Assigning and managing ownership and authentication
- Assisting with the secure storage and preservation of electronic evidence
- Managing notification messaging systems
- Enhancing your ability to analyze and categorize data

When you make the decision, either as an individual or as an organization, to develop the capacity to manage your data and be prepared for whatever need might arise for the production of that information, I offer the following checklist as guidance:

- List and engage your stakeholders: Consider who should be involved in the decision making regarding records retention, litigation holds, and so forth. This might include any or all of this list.
  - Legal counsel and paralegals
  - Auditors
  - Management
  - IT staff and managers
  - Information security professionals
  - Database administrators
  - E-mail administrators
  - Human resources
  - Union representatives

- Executives
- Risk managers
- Records management staff and archivists
- Create a business justification: What are the goals and business reasons for either purchasing or creating this solution? Document the specifications of the solution that will meet those goals, listing the benefits and the risk assessment and mitigation decisions that justify each of those specifications. This important document will both guide your decisions on the best solution and assist with justifying your decisions to business leaders. Some of the possible specifications might be
    - Data-mapping tools that mitigate the risk of compromise of data that could result in data loss, spoliation sanctions, or loss of data integrity
    - Secure transport and storage capabilities that address the risk of a loss of data integrity or compromising of the evidence
    - Authentication and identity management tools that mitigate the risk of mishandling of data or access by nonauthorized personnel
    - Cataloging and indexing features that enhance and expedite your ability to categorize and classify data, thus addressing the risks of inadequately protecting sensitive data, or adversely, spending unnecessary resources to protect publicly available data (this can also mitigate the risk of your producing work product or privileged evidence)
    - Notification and messaging systems that mitigate risks of having failed to adequately protect data through notices to owners and custodians of relevant electronic data, and the possible threat of spoliation sanctions that might result
- Research possible solutions or combinations of solutions that will best meet your compiled list of specifications. These might include
    - Off-the-shelf solutions, some of which we reference in Appendix III
    - Something you are capable of developing in-house
    - A hybrid combination of in-house solutions and off-the-shelf tools

- A tool or system that is physically or logically run from within your organization
- A service located on the Internet or hosted by a contractor
- Assess all of the possible solutions with your stakeholder team, considering
  - Which solution or combination of solutions best addresses your specifications (some specifications might have greater weight than others—these decisions should be made up front by your stakeholder team)?
  - Which gives the most value for its actual costs (do not forget to include training, setup, management, and ongoing operations and maintenance)?
  - Which is the most feasible for deployment in a reasonable time frame?
  - Which will be scalable, robust, and resilient enough to serve you or your organization into the future should you evolve or grow, or when the technology evolves as it is sure to do?
- Finally, document your decision and ensure you have buy-off from all stakeholders, especially the executives and leaders who will be paying the bills.

The purchase, development, and deployment of an automated solution can be of great value in avoiding all of the risks we outlined in this chapter and enhancing your ability to address all of the requirements for keeping your data safe.

It is absolutely worth your time to consider what options are available to automate the procedures necessary to provide for the integrity and security of your electronic information.

7

SHARING IS GOOD

Dissemination and Reporting

7.1 Introduction

In this final chapter, we will discuss the reasons and the methods for sharing the data we have so carefully acquired, preserved, and managed. There are several reasons that we will consider, and each may engender different approaches or procedures appropriate to the specific needs of those situations.

These approaches will include the format in which the data are produced, the content, the timing of release, and the actual physical media and process for delivering the electronic information (Figure 7.1). We also discuss reporting protocols and suggest some ideas to ensure that the reports you create are clear and concise.

Finally, we end this chapter with some tips for participating in depositions or as an expert witness.

7.2 Format Issues: Original or Usable?

One of the first considerations in sharing the data you have collected will be in what format you want to produce the data.

Think about it in terms of your reasons for producing the data in the first place, and this should guide you in your formatting decisions (Figure 7.2). For instance, one reason for producing data is for dissemination to colleagues, relatives, or friends who simply have a nonadversarial interest in the information. In that case, there is little likelihood of their using the data or its metadata in any way that would be harmful to your interests. There will also be no legal or regulatory rules compelling you to ensure the integrity of the data.

If that is the case, you might simply create copies of the pictures, documents, spreadsheets, and so forth, and send them via standard

Figure 7.1 Consider the procedures that you will put into place for disseminating the evidence you collected.

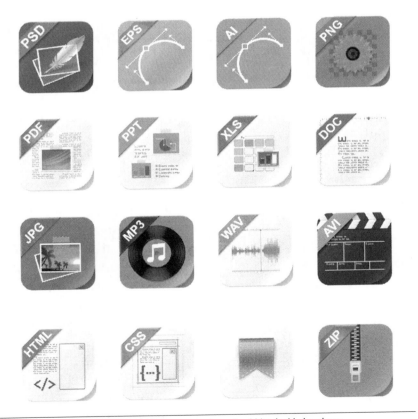

Figure 7.2 The format of the evidence you produce should be decided early on.

e-mail, mail them on a DVD, or store them online on a file sharing tool. You have no responsibility to ensure the data are secure and uncompromised. You do not need to be concerned about what metadata are attached to the data as it is very unlikely that any of those people will even know or care about its existence.

Another reason for producing data could be for a tax audit required by the Internal Revenue Service (IRS) or other taxing authority. You might consider this a somewhat more adversarial situation, and you are legally required to produce any and all relevant records and to be able to prove their integrity. It is unlikely that the IRS would require specific metadata, but if questions arise about the integrity of your records, you could be required to prove the legitimacy of those records. That proof is likely to be enhanced by your ability to refer to metadata and to your careful data handling processes. If this is the case, you will most likely be creating copies of documents, spreadsheets, and so forth, with accompanying metadata or other means of proving their integrity as we discussed earlier (e.g., hashing).

The IRS or other legal auditing authority will be specific about the format in which they expect your documentation to be delivered. It will be to your advantage to not only comply with those requests, but to do all you can to ensure good procedures and data management, including chain of custody and data security practices. That will allow you to address any issues of data integrity with well-documented management practices.

Another likely scenario is the need to produce data for a legal matter. For the most part, as we discussed in Chapter 1, a meeting will be conducted between the parties to discuss the data that will be produced. In that meeting, your legal counsel will make decisions with the other side about specific electronic and physical evidence required to adjudicate the case. The sides will agree in what format they want the evidence produced.

In some cases, they will decide that they want the data produced in its original format, including all metadata. Or they might decide that graphic copies such as TIFF files are appropriate. If that is what they decide, they might also ask for graphic copies of metadata for each file, or they might not require metadata.

Depending on the specific types of data, producing them in original format can have advantages and disadvantages. For instance, if the original data were in a Microsoft Word file, that is relatively common and most organizations will have the applications and tools to be able to read both the document and its attached metadata. Therefore, as long as you are careful not to compromise the document when you transfer it in that Word document format, it will be a simple and relatively secure production of the electronic evidence.

However, if the original data were stored as a Lotus 123 spreadsheet created many years ago, it may be very difficult, first to preserve any metadata when you produce the copy, and second for the recipient to open it with current existing tools. The recipient might also have a hard time being able to access the metadata without specialized tools.

This becomes even more difficult when the original form of the data is in a proprietary database. Database applications can be expensive, and data stored therein might be difficult or impossible to extract or even to view. Without having the correct version of the database software (including required licensing), specific information about the design of the original database, and expertise to re-create the original database architecture, it might be impossible to actually view data in the original context.

All that said, it can be a daunting task to be able to actually gain relevant electronic evidence that will stand up to evidentiary requirements in court. The most important thing that you and your legal counsel can do is to be aware of these issues up front and be specific when requesting data from the other parties during your pretrial meetings.

Being aware of these issues as they relate to your own data will also help to inform you and your legal counsel as to your capabilities for producing relevant electronic evidence in either its original format or in some other format that might be requested.

At times, it may be to everyone's advantage to create different data formats in order to ensure that the evidence is consistent, uncompromised in any way, and most effectively and easily used by all sides. The sides might decide to have all evidence stored in a database online so that it is accessible by all concerned. There are some new online services that offer that possibility.

In the end, it is most important to consider the goals of everyone involved for the production of the data and find the most efficient and effective method to accomplish those goals.

7.3 Mediums for Transfer

The actual physical or logical medium used to transfer produced electronic data will depend on both the goals of the producing parties and any agreements made between them. In many cases, electronic evidence can be copied onto physical media such as DVDs, CDs, tape, or USB devices such as hard drives or flash drives. As long as this copying is done in a forensically sound manner that ensures the integrity of the data, that should be sufficient for most situations (Figure 7.3).

The ways you can ensure a forensically sound copying of data to these media are as follows:

- Create and document at least two different hashes of the data before and after copying (see Chapter 5 for more details).
- Maintain a chain of custody, documenting where the data were originally, who was the custodian, who copied the data, when, and for what purpose.
- Document the tools used to copy the data including their version numbers.

Appendix II includes some sample logging and chain of custody documents.

In other cases, the parties involved might decide on transferring the data using e-mail or an online service. In these cases, you can ensure the integrity of the data by using hashes and maintaining good

Figure 7.3 The type of media on which you store or deliver the evidence will depend on many factors.

logging of all activities involved in copying the data. This should be agreed upon up front between all of the parties.

If you decide to use e-mail as a means of transferring data, you should consider the classification of the information. If it is sensitive in any way, you should look at the possibility of encrypting the e-mail transmissions or possibly encrypting the documents. Most e-mail applications have the capacity to encrypt their contents, or there are third-party add-ins that will allow you to do so. Encrypting the documents or other evidence can also be accomplished with commonplace tools, several of which are referenced in Appendix III.

Should you decide to use an online service, you should ensure that the service provider contract includes the following:

- Information security policies that address the confidentiality of your data, its availability, and its integrity
- Backgrounding of its employees who will have access to your data
- Well-defined procedures for access to the data
- Defined and practiced authentication protocols to ensure data are accessed only by those with the correct and current rights
- Disaster recovery and business continuity policies and practices that are both well documented and auditable
- 24/7/365 access to support and priority assistance
- Effective and timely notification procedures in case any issues affect the confidentiality, integrity, or availability of your data
- Data management, access, retention, and archiving procedures that meet your requirements

These contractual requirements are important in any service that you use online, but when you decide that this is how you are going to disseminate legally relevant electronic evidence, they become paramount to ensuring your data are there when you need them, and that the integrity of the data is unsullied.

Whatever medium makes the most sense to achieve the goals of sharing your data with another party, the most important consideration will always be ensuring the integrity and availability of the data to all concerned. As you consider which solution makes the most sense, always keep this in mind.

7.4 Creating Readable Reports

As the person in your organization who has taken on the task of learning about electronic evidence, or just due to your interest in better managing your own data, you may be in the position to create reports in this regard. These might include data management and retention reports, audit information, or evidence investigation and acquisition reports.

One of the most important things you can do for the sake of your audience is to create reports that are understandable, concise, and complete (Figure 7.4).

The first step in ensuring that your report is complete and contains all of the relevant information is to keep excellent records of everything you do in relation to the data in question. The foundation of that record keeping and of your eventual ability to document your actions will always be a good records retention policy. That policy means little or nothing if it was not properly disseminated and carefully followed by you or your organization.

Beginning with your records management policy, you should have some record or log that illustrates your or your organization's compliance. It should document how you follow the correct records management procedures, where and how the data are preserved, and your process for archiving or destroying the data according to your documented and audited schedules.

Next, you need to carefully log any and all activities undertaken to locate, acquire, and secure any relevant electronic evidence. Using

Figure 7.4   Clear and concise reports will make all the difference.

the samples we give you in Appendix II, or something similar that is appropriate for your organization, you should carefully document all of the following:

- The owner(s) and custodian(s) of the data in question
- The physical and logical locations of the data
- The tools and methods used to acquire the data, including names and versions of acquisition applications and types of hashes or other integrity assurance tools used
- The time and date of acquisition
- The movement of data to or from any type of storage (chain of custody), including who moved it and why
- The security procedures, both physical and logical, used to ensure the data could not have been compromised or accessed by anyone without the correct authority
- The physical and logical medium on which the data is stored or transferred to or from, including the name or type of media and a unique identifier such as a serial number, model number, or label

If you are investigating or analyzing electronic devices or systems to find relevant evidence, you should also log every step of your investigative process. You should include the time and date of each part of the investigation as well as the tools you used and the results of your analysis.

There is an easy way to do this if you are using the Windows operating system. Every Windows OS includes a simple text application called "Notepad." Start up Notepad and create a new file with the first line: 'LOG' (without the quotes) and then close the application. Then when you open it up again it will "automagically" insert a date and time stamp.

I have all of my investigators use this simple tool to log every step of their analyses of devices for forensics investigations or acquisition of data for e-discovery. As they are working they simply open the file, note everything they did, the tools they used, and the results and then close the file again. By doing this we get a nice time-stamped record that is extremely useful in depositions or court appearances by assisting in our recollection of what we did in an investigation.

Depending on the physical and logical location of the evidence in question, you may also need to gather up system or database event logs, ingress and egress records, application logs and metadata, or other detailed information related to the data in question.

Once you begin your reporting process by gathering or creating all of the documentation above, your next step is to winnow it down to the important information for your intended audience.

Take the time to understand who that audience will be and their level of expertise. For instance, perhaps you are creating a report to present to your manager who has a very good understanding of the technical details and language related to the electronic data. In that case, you can use known acronyms and more technical language to describe the work you did, what you found, how and where it was acquired and preserved, and so forth.

However, if you are creating a report to be used in court or for an auditing authority, you should avoid the use of technical terms or acronyms. Instead, create a document that you could easily explain to your grandmother. In Chapter 2 we discussed in detail the idea of translating geek. This is where this skill is most important.

If you need to explain a technical process, try to come up with simple and easy-to-understand metaphors or examples. In Appendix I, we offer some great resources that explain how technical things work in easy-to-understand language.

Should you need to create a report explaining something technical such as how Internet information is stored on a computer, or how data can be fingerprinted using hash algorithms, I recommend reviewing sections in this book that address those ideas or taking the time to research some of the resources offered in Appendix I. These can give you great ideas of ways to make these technical details understandable to people without a technical background.

When creating a report, always begin by having all of the information you need, then consider your audience and tailor your presentation to their level of understanding. In every case, you want to be sure all of the important points are covered while not digressing into information that is not important, not required, or simply too esoteric or technical for the audience.

Very few jurists, judges, or lawyers have studied computer science, so they will neither appreciate nor understand your in-depth explanation of the advantages of the latest version of Linux over the Windows operating system, for example (unless that is germane to your analysis of the evidence).

With written reports, be sure to do a good spell check and reread the report to ensure it is clear and covers all of the important information. There are sample reports in Appendix II.

If you are presenting an oral report, it is important to be comfortable with public speaking. We discuss that in the following section.

7.5 Tips for Depositions and Expert Witness

One of the most challenging and also most rewarding activities that might come from your having used this book and other resources to become an expert in electronic evidence will be the opportunity to share your knowledge as part of a legal matter (Figure 7.5).

This might take the form of simply assisting your legal counsel or your management in understanding the relevant electronic evidence and all of the details and issues that we discussed in this book. In that case, you will probably be dealing with one or only a few people at a time, and it should not be too daunting. Having done a great job in creating the written report as we discussed above, you will simply need to help them understand all of the pertinent details.

However, should you be called upon for a deposition or as an expert witness in a court case, or asked to present your findings to a larger audience, that can be a frightening proposition for some people. The first recommendation I would make is to spruce up your public

Figure 7.5   Delivering your information in court or a deposition can take some special skills.

speaking skills. There are classes and organizations available, some of which are referenced in Appendix I, which can help you with speaking and presentation skills and practice sessions. There are also some online resources with good ideas for creating presentations.

The same ideas apply here as with a written report. Make sure you understand your audience and have all of your information at hand. The actual information you present will depend on the specific requirements and level of expertise of your audience. However, I recommend bringing along any logs or other documentation that you might be questioned about as reference for yourself.

Be concise and ensure you are able to answer any question that might be asked of you. It can be very valuable to sit down with your legal counsel and rehearse possible questions and answers that might be brought forward during the case or deposition.

An important caveat, especially in a court setting, is to only answer the question you are asked. It is not your job to try to figure out what else the questioner might want to know, or to give details that were not specifically requested. It is a common mistake for someone in the witness stand or during a deposition to try to be helpful and to expound on their deep knowledge of a subject without having been asked. This might confuse the actual issue or give opposing counsel information that is not relevant or might even be used against your side. It can lead to your counsel's inability to control the case to their advantage.

Another important tip for appearing in court: Do not allow your questioners to paint you into a corner by insisting on an answer. It is perfectly legitimate for you to reply that you do not know an answer, or that you have provided them with all the information you have. It is a relatively common tactic to try to get the answer they want by insisting that you tell them, "Yes" or "No," or give some other response that leads to the conclusion they want. You can usually avoid this trap by being very careful to answer only with what you know for sure and being ready to say, "I don't know."

Take the time to review all of your data and to go over the possible issues with your own legal counsel beforehand. A mock deposition or trial rehearsal is a great idea if you have the time. It can help to bring up any areas where you might need more information or research. It can also be a way for you and your legal counsel to decide what information is truly relevant and what might be privileged or unnecessary.

Finally, remember that there are specific rules and protocols for expert witnesses and evidence. We discussed those in more detail in Chapter 1, and your legal support will understand and apply those rules as appropriate.

Your responsibility is to be honest, prepared, and respectful. That will mean dressing appropriately, speaking clearly, and being polite and respectful to everyone present. The more prepared you are ahead of time, the less nervous you will be in your presentation.

Presenting to any audience, whether a group of managers, attorneys, a judge and jury, or any other group can be intimidating. However, if you are prepared, have practiced, and have taken the time to hone your presentation skills, you will come off as knowledgeable and reliable.

If it is your job to assist your side of a case, everything might depend on the impression you make. A confident, well-spoken, and clear speaker will be much more believable than someone who is reserved, nervous, and difficult to understand. Even if that nervous person is telling "the whole truth and nothing but the truth," he or she is much less likely to be trusted by a jury or any other audience.

7.6 Conclusion

Well, you made it through to the end. I hope that whether you used this as a reference and skipped around, or worked your way through all seven chapters, you have found this useful in helping to better understand and manage electronically stored information.

The appendices that follow offer many resources for learning more or for further enhancing your understanding of this important subject.

By taking the time to read this book and to better understand these ideas, you have become a more unique and valuable person than you already were, whether just for your own knowledge or for the betterment of your organization. I encourage you to keep learning and to pass on this knowledge to ensure that more people are aware of the data fog we all live in today and all of the important means we have to manage and control that electronically stored information.

Appendix I: Links and References for More Information

The following resources can offer you a vast amount of information that you can use to further enhance your study and expertise about electronically stored information (ESI).

Advice from a Risk Detective, "How can we handle the commonest risks at home, at school, at work, online and on the road?," written by Annie Searle and published by Tautegory Press— This is a very easy to understand book on risk. http://www. advicefromariskdetective.com/.

Considering Third Generation eDiscovery? Two Approaches for Evaluating eDiscovery Offerings—This is another, very inexpensive ($0.99) e-book available in a Kindle version from Amazon. http://www.amazon.com/Considering-Generation-eDiscovery-Approaches-ebook/dp/B002JCSUTK/ref=pd_sim_kinc_3?ie=UTF8&m=AG56TWVU5XWC2.

Discovery Resources—This is another great site with up-to-date information, resources, and news about electronic discovery. http://discoveryresources.org.

e-Discovery for Dummies—This provides a beginner resource for anyone looking to understand the rules and implications of e-discovery policy and procedures, available from Amazon.

http://www.amazon.com/e-Discovery-For-Dummies-ebook/
dp/B002XXGILM/ref=pd_cp_kinc_1?ie=UTF8&m=AG5
6TWVU5XWC2.

EDRM, the Electronic Discovery Reference Model Project—
This organization has done a lot of the work to better understand and document the procedures we discuss in this book.
http://www.edrm.net/.

Electronic Discovery Law—This is an excellent resource published by the law firm K&L Gates for tracking and understanding the evolution of case law. http://www.ediscoverylaw.
com/.

ESI Handbook: Sources, Technology, and Process, 2011, by Adam I.
Cohen and G. Edward Kalbaugh and published by Wolters
Kluwer—This is a good reference book, more geared toward
legal professionals, but with a lot of good information.

KenWithers.com—Mr. Withers' own web page contains a
vast wealth of information on e-discovery issues. http://www.
kenwithers.com/index.html.

LexisNexis® Zimmerman's Research Guide—This resource on
federal court rules covers all of the different rules and has references to other court rule sources. http://law.lexisnexis.com/
infopro/zimmermans/disp.aspx?z=1458

Nixon Peabody—An excellent article on electronic evidence dis-
covery is provided by the Nixon Peabody firm called Electronic
Discovery: What You Need to Know and What It May Cost
If You Don't. http://www.nixonpeabody.com/116735.

Northwestern University—Electronically Stored Information:
The December 2006 Amendments to the Federal Rules of
Civil Procedure by Kenneth J. Withers, Managing Director,
The Sedona Conference®. A comprehensive look by one of the
leading authorities on ESI at the amendments to the FRCP
in 2006. http://www.law.northwestern.edu/journals/njtip/v4/
n2/3/.

The Applied Discovery® Black Letter Book (fourth edition of the
Discovery Book)—This is a relatively inexpensive book that
can be purchased in electronic format (Kindle) and "provides
readers with an essential guide to the latest cases, rules of

civil procedure and evidence, and best practices essential to manage the entire course of electronic discovery in legal proceedings". http://www.amazon.com/Applied-Discovery-Black-Letter-ebook/dp/B004LB5EQ4/ref=sr_1_1?ie=UTF 8&qid=1299725446&sr=8-1.

The Legal and Economic Implications of Electronic Discovery: Options for Future Research—This is a relatively inexpensive e-book available for Kindle that provides an overview of the issues involved and outlines five avenues for future research on the legal and economic implications of e-discovery. http://www.amazon.com/Economic-Implications-Electronic-Discovery-ebook/dp/B001FB68AY/ ref=pd_sim_kinc_6?ie=UTF8&m=AG56TWVU5XWC2.

The Sedona Conference—This organization of attorneys and experts in evidential law has extensive references on interpretation of court rules. http://www.thesedonaconference.org/.

Truth to Power, Information Governance Research Community— This is a site with a comprehensive library of documents and guidelines on information security, governance, and auditing. Some are free and others require membership and payment before you can download them. But they are all excellent. http://www.t2pa.com/.

Windows Incident Response Blog—This excellent blog by Harlan Carvey holds a wealth of knowledge for anyone who needs to delve into the forensic analysis of Windows computers. http://windowsir.blogspot.com/.

Wikipedia is of course an excellent source of information on many different subjects and you will note that it was often referenced in my footnotes. Here are two specific Wikipedia articles that reference issues discussed in the book in much more detail:

Wikipedia—Expert Witness. http://en.wikipedia.org/wiki/ Expert_witness.

Wikipedia—Daubert standard. http://en.wikipedia.org/wiki/ Daubert_Standard.

The following are good resources for understanding how computers work and keeping up with the latest technologies.

Several different websites and books are great references to help you understand computer technology.

http://www.ehow.com/how-computers-work/
http://computer.howstuffworks.com/
https://en.wikipedia.org/wiki/Computer

Derfler, Frank J. and Les Freed, *How Networks Work*, 7th edn., London, England: Que Press, 2004.
Gralla, Preston, *How the Internet Works*, 8th edn., London, England: Que Press, 2006.
White, Ron and Timothy Edward Downs, *How Computers Work*, 9th edn., London, England: Que Press, 2007.

For news and updates on computers and technology, I recommend the following websites:

http://news.cnet.com/
https://www.computerworld.com/
https://www.pcworld.com/news.html
http://gcn.com/
https://www.zdnet.com/
http://www.computerweekly.com/
http://www.cnn.com/TECH/index.html
http://www.pcmag.com/
http://www.theregister.co.uk/
https://www.nytimes.com/pages/technology/index.html
https://www.infoworld.com/
http://www.networkcomputing.com/
http://www.v3.co.uk/
https://www.sans.org/newsletters/

For good resources on presentation skills and tools and expert witness/deposition training, consider the following:

http://www.presentation-skills.biz/
http://www.effective-public-speaking.com/
http://www.presentation-skills.org/
http://prezi.com

http://www.toastmasters.org/
http://expertwitnesstraining.com/
http://www.expertcommunications.com/

Robbins, Judd, *Expert Witness Training: Profit from Your Expertise* [Paperback], Presentation Dynamics, 2010.

Appendix II: Forms and Guides

CHAIN OF CUSTODY FORM

Case Number:
Investigator:
Item Type and Serial Number:

DATE MOVED	NAME	FINAL DESTINATION AND REASON FOR MOVING	DATE RETURNED	NOTES

CONFIDENTIALITY AGREEMENT

As an investigator or in my capacity as support to a digital or telephone data investigation, I understand that I may have access to sensitive or confidential information. By signing this statement, I affirm my understanding of my responsibilities to maintain strict confidentiality and agree to the following:

1. I understand that I may access, read, or handle sensitive or confidential information or records relating to the [Organization], its employees, or constituents to the extent required in, and for the purpose of, performing my assigned duties as an investigator or support person for a digital or telephone data investigation.

2. I agree to limit my investigation to the specifically requested information in the investigation request and to report to the administrator of the investigation process any pertinent information found in the course of those investigations.

3. I agree not to divulge, publish, or otherwise make known to unauthorized persons or to the public any information obtained in the course of an investigation.

4. I understand that:
   a. I may divulge information to the administrator of the investigation, the requesting departmental Authorizing Authorities, and Human Resources staff.
   b. I may divulge information to others only if specifically authorized to do so by statute, law, or court order.
   c. Maintaining confidentiality includes not discussing investigation information outside of the workplace or my usual work area.
   d. After I leave employment with the [Organization], I may not divulge investigation information obtained during my employment.

5. I agree to consult with the administrator of the investigation process on any questions I may have concerning whether particular information may be disclosed.

6. I understand that a breach of confidentiality may be grounds for disciplinary or legal action, and may include termination of employment.

7. I agree to notify the administrator of the investigation process should I become aware of an actual breach of confidentiality or a situation that could potentially result in a breach, whether this be on my part or on the part of another person.

_____

Employee Signature   Date   Printed Name

Electronically Stored Information Preacquisition Planning Meeting Form			Case Number/Name or other Identification:	
Name, title and phone of person managing litigation hold or responding to PDR (attorney, manager, OIS, PD officer, PIO, etc.)			Department	Low org
Name, title, and phone of electronic evidence manager (if different from above)			Case type (litigation hold or PDR)	Date
Item	User ID(s), or Device ID(s), or Locations (Computer Number, Phone Number, etc.)	Name and Phone of Technician Responsible	Specifics (For e-mail: obtain snapshot of post office and/or mailbox? Exempt from expire rules? Block deletion? Remove access to account? Give access to investigator or manager?, etc. For network drives or workstation: obtain image [names of specific folders/files]? Block deletion? Internet access analysis? For phones or other records: specified dates?)	Date Obtained-Delivered (or date block, etc. Is begun/date ended)
E-mail account				/
Network drives				/
Workstation HDD or record				/
Telephone records				/
Cell/Blackberry				/
Access records				/
Video records				/
Database query				/
Other:				/
Other:				/
Other:				/
Other:				/
Other:				/

Other:				/
Other:				/
Other:				/
Other:				/
Other:				/
Other:				/

Signatures

Appointing authority or IT manager for affected department

(Name)	*(department)*	*(title)*

Appointing authority, public disclosure officer, PIO, or attorney managing case

(Name)	*(department)*	*(title)*

Electronic evidence manager (if different from above)

(Printed name)	*(signature)*	*(date)*

FINAL INVESTIGATION REPORT

Case # Format: YYYYMMDD-####

Investigator: Date:

Original Requestor:

Original Date of Request:

Requesting Department Contact (if different from requestor):

Preferred Method of Contact: ☐ E-mail—Address:

                                 ☐ Phone—Number:

Introduction

Methods

Interviews

PERSON INTERVIEWED	PHONE	NOTES

Information Technology Services

PERSON/DIVISION	PHONE	NOTES

Hardware/Software Obtained

HARDWARE/SOFTWARE	NOTES

Hardware/Software Used

HARDWARE/SOFTWARE	NOTES

Other Services

PERSON/DEPT/DIVISION	PHONE	NOTES

Follow-up Interviews

PERSON INTERVIEWED	PHONE	NOTES

Findings

Conclusion

Signatures

_____

Investigator (printed name/signature/date of report submission)

_____

Chief Information Security Officer (printed name/signature/date of receipt and review)

_____

Requesting Department Contact (printed name/signature/date of receipt and review)

SAMPLE LOG FILE (FROM NOTEPAD)

.LOG
Investigation Log—Case # 2009-0711-0111
Requestor: Jane Doe, DRD, 4-4444
Investigator: Dudley Do-Right, 3-3456
Case Overview: Inappropriate Use of Computer Equipment

7/27/11   1651   John Doe contacted me via e-mail regarding Service Desk ticket number 12345. Jane Doe of the Department of Redundancy requested an investigation of a user's computer.

7/28/11   0730   I left a message for Jane Doe asking her to complete an investigation request form. Jane called back shortly thereafter, and I explained what she needed to do and where she could find the form. She e-mailed me at about 1000 to say that the form was completed and on its way in the interdepartmental mail.

7/31/11   Received the investigation request.

8/01/11   Reviewed the request, and contacted Jane Doe for more information on what we should be looking for. She said that Mr. Badboy was suspected of using City equipment for inappropriate Web surfing. She asked that I report on all naughty pictures, plus any evidence of inappropriate use of the Internet, IM chat, personal e-mail, etc.

8/01/11   0956   Received an e-mail from John Doe telling me that he had successfully acquired the image and saved it to a shared folder on his drive.

INVESTIGATION REQUEST

Requestor (Name and Position):

Date of Request:

Requesting Department Contact (if different from requestor):

Preferred Method of Contact: ☐ E-mail—Address:

                                                    ☐ Phone—Number:

Do Not Fill In—To Be Completed by CISO Office: _____

Case # Format: YYYY-MMDD-#####

Investigator:

Reason for Request:

Names of Personnel to Be Investigated (Not required or recommended— preferred method is to only work with phone numbers, computer names, port or cube numbers if this is possible in the context of the request):

Phone numbers, computer names, port or cube numbers to be investigated:

Specific criteria and parameters of investigation:

Departmental IT staff resources available (names and contact information for any department IT staff who will assist in the investigation):

We understand that DoIT will charge back for the necessary work or contract labor required to complete this investigation. Initials _____

Low Org # _____

Case # (if criminal investigation) _____

Signatures:

_____

Requesting Appointing Authority (printed name/signature/date of submittal)

_____

Requesting Department HR Director/Supervisor (printed name/ signature/date of submittal)

Chief Information Security Officer (printed name/signature)

Date of Receipt/Date of Review

☐ Accepted

Date of Acceptance and Assignment to Investigator

☐ Rejected

Date of Rejection and Reason for Rejection

SAMPLE STATEMENT FORM

Case #

Investigator: Date:

Original Requestor:

Original Date of Request:

Requesting Department Contact (if different from requestor):

Preferred Method of Contact: ☐ E-mail—Address:

                                                  ☐ Phone—Number:

Statement of: ☐ Original Requestor ☐ Witness
                        ☐ Investigator ☐ Other

Statement

My name is _____. I am the [organization name] [position title] with over 22 years of experience in the Information Technology field. One part of my responsibilities as the [position title] is the oversight and/or performance of digital investigations. My trained forensics team and I analyze digital equipment, phone and video records, etc., to investigate allegations of policy violations or inappropriate use of the organization's equipment.

Our primary responsibility in this capacity is to retrieve data (evidence) from computers, computer components, or other electronic media in a controlled lab environment. The items being examined are most often property of the [organization name]. However, in some cases we are required to analyze personally owned equipment (with the permission of the owner). Evidence may consist of e-mail, images and documents, chat logs, financial records, Internet history, and event file time/date stamps. Evidentiary data are extracted, analyzed, cataloged, and provided to the requesting party in varying report formats depending on the type and volume of data extracted.

I received hundreds of hours of training in the area of computer forensics, computer hardware and software, and general investigations. I hold certificates in Information Security (CISSP, GSEC), Computer Forensics and Recovery, A+ Software and Hardware, and specific training in forensics software tools (Forensics Toolkit [FTK], and X-Ways/WinHex Forensics). I have also had on-the-job training.

On _____ we received a verbal request for digital investigation of the computer belonging to _____ the [Department] _____. The request was made by _____, (a written request was received on _____). I interviewed _____ over the phone and _____ requested that we analyze the user's hard drive for any evidence of misuse of the organization's equipment.

Another person on my team who is currently certified and able to complete investigations was able to obtain a forensics image of the hard drive on _____, using Forensic ToolKit (FTK) Imager Version 3.2 on the suspect computer #_____ (see attached Case Information Document for specifics and Hash checksums). To ensure the integrity of the evidence, he used a hardware write blocker attached between his acquiring computer and the suspect hard drive.

A write blocker is a hardware device that provides power and connectivity to the source drive (evidence drive) and uses hardware write blocking to ensure that the source drive is not altered in any way during the imaging process.

The image is then placed on a target drive for processing and analysis. The forensics image of the source drive is an exact binary copy of the source drive and identical in every way to the source drive. Before, during, and after the imaging process is complete, several checks are made to ensure the integrity of both the image and the source drive. During those processes, FTK runs Cyclic Redundancy Checks (CRC) of the data stream as it is copied to the target drive. The CRC compares the two data streams using an algorithm to ensure they are the same. Once the image process is complete, FTK runs both an MD5 and a SHA1 hash algorithm to compare the source drive and the resulting image of the source drive.

These hashes serve two purposes: first, they verify that the original source drive was not altered in any way; and second, they verify that the resulting image is identical to the source drive. Both of these types of hashes are large numbers obtained by running an algorithm against the data stream of the drives. These numbers uniquely describe the contents of a file or drive and are essentially a "digital fingerprint" of a file or an entire disk. The odds that two files or disks with different contents will have the same hash value are roughly 1 × 10 to the 38th power (a 1 followed by 38 zeros). By using two different hash algorithms we increase those odds exponentially. The point to be understood from this is that if the hash values of two files or drives match, you can be assured that the file or disk contents match as well.

Once the technician obtained the image of the hard drive, he stored it on his computer and shared the folder out to me, so that I could begin the analysis. Sharing a folder means that he set the permissions on that folder so that I could log into his computer and have read rights to the data on that folder.

I began my analysis by beginning a new case using Forensics Toolkit (FTK) version 1.61a. FTK goes through all of the data on the image and indexes and organizes it for easier analysis. This process can take a considerable amount of time depending on the amount of data.

I first browsed through all of the graphics files. I found a substantial amount of files in some folders labeled _____, that did not seem to be organization business related. I then analyzed the metadata of the photos to gather more information. Metadata are part of the file in a graphic image. When a graphic image is opened in a text or hex editor, you are able to identify metadata that can show if the graphic came from a camera (and if so, the type of camera), and the date that the photo was taken and/or uploaded to the computer. By comparing the metadata of the photos in the _____ folders with other photos taken as part of the user's work, I was able to establish that they were taken with the same camera, a _____. I bookmarked the photos, and exported them for future reference. I also discovered a group of photos taken with a different _____ camera (a _____). I bookmarked and exported them as well. I then went through and bookmarked and exported a sample of all the photos that were taken with either of those cameras.

As a next step, I bookmarked and exported all deleted picture files for reference purposes. I then analyzed some e-mail files and saved one of them for reference.

The next step was to analyze the user's Internet usage. First I looked for and saved any html (Internet) files. Next I extracted all index.

dat files from the image (index.dat files contain Internet cookies, temporary files, and history). I analyzed those files using X-Ways Trace version 2.01. X-Ways parses out the index.dat files and allows you to export them to Excel spreadsheets for further organization and analysis. I did so, and saved the Excel spreadsheets for reference in the report. I found only minimal Internet activities that were not organization business related.

Next, I used FTK to do a search of the hard drive for key words. I searched for _____. I found little new information via this search. I was able to establish that graphics files had been saved to an external device (CD or DVD drive) labeled E:. I also found evidence of graphics files being saved to _____, which seemed to be a legitimate network folder for storage of work-related photographs.

I next browsed through the spreadsheets and documents looking for any that might indicate the user was misusing organization equipment. While doing so, I found a document referencing _____. With that information, I went back to the Search function and searched for the word, _____. That search gave me 43 hits in 5 files. These were all deleted files, but I was able to recover two of them and save them as document files to add to the evidence of the case.

As a final check to make sure nothing was missed, I ran two data carving processes. Data carving is a process that FTK and other forensics applications will run. It goes through all of the unallocated (deleted files, or unused space on a hard drive), and searches for headers that indicate the presence of a particular type of file. If it finds that header, it attempts to piece it together again, and "carves" out that section of data so it can be recovered and analyzed.

I used FTK to carve OLE (Microsoft Office) files, and then used X-Ways Forensic version 13.0 to carve JPEG graphics files. (X-Ways can sometimes do a better job of carving graphics files than can FTK.) These processes take many hours to complete, as they are going through the hard drive bit by bit. When they completed, I did a final review and analysis of the files they had located. There were no new files that had not already been reviewed and bookmarked as evidence.

Finally, I cleaned up some of the evidence in FTK and used its Report Wizard to create a final report, which is included on the accompanying CD.

Signatures

_____

Investigator (printed name/signature/date of report submission)

_____

Chief Information Security Officer (printed name/signature/date of receipt and review)

_____

Requesting Department Contact (printed name/signature/date of receipt and review)

[CAPTION AND NAMES OF PARTIES]

1. Pursuant to Fed.R.Civ.P. 26(f), a meeting was held on ___(date)___ at ___(place)___ and was attended by:

   ___(name)___ for plaintiff(s)
   ___(name)___ for defendant(s) ___(party name)___
   ___(name)___ for defendant(s) ___(party name)___

2. Pre-Discovery Disclosures. The parties [have exchanged] [will exchange by ___(date)___] the information required by [Fed.R.Civ.P. 26(a)(1)] [local rule _____].

3. Discovery Plan. The parties jointly propose to the court the following discovery plan: [Use separate paragraphs or subparagraphs as necessary if parties disagree.]

Discovery will be needed on the following subjects: ___(brief description of subjects on which discovery will be needed)___

All discovery commenced in time to be completed by ___(date)___. [Discovery on ___(issue for early discovery)___ to be completed by ___(date)___.]

Maximum of _____ interrogatories by each party to any other party. [Responses due _____ days after service.]

Maximum of _____ requests for admission by each party to any other party. [Responses due _____ days after service.]

Maximum of _____ depositions by plaintiff(s) and _____ by defendant(s). Each deposition [other than of _____] limited to maximum of _____ hours unless extended by agreement of parties.

Reports from retained experts under Rule 26(a)(2) due:

   from plaintiff(s) by ___(date)___
   from defendant(s) by ___(date)___

Supplementations under Rule 26(e) due ___(time(s) or interval(s))___.

4. Other Items. [Use separate paragraphs or subparagraphs as necessary if parties disagree.]

The parties [request] [do not request] a conference with the court before entry of the scheduling order.

The parties request a pretrial conference in __(month and year)__.

Plaintiff(s) should be allowed until __(date)__ to join additional parties and until __(date)__ to amend the pleadings.

Defendant(s) should be allowed until __(date)__ to join additional parties and until __(date)__ to amend the pleadings.

All potentially dispositive motions should be filed by __(date)__

Settlement [is likely] [is unlikely] [cannot be evaluated prior to __(date)__] [may be enhanced by use of the following alternative dispute resolution procedure: [____].

Final lists of witnesses and exhibits under Rule 26(a)(3) should be due:

   from plaintiff(s) by __(date)__
   from defendant(s) by __(date)__

Parties should have _____ days after service of final lists of witnesses and exhibits to list objections under Rule 26(a)(3).

The case should be ready for trial by __(date)__ [and at this time is expected to take approximately __(length of time)__].

[Other matters]

Date: _____

_____

/signed by all counsel

Appendix III: Links to Technical Software Solutions

The following links are to sites with tools and applications that can assist with the safe acquisition, storage, and management of electronically stored information:

- 7-Zip—A simple-to-use tool that will allow you to encrypt single files or folders in Windows operating systems. http://www.7-zip.org/.
- AxCrypt—Another free tool that integrates with Windows to allow you easy one-click encryption of files. http://www.axantum.com/axcrypt/Downloads.aspx.
- BitLocker Encryption Overview—In our first edition we pointed you toward TrueCrypt, but Microsoft has since replaced that with BitLocker on all of its operating systems. This is a good overview article. http://windows.microsoft.com/en-us/windows-vista/bitlocker-drive-encryption-overview.
- Crytophane A GUI for GnuPG. https://code.google.com/p/cryptophane/.
- EnCase by Guidance Software—This is perhaps the most used and best known of the forensics application suites. They also have e-discovery and management tools. They are some of

the best you can buy and can again be costly. http://www.guidancesoftware.com/.

FTK by AccessData—These are the creators of FTK (Forensic Tool Kit) and many other products for forensic analysis, e-discovery, and management of electronic records. Some of them can be a little pricey, but they are well known and proven in the marketplace and by the courts. Their "Imager" product is free and has some great features for taking a first look at evidence, creating forensically sound images, and mounting those images as a drive. http://accessdata.com/.

GNU Privacy Guard (GnuPG)—An open-source version of PGP (Pretty Good Privacy) which is also good but must be paid for. This is a command line tool, but there are graphical user interfaces that can be added to make it more user-friendly. http://www.gnupg.org/.

Microsoft SharePoint—One of the best-known and well-regarded applications for managing records and workflow is Microsoft's SharePoint application. https://products.office.com/en-us/SharePoint/collaboration.

P2 eXplorer by Paraben—This is a tool for mounting forensic images or hard drives in read-only mode so that you can examine them for evidence, including deleted files (demo version available). http://www.paraben.com/p2-explorer.html. Paraben also has a suite of tools for forensics work and is well known for its mobile forensics tools. http://www.paraben.com/.

X-Ways Software—For those of a little more technical bent, the forensics analysis products provided by X-Ways are excellent and relatively inexpensive. http://www.x-ways.net/.

These are only a few of many new products out on the market currently. Depending on your budget constraints and risk decisions, you can find a wide variety of excellent products that should meet your needs.

There are also many online and professional services available to assist you with your e-discovery and records management processes.

Once you have completed this book and considered what you really need, you should be well prepared to select from the many available products and services available.

Index

A

ABA Journal, 61, 68

Access card, 70

Access control, and management, 226–232

Active Directory, 96

American Bar Association, 52

American Standard Code for Information Interchange (ASCII), 84

American Telephone and Telegraph Company (AT&T), 115

Archival information, 8, 9

Archival tools, e-mail–based, 237

ASCII, *see* American Standard Code for Information Interchange (ASCII)

AT&T, *see* American Telephone and Telegraph Company (AT&T)

Attorney competence cases, 48–49
    Brown v. Tellermate Holdings, Ltd., 49

    Chen v. Dougherty, 48–49

Auditors, 163–164

Audits, 238–241

Authentication, 90, 227–228

Automated technical solutions, 250–253

B

"Baby Bells", 116

Back-end database, 182

Backup
    procedure, 242
    systems, 244, 245
    tapes, 38

Bass v. Miss Porter's School, 20–21

Bell, Alexander Graham, 109

BES, *see* BlackBerry Enterprise Server (BES)

Binary
    language, 81
    mathematical algorithm, 175

Bit, 80

BitLocker, 188

BlackBerry Enterprise Server
    (BES), 120
"Blue screen of death", 151–152
*Brown v. American Home Products
    Corporation Diet Drugs*, 23
*Brown v. Tellermate Holdings,
    Ltd.*, 49
Buddy List, 100
Business organizations, 59–60
Byte, 80

C

Cache file, 133
CCTV, *see* Closed-circuit television
    (CCTV)
Cellular devices, 119–126
Centers for Disease Control and
    Prevention, 62
Central processor, 150–151, 152
Checksum, 218
Chen v. Dougherty, 48–49
Citco Defendants, 32, 33, 34
Claw-back
    and privilege cases, 41–44
        *Holmes v. Petrovich
            Development Company,
            LLC*, 43
        *Kyko Global Inc. v. Prithvi Info.
            Solutions Ltd.*, 43–44
        *Pacific Coast Steel, Inc. v.
            Leany*, 42–43
        *Williams v. District of
            Columbia*, 41–42
    provision, 9
    rules, 4
Closed-circuit television (CCTV),
    70, 126–127, 129
Cloud computing, 124
Cloud services, 242, 243
Cloud storage, *see* Cloud computing
Coleman v. Morgan Stanley, 23
Computer forensics, 215–221

Computer Fraud and Abuse Act, 48
Confidential information, 200, 201
Cookies, 139, 185
Corruption, of file, 190
Cost shifting, 7, 37–38, 202
Court of Appeals, 41
Crews v. Avco Corp., 28–29
Crispin v. Christian Audigier, Inc., 21

D

Database systems, 87–91
Data map, 168–170
Data preservation, and management,
    223–253
    access control and, 226–232
    automated technical solutions,
        250–253
    litigation hold, 246–248
    organization and file
        management techniques,
        232–241
        day-to-day, 232–236
        management of data over time,
            236–238
        response to litigation/audits,
            238–241
    safe storage issues and
        considerations, 241–246
    securing data, 223–226
    spoliation, 248–250
Data recovery, and acquisition,
    177–221
    applications as vital user interface,
        178–183
    computer forensics, 215–221
    deleted/corrupted data, 190–191
    encrypted data, 188–190
    hidden/restricted access data,
        183–188
    obsolete media, data stored on,
        191–196
    ownership and integrity, 203–211

privileged, sensitive, and inaccessible data, 196–203
proprietary data, 191–196
time recording and integrity, 211–214
Data; *see also* Data preservation, and management; Data recovery, and acquisition
acquisition, 238–239
carving, 191
centers, 95
classification, 233
cloud, 143
control considerations, 170–173
dissemination and reporting, 255–266
creating readable reports, 261–264
format issues, 255–258
mediums for transfer, 259–260
tips for depositions, 264–266
storage, 233
Day-to-day organization, 232–236
Decimal language, 81
Deleted/corrupted data, 190–191
Deloitte Forensic Center, 6
Department heads, 164
Desktop computer, 149–153
Digital computer, 110
Digital Evidence Committee, 52
Digital video, 126–130
Directory service, 96
Discovery master, 23–24
Dissemination and reporting, data, 255–266
creating readable reports, 261–264
format issues, 255–258
mediums for transfer, 259–260
tips for depositions, 264–266
DOS prompt, 195
Duke Today, 57
Duty of Disclosure Rule 26, 4–11

E

Economist Intelligence Unit (EIU), 6
Edelson McGuire, 52
E-discovery process, 4, 6, 10
EEPROM, *see* Electronically erasable programmable read-only memory (EEPROM)
EIU, *see* Economist Intelligence Unit (EIU)
"Elaborate spoliation", 27
Electronically erasable programmable read-only memory (EEPROM), 147
Electronically stored information (ESI), 1–62, 79–157
affecting business organizations, 59–60
case law examples, 18–50
attorney competence, 48–49
claw-back and privilege, 41–44
metadata, 40–41
preservation/production, 44–48
reasonably accessible, 36–40
rulings of Judge Scheindlin, 29–36
social media cases, 20–23
spoliation cases, 23–29
cellular devices, 119–126
changes to Federal Rules of Civil Procedure, 3–16
Form 35, 15
Rule 1, scope and purpose, 3
Rule 16(b) (5) and (6), 3–4
Rule 26, 4–11
Rule 33(d) interrogatories to parties, 15
Rule 34(b) producing documents procedures, 13–15

Rule 37 safe harbor, 11–13
Rule 45 subpoena, 15
database systems, 87–91
description, 80–87
desktop computer facts, 149–153
as discoverable evidence, 50–55
digital video, 126–130
effects on government entities, 60
e-mail systems, 91–94
event and system logs, 148–149
Federal Rules of Evidence
    (FREs), 16–18
  502, 17
  802, 18
  901, 17–18
federal rules affecting electronic
    data, 49–50
file and print servers, 94–99
instant messaging services,
    99–101
Internet of Everything (IOE),
    147–148
Internet of Things (IOT),
    147–148
Internet/online data, 130–144
metadata and other nonapparent
    data, 154–157
mobile devices, 101–105
physical access records, 105–109
practice of law, 55–59
problems with, 50–55
storage media, 144–147
telecommunications, 109–119
Electronic Communications Privacy
    Act, 48
Electronic discovery, *see* E-discovery
    process
Electronic evidence, 17–18, 19, 41,
    42, 56–57, 208, 240, 258
E-mail
  applications, 179, 180
  -based archival tools, 237
  destruction policies, 239

records, 240
systems, 91–94
transmissions, 260
Emojis, 47
Encryption, 188–190,
    228–229, 260
ESI, *see* Electronically stored
    information (ESI)
Event, and system logs, 148–149
Executives, 164

F

Facebook, 20, 22
Family Stuff folder, 180
Federal Rules of Civil Procedure
    (FRCPs), 3–16
  Form 35, 15
  Rule 1, scope and purpose, 3
  Rule 16(b)(5) and (6), 3–4
  Rule 26, 4–11
  Rule 33(d) interrogatories to
    parties, 15
  Rule 34(b) producing documents
    procedures, 13–15
  Rule 37 safe harbor, 11–13
  Rule 45 subpoena, 15
Federal Rules of Evidence (FREs),
    16–18
  502, 11, 17
  802, 18
  901, 17–18
Federico v. Lincoln Military Housing,
    46–47
FIFO, *see* First in–first out (FIFO)
File, and print servers, 94–99
First in–first out (FIFO), 121
Flash memory, 146
Floppy disks, 146, 193
FOIA, *see* Freedom of information
    act (FOIA)
Forensic imaging software, 219
Format issues, 255–258

FRCPs, *see* Federal Rules of Civil Procedure (FRCPs)
Freedom of information act (FOIA), 34, 35, 172
FREs, *see* Federal Rules of Evidence (FREs)
Front-end application, 90, 182
FTK (Forensic Tool Kit) Imager, 220

G

Gates, Bill, 84
Geek, 77–78
General Provisions Governing Discovery, 4–11
Gigabytes, 85
Government entities, 60
Greenwich Mean Time (GMT), 213

H

Hard disk drive, 144–145
Hash algorithms, 175, 217, 218, 209
Hearsay Rule, *see* FRE 802
Hexadecimal code, 156
Hexadecimal mathematical language, 81, 82
Hidden/restricted access data, 183–188
Holmes v. Petrovich Development Company, LLC, 43
"Home" directory/drive, 95
HTML, *see* Hypertext Markup Language (HTML)
Human resources, 164
Hypertext Markup Language (HTML), 134
Hypervisor, 97

I

ICE, *see* Immigrations and Customs Enforcement (ICE)

Identity management, 229–230
Immigrations and Customs Enforcement (ICE), 34
Inaccessible data management, 202–203
Information technology (IT), 5
 vs. everyone else, 63–78
 as ally, 76–77
 information technologist's perspective, 72–76
 role of, 63–72
 translating geek, 77–78
 professionals, 159–162
In re Domestic Drywall Antitrust Litig., 46
Instant messaging services, 99–101
Integrity, of time, 211–214
Intellectual property (IP), 225
Internal Revenue Service (IRS), 257
Internet
 browsing, 124
 data, 130–144
Internet of Everything (IOE), 147–148
Internet of Things (IOT), 147–148
Intranet, 143
IOE, *see* Internet of Everything (IOE)
IOT, *see* Internet of Things (IOT)
IP, *see* Intellectual property (IP)
IRS, *see* Internal Revenue Service (IRS)
IT, *see* Information technology (IT)

J

Jaz drive, 194
Junk Mail folder, 180

K

KCHServs., Inc. v. Vanaire, Inc., 25–26

Keywords, 240
Kilobyte, 84
Kipperman v. Onex Corp., 27
*Kyko Global Inc. v. Prithvi Info.
   Solutions Ltd.*, 43–44

L

Legal staff, 162–163
Lester v. Allied Concrete Company,
   22–23
Library of Congress, 210
License capture cameras, 68
Linux, 218
Litigation
   hold, 246–248
   response to, 238–241
*LordAbbettMun. Income Fund., Inc.
   v. Asami*, 45
Loyalty card, 71

M

"Ma Bell", *see* American Telephone
   and Telegraph Company
   (AT&T)
McCullough, Mike, 52
Magnetic tape, 146
Management, of data
   preservation and, 223–253
      access control and
         management, 226–232
      automated technical solutions,
         250–253
      litigation hold, 246–248
      organization and file
         management techniques,
         232–241
      safe storage issues and
         considerations, 241–246
      securing data, 223–226
      spoliation, 248–250

privileged, sensitive, and
   inaccessible, 196–203
Mapping, 96
Master File Table (MFT), 153, 186,
   204
Medcorp, Incv. Pinpoint Tech., Inc.,
   24–25
Megabytes, 85
Memory cards, 124–125
Memory sticks, 86
Metadata, 35, 51, 86, 179, 257, 258
   cases, 40–41
   of electronic record, 204
   and other non-apparent data,
      154–157
MFT, *see* Master File Table (MFT)
Mirror image, 219
Mirroring, database, 90
MMS, *see* Multimedia Message
   Service (MMS)
Mobile devices, 101–105
Mock deposition, *see* Trial rehearsal
Moore's law, 85
*Mosaid Technologies, Inc. v. Samsung
   Electronics Corporation*, 11
Motion to compel, 7
MSNBC, 52
Multimedia Message Service
   (MMS), 141
MySpace, 21, 22

N

*National Day Laborer Organizing
   Network v. U.S.
   Immigration and Customs
   Enforcement Agency*,
   34–36, 44
National Rifle Association
   (NRA), 202
Near-line data, 7
The New York Times, 225
Nibbles, 80

Nonrepudiation, 203
Notepad, 262
NRA, *see* National Rifle Association (NRA)

O

Obsolete media, data stored on, 191–196
Off-site storage, 245
Olson v. Sax, 26–27
O'Neill v. the City of Shoreline, 40–41
Online data, 130–144
Online services, *see* Cloud services
Open Channel, 52
Optical storage media, 145
Organization, and file management techniques, 232–241
  day-to-day, 232–236
  management of data over time, 236–238
  response to litigation/audits, 238–241
Ownership
  of data, 165–170
  and integrity, 203–211

P

Pacific Coast Steel, Inc. v. Leany, 42–43
Payment Card Industry (PCI), 59
Peck, Andrew, 240
Pension Committee of the University of Montreal Pension Plan v. Banc of America Securities, LLC, 28, 32–34
Personal health information (PHI), 200
Personally identifiable information (PII), 200
PHI, *see* Personal health information (PHI)

Physical, and information security personnel, 165
Physical access records, 105–109
PII, *see* Personally identifiable information (PII)
Pippins v. KPMG LLP, 44
Plain Old Telephone System (POTS), 110, 111
Plausible deniability, 203
POTS, *see* Plain Old Telephone System (POTS)
Practice of law, 55–59
Preservation and management, data, 223–253
  access control and management, 226–232
  automated technical solutions, 250–253
  litigation hold, 246–248
  organization and file management techniques, 232–241
    day-to-day, 232–236
    management of data over time, 236–238
    response to litigation/audits, 238–241
  safe storage issues and considerations, 241–246
  securing data, 223–226
  spoliation, 248–250
Preservation/production cases, 44–48
  Federico v. Lincoln Military Housing, 46–47
  In re Domestic Drywall Antitrust Litig., 46
  LordAbbettMun. Income Fund., Inc. v. Asami, 45
  National Day Laborer Organizing Network v. U.S. Immigration and Customs Enforcement Agency, 44

new cases regarding emojis, 47

Pippins v. KPMG LLP, 44

Procaps S.A. v. Patheon Inc., 45–46

Rajaee v. Design Tech Homes, Ltd., 47–48

United Corp. v. Tutu Park Ltd., 44–45

Privileged data management, 196–200

Procaps S.A. v. Patheon Inc., 45–46

Proprietary data, 191–196

Proprietary programming, 180

PST file, 182, 183

Pulse dialing, 111

Q

"Quantum" encryption, 229

R

Rajaee v. Design Tech Homes, Ltd., 47–48

RAM, *see* Random-access memory (RAM)

Random-access memory (RAM), 86, 145, 151

Readable reports, 261–264

Reasonably accessible cases, 36–40

   Spieker v. Quest Cherokee, LLC, 36

   Takeda Pharm. Co., Ltd. v. Teva Pharm. USA, Inc., 37–38

   United States ex rel. Carter v. Bridgepoint Educ., Inc., 305 F.R.D. 225, 38–39

   United States ex rel Guardiola v. Renown Health, 40

   Valeo Electric Sys., Inc. v. Cleveland Die and Mfg. Co., 37

'Recent' folder, 185

Records

   management policy, 215, 216, 217, 261

   managers, 163

   retention laws, 237

Recovery, and acquisition, data, 177–221

   applications as vital user interface, 178–183

   computer forensics, 215–221

   deleted/corrupted data, 190–191

   encrypted data, 188–190

   hidden/restricted access data, 183–188

   obsolete media, data stored on, 191–196

   ownership and integrity, 203–211

   privileged, sensitive, and inaccessible data management, 196–203

   proprietary data, 191–196

   time recording and integrity, 211–214

Registry, 183, 184

Relevant data, loss of, 248–250

Restore file, 186

Restore function, 104

Ritvo, Dalia Topelson, 47

Rollback, 104

Romano v. Steelcase, 21–22

Rowe Entertainment, Inc. v. The William Morris Agency, 30

Royal Greenwich Observatory, 213

S

Safe Harbor rule, 12, 25, 26

Safe storage issues, and considerations, 241–246

SANS, *see* Storage area networks (SANS)

Saturday Night Live, 115

Scheindlin, Shira, rulings of, 29–36

National Day Laborer Organizing Network v. U.S. Immigration and Customs Enforcement Agency, 34–36
Pension Committee of the University of Montreal Pension Plan v. Banc of America Securities, LLC, 32–34
Zubulake v. UBS Warburg, 29–32
"Secure Communities" program, 34
Securing data, 223–226
Sensitive data management, 200, 201
Shadow Copy, *see* Restore file
Short Message Service (SMS), 120
Silk Road, 47
Single sign-on system, 230
Skill sets, and tools, 173–176
Smart phones, 70
SMS, *see* Short Message Service (SMS)
Social media cases, 20–23
Bass v. Miss Porter's School, 20–21
Crispin v. Christian Audigier, Inc., 21
Lester v. Allied Concrete Company, 22–23
Romano v. Steelcase, 21–22
Solid-state memory, *see* Flash memory
Southwestern Association of Technical Accident Investigators, 52
Spieker v. Quest Cherokee, LLC, 36
Spoliation, 11
cases, 23–29
Brown v. American Home Products Corporation Diet Drugs, 23
Coleman v. Morgan Stanley, 23
Crews v. Avco Corp., 28–29
KCHServs., Inc. v. Vanaire, Inc., 25–26

Kipperman v. Onex Corp., 27
Medcorp, Incv. Pinpoint Tech., Inc., 24–25
Olson v. Sax, 26–27
Pension Comm. of Univ. of Montreal Pension Plan v. Bank of Am. Secs., LLC, 28
United Central Bank v. Kanan Fashions, Inc., 27–28
Wachtel v. Health Net, Inc., 23–24
Zubulake v. UBS Warburg, 24
loss of relevant data, 248–250
Stakeholders, list of, 159–165
auditors, 163–164
department heads, 164
executives, 164
human resources, 164
information technology professionals, 159–162
legal staff, 162–163
physical and information security personnel, 165
records managers, 163
vice presidents, 164
Steganography, 155
Storage area networks (SANS), 95
Storage media, 144–147
Stored Communication Act, 21
Subpoenas, 15
Supreme Court and Congress, 2
"Swipe a Loyalty Card, Help a Food Detective", 62

T

Takeda Pharm. Co., Ltd. v. Teva Pharm. USA, Inc., 37–38
Telecommunications, 109–119
Teppler, Steven, 52
"Textbook case of discovery abuse", *see Kipperman v. Onex Corp.*
Text messaging, 120, 121

Time recording, 211–214
T-Mobile, 123
Tracking cookies, 185; *see also*
    Cookies
Tracking, time, 212
Transit card, 69
Trial rehearsal, 265–266
Twitter, 141

U

Ulbricht, Ross, 47
Uniform Electronic Legal Material
    Act, 210
*United Central Bank v. Kanan
    Fashions, Inc.*, 27–28
United Corp. v. Tutu Park Ltd., 44–45
*United States ex rel. Carter v.
    Bridgepoint Educ., Inc., 305
    F.R.D. 225*, 38–39
*United States ex rel Guardiola v.
    Renown Health*, 40
Universal Coordinated Time
    (UTC), 213
Unix, 218, 219–220
USB flash drives, 147
U.S. Congress, 210
U.S. Justice Department, 116
U.S. Naval Observatory, 213
UTC, *see* Universal Coordinated
    Time (UTC)

V

*Valeo Electric Sys., Inc. v. Cleveland
    Die and Mfg. Co.*, 37

Verified copy, 218
Verizon, 123
Vice presidents, 164
Video surveillance cameras,
    127–128
Videotapes, 12
Virtual machines (VMs), 97, 231

W

Wachtel v. Health Net, Inc., 23–24
Washington State Supreme
    Court, 41
"Was This Web Photo
    Altered?", 57
Web 2.0, 141, 142
Web logs, 141
*West v. The Goodyear Tire and Rubber
    Company*, 249
Williams v. District of Columbia,
    41–42
Windows operating system, 262
Wired, 123
Word Perfect, 194, 195
Word processor, 86
Work product doctrine, 199
Write blockers, 175, 219
Writ of Execution, 43

Y

YouProve, 57

Z

Zubulake v. UBS Warburg, 24, 29–32